KOREA

HOT SPOTS IN GLOBAL POLITICS

Published

Christoph Bluth, *Korea*
Alan Dowty, *Israel/Palestine* – 2nd edition
Amalendu Misra, *Afghanistan*
Gareth Stansfield, *Iraq*
Jonathan Tonge, *Northern Ireland*

KOREA ———————————

CHRISTOPH BLUTH

polity

First published in 2008 by Polity Press

Polity Press
65 Bridge Street
Cambridge CB2 1UR, UK

Polity Press
350 Main Street
Malden, MA 02148, USA

ISBN-13: 978-07456-3356-5
ISBN-13: 978-07456-3357-2 (pb)

A catalogue record for this book is available from the British Library.

Typeset in 10.5 on 12 pt Sabon
by Servis Filmsetting Ltd, Manchester
Printed and bound in India by Replika Press PVT Ltd, Kundli, India

The publisher has used its best endeavours to ensure that the URLs for external websites referred to in this book are correct and active at the time of going to press. However, the publisher has no responsibility for the websites and can make no guarantee that a site will remain live or that the content is or will remain appropriate.

Every effort has been made to trace all copyright holders, but if any have been inadvertently overlooked the publishers will be pleased to include any necessary credits in any subsequent reprint or edition.

For further information on Polity, visit our website: www.polity.co.uk

Contents

Foreword

When North Korea tested a nuclear weapon on 9 October 2006, the world was reminded once again of the dangerous situation on the Korean peninsula. This action, which was roundly condemned by the international community, destroyed many illusions about the alleged achievements of diplomacy and the inter-Korean dialogue.

The dangers of the military conflict on the Korean peninsula are obvious for the world to see. North Korea has an army of 1.1 million troops, 70 per cent of which is deployed within 100 km of the demilitarized zone that has separated the two Korean states since the end of the Korean war. It has deployed thousands of artillery pieces, tanks, hundreds of ballistic missiles and a significant number of chemical weapons. On the other side of the DMZ, referred to by former US President Bill Clinton as 'the scariest place on earth', forces of the United States and the Republic of Korea are deployed to counter any North Korean attack. According to the American specialist Michael O'Hanlon, the area between the South Korean capital Seoul and the North Korean capital Pyongyang has a higher concentration of military firepower than central Europe during the Cold War. The armed forces of North Korea are not configured for defence, but for offence, meaning that if a conflict should start armoured columns will immediately move south and Seoul will come under heavy artillery bombardment. In this context, North Korea's growing ballistic missile and nuclear capabilities appear to raise the military threat to a new level.

But how are we to understand the nature of this threat? In the popular literature, North Korean leader Kim Jong-il is often portrayed as an irrational dictator ruling over an isolated 'hermit kingdom' and out of touch with the outside world. Of course this image is a caricature. In the Republic of Korea, there is a palpable division within society about how to understand and deal with North Korea. The traditional position of the political and military elite in South Korea has been defined by a staunch rejection of communism and the portrayal of North Korea as the enemy that must be deterred by the security cooperation with the United States. North Korean belligerence was explained as based on the desire by the Pyongyang regime to unite the Korean peninsula on Northern terms and extend communist rule over all of the Korean people. The alliance with the United States was essential to safeguard the security of free Korean people. Although in the decades following the Korean War this view found broad acceptance within South Korean society, there was growing opposition to the authoritarian government and a desire for social change and the movement towards democracy. Some of the younger generation who did not witness the devastating Korean War (1950–3) and who were involved or witnessed the struggle for democracy in the South have a more benign view of North Korea. They are yearning for unification of the divided nation and believe that interference from outside powers is prolonging the division. Such views were reinforced by President Kim Dae-jung's so-called 'sunshine policy' of engaging the North Korean regime with political dialogue, economic assistance and joint economic projects. His successor, President Roh Moo-hyun, inherited the same policy line under the banner of 'peace and prosperity' policy towards North Korea. But the nuclear test in October 2006 represents the culmination of trends in relations with North Korea that have raised grave doubts about the results of these policies. Thus President Roh has been criticized for continuously meeting North Korea's demands for aid without any concessions from North Korea's leaders. Moreover, the Roh government has allowed relations with the United States to drift apart. For example, it proposed that the Republic of Korea should assume the role of 'balancer' between major powers in

Asia, suggesting an almost neutral position in regional security. For a small country like South Korea which is at the frontline of a major geopolitical confrontation, that is simply not a feasible position to adopt. Even more controversial is the transfer of 'wartime command' from the United States to the Republic of Korea. Previously in the event of war, South Korean armed forces would have been under the Combined Forces Command (CFC) led by the commander of US forces under the aegis of the United Nations. In the future South Korea will be responsible for securing the armistice, raising doubts about the extent of support from the United States.

At the time of writing, the situation on the Korean peninsula has entered a new and particularly uncertain phase. The North Korean state has reached a point where it is politically, socially and economically bankrupt. The regime cannot guarantee minimal food provision for its people, its industry is largely idle and it relies on food and energy supplies from other countries. It uses its military and especially its weapons of mass destruction programmes to extort economic support and political concessions. In short, the apparent stability on the Korean peninsula is fragile. The sudden collapse of the North Korean state or the outbreak of military hostilities could have catastrophic consequences for the Korean people north and south and would affect the security of the entire region.

The situation on the Korean peninsula is complex and often misunderstood. North Korea is a very secretive and isolated country, and there is much that is unknown about its internal politics and decision-making processes. At the same time, an understanding of the factors that drive North Korean foreign policy behaviour is crucial. It is therefore very important that scholars, students, policymakers and the general public develop a deep understanding of the crisis on the Korean peninsula which is steeped in the knowledge of the history of the two Koreas since their division and an appreciation of their development into the post-Cold War era. It is for this reason that I welcome this book, which provides an excellent background on the security dilemma in Korea and makes a vital contribution to the international dialogue on the future of the Korean peninsula.

Acknowledgements ————

The author benefited from the help, support and advice of many institutions and people during the writing of this book. The Korea Institute for Defence Analyses (KIDA) under the directorship of Dr Hwang Dong-joon awarded me the so far unique honour of being the only non-American non-military visiting research fellow so far in 2005. I owe a great deal to the expertise and friendship of my colleagues at KIDA, especially Kim Chang-su, Kim Tae-woo, Hwang Jae-ho and Nam Man-kwon. During my period as Visiting Professor at the Department of Political Science and Diplomacy at Yonsei University in 2005, I benefited especially from advice from Kim Woo-sang and Moon Chung-in. The support and friendship of Dr Park Jin, member of the National Assembly, made an essential contribution to my work in Korea. Daniel Pinkston and William Potter from the Monterey Institute of International Studies gave me the opportunity to present the preliminary results of my research and have been a source of advice and encouragement. Others who shared their expertise with me include Professor Choi Jung-hul (National Defense University Seoul), Choi Soung-ah (*Korea Herald*), Brendan Howe (Ewha Women's University), Kim Hannah, Lee Shin-wha (Korea University), Park Chan-bong (Unification Ministry), Gary Samore (International Institute for Strategic Studies), Scott Snyder (Asia Foundation), Seo Hyun-jin (*Korea Herald*), James Strohmaier (Pusan National University), Adam Ward (International Institute for Strategic Studies),

Yoon Young-kwan (Foreign Minister, now at Seoul National University) and Yu Yong-weon (*Chosun Ilbo*). The opportunity for exchanges with North Korean diplomats, including Ambassador Ri Yong-ho, Thae Yong-ho, Hwang Ik-hwan and Kim Chun-guk (Director of the European Department at the Ministry of Foreign Affairs in Pyongyang) enabled me to get a first-hand view of the North Korean perspective. The advice, encouragement and friendship of Kim Hyun-sook was invaluable. My old friend, Chun Hong-chan from Pusan National University, acted as my mentor during my first research trip to Korea. Park Min-hyoung checked the Korean transliteration in conformity with the new government-approved spelling (although the traditional spelling of some names has been retained). I am also grateful for the support of the British Academy in conducting fieldwork in the Republic of Korea. All errors and omissions in the book are of course my responsibility alone.

Chronology

1945

February 8   Yalta Conference between the Allies of World
               War II

July 26   Potsdam Conference. An agreement is made
               to divide the Korean peninsula into zones
               of Soviet and US operation along the 41st
               parallel

August 15   Japan surrenders and Korea is liberated

August 26   Soviet armed forces enter northern Korea

September 8   US troops arrive in southern Korea

1948

May 31   After elections in the south of Korea, a
               National Assembly is formally established
               with Rhee Syngman as chairman

July 17   The National Assembly adopts a constitution
               for the Republic of Korea. Rhee Syngman is
               elected President and the ROK is recognized
               by the United States

August 15   The Republic of Korea takes over the gov-
               ernment of South Korea from the US military
               government

September 9   The Democratic People's Republic of Korea
               is established under Kim Il-sung

December 12   The UN recognizes the Republic of Korea as
               the sole legal government of Korea

1950

June 25	North Korean forces invade South Korea
July 8	General MacArthur is appointed UN commander-in-chief
September 15	UN forces land at Inchon
October 14	Chinese troops enter North Korea

1951

January 4	Chinese and North Korean forces capture the capital of the ROK (Seoul)
March 15	The UN forces retake Seoul

1953

July 27	The armistice agreement signed by the US (on behalf of the UN), North Korea and China. Rhee refuses to sign

1960

April	After student protests Rhee Syngman is forced to resign and leave the country

1961

May 16	Major General Park Chung-hee seizes power in a military coup

1965

June	South Korea signs normalization treaty with Japan

1968

January 23	The US 'spy ship' *Pueblo* is seized by the North Korean navy in international waters off the eastern coast of the DPRK. The crew is released one year later

1973

June 8	Opposition leader Kim Dae-jung is kidnapped by agents of the Korean Central Intelligence Agency in Tokyo. He is kept under house arrest in Seoul

1979

October 26   Park Chung-hee is assassinated by the head of the KCIA. Major General Chun Doo-hwan takes control of the government

1980

May 18   Gwangju massacre. After mass protests, the armed forces kill 240 people. For the period of Chun Doo-hwan's administration, the incident is officially regarded as a rebellion inspired by Communists, but after civil rule the protests receive recognition as an effort to restore democracy from military rule

1983

October 9   North Korean commandos launch a bomb attack on a South Korean government delegation during an official visit to Rangoon, Myanmar, headed by the President Chun Doo-hwan. The president is unhurt, but 21 people are killed including four South Korean cabinet ministers

1986

January   A nuclear reactor (the 5 MW(e) reactor) begins operation at Yongbyon, North Korea

1988

February   Roh Tae-woo is inaugurated as president of the Republic of Korea

October   The Olympic Games are held in Seoul

1990

June 1   Soviet President Mikhail Gorbachev visits South Korea

September 11   Diplomatic relations are established between the Soviet Union and the Republic of Korea

1991

September 17   The DPRK and the ROK are admitted into membership of the United Nations

September 27   President G. Bush announces the withdrawal of all US nuclear weapons from the Korean peninsula

December   North and South Korea announce a Joint Declaration on the denuclearization of the Korean peninsula and a non-aggression agreement

1992

January   South Korea announces the suspension of the 'Team Spirit' joint exercises with the US and the DPRK signs the IAEA safeguards agreement

December   Kim Young-sam is elected president, the country's first democratically elected civilian president in 30 years

1993

February 25   The IAEA Board of Governors passes a resolution requiring North Korea to accept special inspections

March 12   The DPRK announces that it intends to withdraw from the NPT

April 1   The IAEA Board of Governors finds North Korea in non-compliance with its safeguards obligations

May 11   UN Security Council Resolution 825 is passed. It calls on North Korea to comply with safeguards

1994

March 19   North Korea walks out of negotiations with the US after one delegate threatens to 'turn Seoul into a sea of fire'. Plans for 'Team Spirit' 1994 are reactivated

April 28   The DPRK declares that the 1953 Armistice Agreement is invalid

May 4	North Korea begins to discharge fuel from the 5 MW(e) reactor, affecting the IAEA's capacity to measure spent fuel
June 13	North Korea withdraws from the NPT
June 15	Former US President Jimmy Carter travels to Korea and meets with Kim Il-sung. The North Korean leader agrees to permit IAEA inspections, to cooperate with the recovery of American soldiers 'missing in action' from the Korean War, and to hold an inter-Korean summit with President Kim Young-sam in return for improved political relations and economic support
July 8	North Korean leader, Kim Il-sung dies of a heart attack. His son, Kim Jong-il, succeeds him as General-Secretary of the Korean Workers Party, but does not take the title of president
October 21	North Korea agrees with the US to dismantle nuclear development programme in return for 2 light water reactors and economic aid (Geneva Agreed Framework)
December 6	North Korean diplomats visit Washington, DC, in relation to the establishment of consular offices

1995

January 19	The first shipment of heavy fuel oil as part of the Agreed Framework arrives in Sonborg, North Korea
January 20	US announces easing of sanctions on North Korea relating to telecommunications, financial transactions, North Korean magnesite exports and energy projects
February	Joint US–ROK exercises 'Team Spirit' cancelled
March 9	KEDO is established as an international organization

August   Torrential rain and flooding causes a major natural disaster in North Korea

September   International aid sent to North Korea

December 15   The contract to supply LWR signed in New York

1996

July   The US and North Korean army begin to conduct joint operations to recover remains of American soldiers missing in action in the Korean War

September   A North Korean submarine transports commandoes to land on South Korea's east coast, provoking a major crisis on the peninsula

1997

February   Leading North Korean ideologue Hwan Chang-yop defects to South Korea

August   The groundbreaking ceremony for the construction of the light water reactors takes place in Sinpo, North Korea

August   The first preliminary round of the four-party talks to resolve the outstanding issues on the Korean peninsula takes place

December   Former opposition leader Kim Dae-jung is elected president. He goes on to pursue the 'sunshine policy' to engage North Korea

1998

August 1998   North Korea launches a long-range missile to launch a satellite. The partially successful launch appears to threaten Japan, provoking a serious reaction from Tokyo

1999

January   The last round of the Four-Party Talks ends inconclusively

September   On the basis of the Perry Report, the United States eases sanctions on North Korea

2000

February 9	The Russsian Federation and the DPRK sign a new Treaty of Friendship, Good-Neigbourliness and Cooperation
June 12	The first summit between North and South Korean leaders takes place in Pyongyang
October 9	North Korea's senior military leader, Cho Myong-rok (Vice-Chairman of the National Defence Committee), visits Washington and meets with President Clinton
October 23	Summit meeting between US Secretary of State Madeleine Albright and North Korean leader Kim Jong-il
November 3	Talks on North Korea's missile programme end inconclusively

2001

January 21	Inauguration of US President G. W. Bush
March 7	South Korean President Kim Dae-jung meets President Bush
June 6	President Bush announces the completion of the review of policy on North Korea

2002

January 29	President Bush includes North Korea as part of the 'axis of evil' in his State of the Union speech
October 3	While the US special envoy, James Kelly, visits North Korea, North Korea first denies and then apparently admits to having a programme to produce HEU (highly enriched uranium)
October 26	The United States, the Republic of Korea and Japan call upon North Korea to dismantle its HEU programme and comply with all its international commitments
November 14	KEDO suspends the shipment of Heavy Fuel Oil to North Korea

December 19   The Millennium Democratic Party Candidate Roh Moo-hyun is elected president of the Republic of Korea

December 22   North Korea announces that it will restart the nuclear reactor at Yongbyon and resume the reprocessong of plutonium

December 27   North Korea announces the expulsion of IAEA inspectors and ends all IAEA monitoring of its nuclear facilities

2003

January 10   North Korea announces its withdrawal from the nuclear non-proliferation treaty

May 12   North Korea declares the Agreed Framework to be nullified

April 23   Delegates from the United States, China and North Korea meet in Beijing to discuss the North Korean nuclear programme

August 27   The first round of Six-Party Talks, which includes North Korea, South Korea, the US, China, Russia and Japan, to solve North Korea nuclear crisis is convened in Beijing, China

2004

February 24   Second round of Six-Party Talks begins in Beijing

February 25   Bilateral meeting between DPRK and US delegates to the Six-Party Talks

February 28   Six-Party Talks end with agreement for a further round, but no progress in the substance

March 12   The National Assembly impeaches President Roh Moo-hyun. The impeachment is overturned two months later by the Constitutional Court

June 26   Third round of Six-Party Talks ends inconclusively after the US presents a comprehensive proposal including energy provision and

	a security guarantee in return for the dismantlement of North Korea's nuclear programme
September	North Korea postpones the next round of talks indefinitely

2005

May 11	North Korea announces it has completed the extraction of fuel rods from the nuclear reactor at Yongbyon
July 15	Fourth round of Six-Party Talks begins in Beijing
September 15	US bans all transactions with Banco Delta Asia Bank that is accused of handing illicit North Korean funds linked to money laundering, drug trafficking and counterfeiting of US currency, and freezes North Korean assets
September 19	In an agreed joint statement. North Korea agrees to give up its entire nuclear programme in exchange for energy assistance and security guarantees
September 20	North Korea states that it will only give up its nuclear programme if it gets a civilian nuclear reactor, in seeming contradiction to the joint statement

2006

January 3	North Korea states it will not return to talks unless the US releases frozen North Korean assets from Banco Delta Asia Bank
July 5	North Korea launches seven missiles including a long-range missile, *Taepodong-2*
July 15	The UN Security Council imposes sanctions on North Korea in response to the missile launches
October 9	North Korea conducts a test of a nuclear fission device
October 14	The UN Security Council imposes further sanctions on North Korea in response to the nuclear test

December 18   Six-Party Talks resume in Beijing

2007

February 13   North Korea pledges to dismantle nuclear weapons development programme in return for diplomatic recognition and economic aid

March 15   US enables the release of frozen North Korean bank accounts

April 14   North Korea misses the deadline to close down its reactor, but is given more time by the other parties

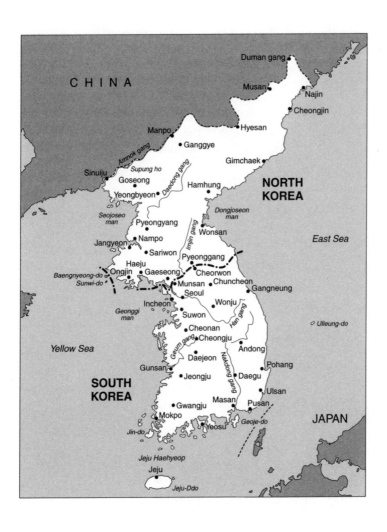

1 The Crisis on the Korean Peninsula

Early on the morning of 5 July 2006, seven missiles were launched from North Korea over the Sea of Japan. The launches were timed to take place shortly after the United States launched the space shuttle *Discovery* to celebrate Independence Day. One of the missiles, called the *Taepodong-2*, is presumed to be a prototype intercontinental range delivery system for nuclear weapons that may in future reach the territory of the United States. Its capabilities could not be assessed because it blew up shortly after launch, although some inferences can be made from previous launches. The announcement by the North Korean news agency KCNA on 9 October 2006 that the Democratic People's Republic of Korea (DPRK) had carried out an underground nuclear test marked a further escalation of the North Korean military threat and the culmination of a long confrontation over its nuclear programme. Once again the world was reminded that Korea is one of the critical flashpoints of international security today.

The division of Korea goes back to World War II when the Korean peninsula was partially occupied by Soviet troops. The southern part was under US occupation for three years. Efforts through the UN to end the occupation and create a unified Korea were rejected by the Soviet Union and thus the Democratic People's Republic of Korea in the North as well as the Republic of Korea (ROK) in the South were established in 1948. In 1950 North Korean armed forces, with the support of the Soviet Union, invaded the South. The Truman administration perceived this conflict as an act of communist aggression and quickly committed forces under the aegis of the UN which restored the status quo by 1953. The current division of Korea is a legacy of these events.

The Korean War was a devastating setback for the ambitions of North Korean leader Kim Il-sung with regard to the reunification of Korea as a socialist state. The US military presence in the ROK made this objective unachievable in the short term, so the DPRK focused on the reconstruction and development of the North Korean economy, without however abandoning the goal of unification. Between 1953 and 1962, the North Korean economy experienced a rapid growth in output. The emphasis was on heavy industry to fulfil the requirements of a military-industrial base, rather than consumer goods. North Korean GDP per head exceeded that of South Korea until the 1970s. North Korea nevertheless received grants and loans from the Soviet Union, China and various European socialist countries. The presence of Chinese forces in North Korea until the late 1950s relieved pressure on military expenditures.

The North Korean economy was a centrally planned economy similar to that of other socialist countries. It was organized on the principle of *juche*, national self-reliance. Even though North Korea did rely to some extent on foreign economic assistance and trade, it developed the world's most autarkic economy and did not even join the Council for Mutual Economic Assistance. Although an ally of the Soviet Union, the DPRK sought to reduce reliance on the Soviet Union and create a balance between relations with China and with the USSR.

In the 1960s, the DPRK embarked on a sustained military build-up in support of a more aggressive pursuit of reunification. The size of the armed forces grew from 300,000 to about a million by the end of the 1970s, and military preparedness was absorbing an increasing share of national output. As support from its traditional allies weakened, the correlation of forces on the Korean peninsula slowly changed.

The security dilemma of the Republic of Korea derives from the contest for the 'Korean nation' and the battle for legitimacy between North and South Korea. In the early years the Republic of Korea suffered from political factionalism and uneven economic growth, misallocation of resources and rent-seeking behaviour. Politically, militarily and to an extent economically it was dependent on the United States.

The authoritarian government of President Park Chung-hee (1961–1979) maintained societal stability and presided over a period of economic development and industrialization. At the same time there was considerable discontent with the authoritarian nature of the regime. Relations with the US deteriorated as human rights violations raised concerns and President Carter proposed the withdrawal of US forces from Korea. In 1979 President Park was assassinated by the director of the Korean Central Intelligence Agency. After a period of government dominated by the military under Chun Doo-hwan, pressure to move towards democracy increased in the wake of major civil society democratic movements in early 1987 and the 'Declaration of Democratization and Reforms' (29 June 1987). The political struggles culminated in the new constitutional arrangement with the presidential elections in 1987 and the election of the National Assembly in 1998.

The end of the Cold War heralded a reversal of the security dilemma on the Korean peninsula, which was the result of long-term political and economic trends. South Korea had become a prosperous country, with increasingly stable democratic political institutions. The economy of North Korea, on the other hand, was in serious decline. The main feature of the post-Cold War period is the weakness of the North Korean state. The principal factor determining North Korea's foreign policy is regime survival.

The collapse of communism in Russia and eastern Europe was a tremendous blow to Kim Il-sung and the elite of the DPRK. Already during the Gorbachev period in the 1980s, Soviet interest had begun shifting towards closer relations with the Republic of Korea. Since the end of the Cold War Russia has lost both the incentive and the capacity to provide assistance to North Korea, nor is sufficient assistance forthcoming from China. By 1992, both China and Russia had officially recognized the Republic of Korea.

Consequently, the economy of North Korea has virtually collapsed with the loss of cheap energy imports, the lack of manufactured goods from Russia and of other aid. In the years 1990–97, the North Korean economy decreased by 42.2 per cent. In addition to its basic inefficiency, agriculture was hit by natural disasters resulting in serious food shortages and starving people leaving North Korea for China. Material conditions of life for ordinary people have become almost unbearable.

The economic predicament is at the root of the problems of the North Korean regime. The options for halting, never mind reversing, the economic decline are extremely limited. Effectively it requires North Korea to obtain external support through trade and aid or credits. This is difficult because North Korea continues to represent a very unfavourable investment climate.

In response to this situation, North Korea has adopted what came to be called 'the triple survival strategy' of improving relations with the United States, Japan and other major capitalist countries, strengthening North Korea's 'own way of socialism' in domestic policy, and gradually opening up to the outside world.

Initial contacts with the United States, however, precipitated a major crisis over North Korea's nuclear programme. The United States suspected that North Korea was producing plutonium using a research reactor and concealing some of the nuclear material from international inspectors. In other words, the DPRK was pursuing nuclear weapons. As a result of negotiations with the United States, North Korea agreed to give up its plutonium programme in return for a range of political and economic concessions, including the provision of two light water reactors for electricity production. However, after George W. Bush assumed the presidency, the so-called Agreed Framework collapsed over allegations that North Korea was pursuing a second nuclear programme based on uranium enrichment technology. Since then North Korea is believed to have accumulated enough plutonium for about eight nuclear warheads and claims to possess nuclear weapons, and conducted a nuclear test in October 2006 which resolved any doubt about its capability to produce a nuclear detonation.

The perception of the North Korean threat is heightened by its ballistic missile industry based on Soviet-designed missiles, especially the so-called *Rodong* and *Taepodong*. Missile engineers in the DPRK have improved rocket engines and guidance systems and thereby increased the range of their missiles. North Korea has exported its missiles to countries like Pakistan, Iran, Iraq, Egypt and Libya and thereby has become one of the major proliferators of missile technology. This fact alone is a major issue of contention between the DPRK and the United States. But North Korea has also used its missile capability to threaten Japan. It has demonstrated the capability of building three-stage missiles which may in future provide the basis for an intercontinental missile capability.

The dynamics of the confrontation on the Korean peninsula

The crisis on the Korean peninsula has acquired a paradigmatic character for the sources of insecurity between states in the twenty-first century, when the confrontation between major powers has diminished and the principal threat to international security stems from crisis regions, such as South Asia or the Korean peninsula, so-called 'rogue states', or non-state actors, i.e. ethnic conflicts, civil wars in less developed regions and international terrorism. In this context, the threat of the proliferation of weapons of mass destruction (especially nuclear weapons) and ballistic missiles has become a central concern. Thus Korea presents an excellent case study of the sources of proliferation, the effectiveness of instruments of counterproliferation, and of dealing with 'rogue states' that have not integrated into the international community.

But the dynamics and the persistence of the confrontation on the Korean peninsula defies simple analysis. North Korean behaviour often *seems* irrational and unpredictable. The different perceptions of North Korea range from that of a brutal, dangerous dictatorship that must be contained and ultimately removed from power, to that of a small, desperate state that considers itself besieged by the most powerful country in the world. In the latter view, North Korea's seemingly aggressive behaviour is based on its search for security in a hostile world. The dilemma for scholars and policymakers alike is that there is a paucity of data that makes it very hard to know what is really going on in North Korea. There are persistent rumours about internal dissent and disagreements within the ranks of the military, military leaders and political leaders, but little hard evidence. On the other hand, the analysis of what drives the confrontation on the Korean peninsula is not just of theoretical interest. It has profound implications for policy and determines the risks that the Republic of Korea and other states in the region face and how they should deal with them. While some like China and South Korea actively pursue a policy of engaging the North, others like the United States and Japan favour a policy of containment and isolation.

This study is designed to provide an analytical historical account of the relations between the two Koreas since the Korean War, the domestic political and economic development of the two Korean states, their policies towards national security and unification, and the international context. It will present an analysis of the political systems and the development of state identities in Korea with a view to explaining perceptions of threats and security. In order to achieve this task, chapter 2 provides a brief history of the division of Korea, the origins of the Democratic People's Republic of Korea in the North and the Republic of Korea in the South, the Korean War and its aftermath. Chapter 3 is concerned with the evolution of the political system in the DPRK, the consolidation of the rule of Kim Il-sung and the succession of his son Kim Jong-il. It shows how the centrally planned economy of the DPRK developed in the 1950s with a primary emphasis on heavy industry, aided by support from the Soviet Union and China. The failure to reform and modernize as well as the excessive reliance on the support and the markets of other communist countries resulted in a precipitate decline of the economy when the Soviet Union and China withdrew their support as the Cold War came to an end to the point where

North Korea experienced serious and chronic food shortages. The chapter discusses the dilemma of economic reform in the North and assesses the reforms introduced in recent years, and examines the development of North Korea's policy with regard to the unification of Korea.

Chapter 4 traces the development of the Republic of Korea from the early period of military dictatorship to the emergence of a vibrant democracy and highly developed industrialized economy after years of social unrest. Chapter 5 discusses US policy towards North Korea and the crisis that resulted from the emergence of North Korea's nuclear programme. It analyses the various steps that led the DPRK to refuse demands from the International Atomic Energy Agency to conduct special inspections of its nuclear facilities that almost led to US military strikes against North Korea. A meeting between former President Jimmy Carter and Kim Il-sung marked the beginning of a process of negotiations resulting in the so-called Agreed Framework that froze North Korea's nuclear programme in return for economic support (including the provision of civil nuclear reactors), the development of political relations between the United States and the DPRK and security guarantees. The chapter assesses the achievements and weaknesses of the Agreed Framework and discusses possible lessons for the future.

Chapter 6 is concerned with the development of inter-Korean relations in the current era. It discusses the origins of a South Korean policy of engaging the North, dubbed the 'sunshine policy' by its architect, President Kim Dae-jung, and continued by his successor, Roh Moo-hyun. This policy represents a substantial shift from earlier policies towards the North which were predicated on deterring any aggression and isolating the DPRK as a non-legitimate entity. It resulted in the first-ever summit between North Korea's leader and South Korea's president. However, after the Bush administration came into office, relations with North Korea deteriorated as the Agreed Framework collapsed and North Korea resumed its nuclear programme. Chapter 7 discusses the renewed confrontation over the nuclear programme and the efforts to resolve it through the so-called Six-Party Talks, assesses the reason for the failure to achieve their objective so far and discusses the prospects for the future.

How can we assess the threat of the crisis on the Korean peninsula to international peace and security in the region and beyond? The threat has both a military and a political dimension. Chapter 8 provides a thorough assessment of the military dimension. This includes an analysis of the conventional military balance on the Korean peninsula as well North Korea's missile, nuclear, chemical and biological weapon capabilities. The political dimension is covered in chapter 9 which seeks to get to the core of the security dilemma in Korea, the threat perceptions that drive North Korean foreign policy behaviour, and the dilemmas facing the other powers in the region as they seek to avert conflict and consider the longer-term future of the Korean peninsula. Korea plays a crucial role in the geopolitics of North East Asia. At the same time, the prevention of the proliferation of nuclear weapons is a key issue in global international security and the North Korean case therefore has great significance as a test case for global counterproliferation policies. For all these reasons, the case of 'Hotspot Korea' provides valuable insights for the debate about the nature of the international system and approaches to international security in the twenty-first century.

2 | Korea: A Nation Divided

The origins of the Korean people can be traced far back into prehistoric times. There is evidence of human activity in the territory now known as the Korean peninsula about 500,000 years ago. According to legend, the origins of Korean history date back to 2333 BCE when the first kingdom called Joseon ('land of the morning calm') is said to have been established by King Tangun. Although the existence of Tangun remains disputed, it is believed by scholars that ancient Korea was composed of clan communities that joined to form small town-states. These gave rise, by the first century BCE, to three kingdoms on the Korean peninsula and part of a region that today is called Manchuria. These three kingdoms were called Paekche (18 BCE–660 CE) (in the south-east), Koguryo (31 BCE–688 CE) (in the north) and Shilla (57 BCE–935 CE)(in the south-west). In 668 CE, Shilla united most of the territory on the peninsula. After the end of Koguryo, Dae Jo-yeong, who had been a general in the Koguryo dynasty, founded the Balhae kingdom in the Jilin area of Manchuria in 698. The Balhae at their peak occupied a sizeable territory, but in 926 were destroyed by the Khitans (whose name is the origin of the Russian word for 'Chinese'). When the Shilla dynasty weakened, a warlord took over the entire state and established the Koryo dynasty (918–1392). The end of the Koryo dynasty came after almost five hundred years when a General Yi Seong-gye was sent to attack the forces of the Ming dynasty by the Korean court loyal to the Chinese Yuan dynasty.

General Yi turned against his own government, sided with the Ming and became the first king of the new dynasty that adopted the name Joseon in reference to the first kingdom in Korea's history. The Joseon dynasty lasted for over five hundred years (1392–1910). One of its notable figures was King Sejong the Great (1397–1450) who was an effective military planner and is best known for introducing *Hangul*, the Korean writing system which is still used today. Between 1492 and 1598, Korea suffered Japanese invasions which were finally repelled with help from China, and in the following century the Manchu Qing Dynasty invaded the peninsula. In the nineteenth century, Korea became a pawn in the power-game between the great imperialist nations (Russia, China and Japan) and was finally annexed and occupied by imperial Japan in 1910 (Han 1970; Palais 1975).

In addition to establishing political control over Korea and developing its economy to serve its own needs, Japan sought to dominate Korea socially and culturally, effectively seeking to destroy Korean culture. Koreans were required to learn Japanese, which became the official language of government, commerce and education, and had to adopt Japanese-style names. This went as far as forcing Koreans (even Korean Christians) to worship at Shinto shrines. Even though the Japanese modernized Korea's industry, their 35-year rule of Korea left a legacy of hatred of the oppressors that to some extent persists to the present day. Even though politically and even culturally the Republic of Korea is closer to Japan than any other country in the region, the past still makes it difficult for these countries to be the close allies that logically they should become. The experience also engendered a strong feeling of nationalism that is especially evident in North Korea today.

The occupation provoked the formation of a Korean independence movement which the Japanese tried ruthlessly to suppress. Some of the principal leaders formed the provisional government of Korea in Shanghai on 9 April 1919. They included Rhee Syngman, a conservative nationalist who later became the first president of the Republic of Korea, Kim Gu, who represented the moderate left, and Lee Dong-hwi, the father of the Korean communist movement. Kim Gu returned to Korea as President of the provisional government in August 1945 after World War II ended and the Japanese had been forced to leave Korea. The US Army occupation government disbanded his political coalition called the Democratic League (*Minjuuiwon*).

Although Lee Dong-hwi was the first premier of the provisional government, he resigned as the Korean communist movement was developing closer links with Russian communists. In 1918 the Korean People's Socialist Party (*Hanin Sahoedang*) was formed in Khabarovsk, Siberia. Moscow supported it financially and Lee returned to Manchuria in 1921 to organize armed raids into northern Korea. He eventually died in Siberia in 1928. Kim Il-sung (1912–1994) (birth name Kim Song-ju) portrayed himself as the father of the communist resistance movement against Japanese rule, but in fact he did not play a prominent role in either the independence movement or the Communist Party until 1934. In 1929 he was arrested by the Japanese just after joining the underground communist youth group. The official history promulgated by the Korean People's Army states that Kim Il-sung formed the army on 25 April 1932, but like much of the official version of Kim Il-sung's role in the communist movement and the anti-Japanese resistance, this bears little relation to reality. The anti-Japanese armed movements in Southern Manchuria were organized and led by Chinese fighters who had been trained by communists. It is true that Kim Il-sung created a sufficient profile as a successful military leader to catch the attention of some high-ranking Soviet officers and eventually he ended up in the Soviet Union. There he and his men were inducted into the Soviet Army and he was trained in preparation for a political role in post-war Korea (Quinones and Tragert 2003, p. 113). The task of defeating the Japanese fell to Soviet and American forces, and Kim Il-sung did not play an active role in the military campaign. After the detonation of the atomic weapons over Hiroshima and Nagasaki, Japan surrendered and, although the Soviet Union entered the war against Japan, Soviet forces were no longer required to intervene in the battle over the Japanese mainland.

According to an agreement with the United States, Soviet forces occupied the Korean peninsula north of the 38th parallel, whereas American forces occupied the more populous South, including the capital Seoul.

Kim Il-sung returned to Pyongyang on 19 September 1945. He and his fighters returned on the Soviet naval ship *Pugachev* that landed at the east-coast port of Wonsan. He was not exactly a national hero, but one Korean guerrilla fighter among many. Soviet leader Stalin had delegated the organization of a pro-Soviet government to the local officials in the Soviet Maritime Province. The Soviet occupation leaders had an important role in mind for Kim Il-sung, possibly minister of defence. O Jin-u was made police chief of Pyongyang and later became the top military leader of North Korea until his death in 1995. The first choice of leader for a Soviet-controlled government in North Korea was Cho Man-sik who had been the leader of the non-violent reformist movement. The Soviets supported the idea of a trusteeship by the Allied powers (the Soviet Union, the United States, Nationalist-ruled China and Britain) for five years rather than immediate independence for Korea. This plan, initially proposed by the United States, would maintain Korea as one unit rather than dividing it into independent zones. But among Korean leaders, North and South, this plan met with widespread opposition, and the United States began to distance itself from its own proposal. Cho Man-sik likewise opposed trusteeship and demanded immediate independence. Cho was increasingly at odds with the Soviet occupation authorities and was eventually placed into custody, as the Soviets put communists in charge of Korean administrative organs.

Why did the Soviet Union insist on a trusteeship for Korea? Research based on archival documentation that has become available since the dissolution of the Soviet Union shows that the authorities in Moscow did not really want a trusteeship. Their support for this policy was simply designed to gain time in order to establish a communist satellite regime loyal to the Soviet Union in the North. Kim Il-sung followed the Soviet line of the rejection of immediate independence or unification. Instead, he proposed that favourable conditions existed for building a new country in the North. This position was in diametrical opposition to that of the leader of the home-grown communist movement, Park Heon-young, who was based in Seoul and advocated a Korean People's Republic. In December 1945 Kim Il-sung became chairman of the North Korean branch of the Korean Communist Party and on 8 February 1946 chairman of the Interim People's Committee, thereby assuming the top Korean administrative position in the North (Martin 2004, p. 56). Although Kim supported Soviet policy, this does not mean that he expected Korea to be divided for long. On the contrary, as we will see, the unification of Korea under his leadership became a high priority for him once the North Korean state had established itself.

In the South, there was considerable opposition to the idea of a trusteeship among Korean political leaders. Conservative nationalists such as Rhee Syngman and the leader of the moderate left, the leader of the Korean provisional government (soon disbanded by the United States) Kim Gu found the idea that Korea should remain divided and under foreign rule unacceptable. The effort to establish a multilateral temporary trusteeship to govern Korea ran into the ground. The United States brought a proposal before the United Nations General Assembly (UNGA) to establish a UN Temporary Commission on Korea. This was adopted by the UNGA alongside a resolution for elections to be held by 31 March 1948 to choose representatives that would ultimately constitute a National Assembly and lead to a form of Korean national government. The North refused to participate, would not admit UN observers and was accused of launching a terrorist campaign in the South to prevent the elections from taking place. In fact, the North gave guerrilla training to 2,000 Southerners who were then sent back to start a terrorist campaign. The elections were held in the South finally on 10 May 1948. Even before the votes had been counted, a National Assembly was formed that elected Rhee Syngman as its chairman. The UN ratified the elections on 25 June as a proper expression of the will of two thirds of the Korean people. On 17 July, the National Assembly adopted a constitution for the Republic of Korea which the United States recognized as the sole legitimate government of the people of Korea. Rhee Syngman was elected president of the ROK by the National Assembly. Soon after that, on 10 September 1948, the North Koreans proclaimed the Democratic People's Republic of Korea (DPRK) which claimed to have jurisdiction over the whole of Korea. Thus two Korean states came into being, both of which claimed to be the sole legitimate Korea. Kim Il-sung became chairman of the Supreme People's Council of the DPRK and thus premier of the country.

Until recently, various theories have been advanced about the origins of the Korean War in 1950 and in particular the role played by the Soviet Union. American leaders were convinced that the attack by North Korean forces in June 1950 represented an expansionist move by the Soviet Union. The standard historical accounts, such as those by David Rees and David Dallin, asserted that the war was planned and initiated by the Soviet Union (Rees 1964; Dallin 1961). Revisionist historian Bruce Cumings (1981, 1990) on the other hand raised doubts about the Soviet role and claimed that the Soviet hold over North Korea was tenuous and Kim Il-sung did not need to ask Stalin for permission. He even claimed that it was uncertain whether North or South Korea was to blame for the outbreak of the Korean War. Indeed the North has always claimed that it was responding to an attack from the South that was a provocation it could not ignore.

However, Soviet documents that have been found in archives opened since the end of the Cold War have shown both the traditional and the revisionist accounts to be unsustainable. These documents include various telegrams which report meetings between Kim Il-sung and Soviet or Chinese officials and leaders, as well as a complete, top-secret internal Soviet history of the origins of the Korean War (Weathersby 1993). The following account is based on these documents.

Although the division of Korea was complete, it was not accepted by the leaders in the North or the South. Rhee Syngman announced in March 1950 that South Korean forces would cross the 38th parallel to respond to South Korea's brothers who were 'crying in distress'. The problem for the South Korean government was the relative weakness of the

South Korean armed forces and the total opposition of the US government to any move northwards. The United States refused to grant the Koreans access to heavy weapons and aircraft and even restricted their supply of ammunition in order to prevent any military adventures. In the meantime, Kim Il-sung made a tremendous effort to build up the armed forces of the DPRK with support from the Soviet Union. In March 1949, Kim Il-sung asked Stalin to support his plan to unite the peninsula. He was going to 'prod the South with the point of a bayonet'. He believed there would be an uprising against the US puppet government and that the people's power would triumph. Stalin opposed any move south of the 38th parallel except in response to a South Korean attack and Kim Il-sung left empty-handed. Soviet troops were withdrawn from North Korea in 1948. Later in 1949, during August and September, Kim had another go. This time he claimed the South was planning to attack the North but pledged to send his troops only in response to an attack from the South. General Shyktov, Soviet Ambassador to the DPRK, was instructed to deliver the following message to Kim Il-sung:

From the military side it is impossible to consider that the People's Army is prepared for such an attack. If not prepared for in the necessary manner, the attack can turn into a prolonged military operation, which not only will not lead to the defeat of the enemy but will also create significant political and economic difficulties for North Korea, which, finally, cannot be permitted. Since at present North Korea does not have the necessary superiority of military forces in comparison with South Korea, it is impossible to acknowledge that a military attack on the south is now completely prepared for and therefore from the military point of view it is not allowed.

From the political side, a military attack on the south by you is also not prepared for. We, of course, agree with you that the people are waiting for the unification of the country and in the south they, moreover, are waiting for liberation from the yoke of the reactionary regime. However, until now very little has been done to raise the broad masses of South Korea to an active struggle, to develop the partisan movement in all of South Korea, to create there liberated regions and to organize forces for a general uprising. Meanwhile, only in conditions of a people's uprising which has begun and is truly developing, which is undermining the foundations of the reactionary regime, could a military attack on the south play a decisive role in the overthrow of the South Korean reactionaries and provide the realization of the task of the unification of all Korea into a single democratic state. Since at present very little has been done to develop the partisan movement and prepare for a general uprising in South Korea, it is also impossible to acknowledge that from a political side an attack by you on the south has been prepared . . . Moreover, it is necessary to consider that if military actions begin at the initiative of the North and acquire a prolonged character, then this can give to the Americans cause for any kind of interference in Korean affairs. (APV-RF 1949, cited in Weathersby 1993)

During a visit to Moscow in March/April in the same year, Kim finally managed to persuade Stalin to support his plan. Kim then went to see Mao in May 1950 to get his approval. According to the internal Soviet history, Kim made the case that the United States was not going to intervene in such a conflict. He argued that the military balance was such that North Koreans would overwhelm the South within three days, not giving the United States any time to intervene, that the 200,000 Communist Party members in the South would take part in an uprising against the hated regime led by Rhee Syngman and that North Korean forces would be supported by guerrillas in the South. The perception that the United States would not intervene may have arisen in part because, due to domestic political pressures, the United States engaged in a global reduction of forces. US forces had been withdrawn entirely from the Korean peninsula by June 1949. In January 1950, President Truman made a remark to the effect that at the present time there would be no American defence of Taiwan. There is no doubt that this statement was overinterpreted, given that Truman was strongly committed to the worldwide containment of communism. Indeed the official policy of the US government, as it was understood by officials, was that containment did apply to Korea and the Pentagon was considering the contingencies for reintroducing American troops under the aegis of the United Nations should an attack be launched. But in Seoul Truman's statement was read as suggesting that the US would not come to the defence of the Republic of Korea in the event of an attack from the North, and Stalin and Mao Zedong likewise seem to have concluded that the United States would not take any risks for Korea. Secretary of State Dean Acheson strengthened this impression when, in his description of the US defence perimeter, various Asian-Pacific countries were included, but Korea was not mentioned. The United States was downplaying its commitment to Korea because they did not want to encourage any belligerence on the part of the Rhee government which was straining at the bit to have a go at the North. The evidence now available leads to the conclusion that the outbreak of the Korean War constituted a massive failure of deterrence.

All North Korean requests to its allies for the supply of arms and equipment to increase the size of the army were met. China sent a division of soldiers formed from ethnic Koreans who had been serving in the Chinese army. Kang Kon, the Chief of the General Staff of the Korean People's Army (KPA), announced at the end of May with the concurrence of Soviet advisors that the army was ready. The 'Pre-emptive Strike Operational Plan' on which the invasion of the South was based had been drawn up by Soviet military planners and translated into Korean. Soviet military advisors in North Korea were replaced by experienced military specialists, led by Lieutenant General Bashilev who had made his reputation in the Soviet–German war. As they were getting ready for war, the armed forces of the DPRK enjoyed substantial superiority over the South. According to Soviet data, they had twice the number of troops, six and a half times the number of tanks and six times the number of planes.

The North Korean offensive began on 25 June 1950 at 4 a.m. Southern forces were caught by surprise as seven divisions moved towards Seoul. They managed to stall the Northern army for two days to allow people to flee south. But on the third day resistance collapsed and the KPA entered Seoul. The ease with which they accomplished this objective surprised North Korean military leaders. Due to the central importance of the capital, they thought the war was all but won. Not everything went according to plan, however. In particular, the expected uprising in the South never materialized. Whatever support there may have been for the North seemed to vanish as North Korean soldiers started rounding up and shooting 'reactionaries'. More importantly, the United States immediately decided to support South Korea and sent aircraft and anti-tank weapons while Truman went to the United Nations to get a Security Council resolution in support of South Korea. As the Soviet Union was boycotting the Security Council at the time over the issue of the admission of Mongolia into the UN, it was unable to veto the resolution which then took effect and UN forces led by the United States were sent to Korea. The North Korean forces facilitated the regrouping of Southern forces and the external intervention by halting their advance for two days after capturing Seoul.

The entry of UN forces into the war did not immediately turn the situation around. The KPA continued its advance and about a hundred miles south of Seoul defeated an entire US Army division. Six weeks into the war, the North Korean forces had occupied all of the Korean mainland except for a defence perimeter around the southern port of Busan. Kim Il-sung gave his troops a strict deadline to conquer Busan, but the massive use of American airpower defeated this effort and deprived the North Korean forces of their logistical support. The entire communications network of the KPA collapsed, making it impossible to pass down orders. General MacArthur launched his counter-attack with a daring and controversial amphibious assault at Incheon on the coast west of Seoul, 200 km behind enemy lines. The KPA troops in the South were cut off from their logistic support. The operation was a success and three weeks later North Korean forces had been expelled from the South. MacArthur persuaded Washington that the objectives of the war should be widened and UN forces moved across the 38th parallel into the North, soon occupying Pyongyang. MacArthur called upon the defeated KPA to surrender, but Kim Il-sung ordered them to fight to the death. Meanwhile he pleaded to Stalin and Mao for help. The Chinese were ready. They had watched the progress of the war with great anxiety and it was clear to them that the KPA was not strong enough to achieve its goals. After the landing at Incheon, Mao had concluded that China needed to intervene. The crossing of the 38th parallel raised the prospect of a unified Korea occupied by the United States that was considered an unacceptable situation from the standpoint of China's national security. Once again both deterrence and reassurance were ineffective – Mao was convinced that the United States would not resort to nuclear weapons, but he rejected US Secretary of State Dean Acheson's reassurance that the United States had no intention of attacking China. China also came under Soviet pressure to intervene, as the Soviet Union did not want to send its own troops but nevertheless wanted to avert a total defeat by the North Koreans. Although the liberation of Taiwan was China's priority, the Politburo decided on 2 October 1950 to come to the aid of the North Koreans. In October and November, hundreds of thousands of Chinese troops entered Korea to join the fighting. Kim Il-sung effectively lost control over the military command which was in the hands of Chinese commanders. Soon UN troops were pushed back south and Chinese and North Korean forces reoccupied Seoul on 4 January 1951. They in turn were beaten back by three months of intensive and bloody combat and eventually retreated across the 38th parallel.

MacArthur wanted to defeat the Chinese by carrying the war onto Chinese territory. His plan was for Chinese nationalists based on Taiwan to attack the mainland while supported by US air attacks, including the use of atomic weapons. President Truman himself had discussed the use of atomic weapons at a press conference on 30 November 1950, but he made it clear to MacArthur that he would only support limited objectives for the war. This meant no attempt to reoccupy North Korea and no attack on China. The disagreement between the general and the president became public and so bitter that Truman sacked MacArthur on 10 April 1951 for insubordination. On 27 June 1951, the Soviet Union proposed negotiations for an armistice. Such negotiations began on 10 July but dragged on while fighting continued. The issue of the exchange of prisoners of war became especially contentious as the US insisted that POWs should be free to stay in South Korea if they did not want to return to the North or China. Truman's successor, Dwight Eisenhower, eventually threatened to widen the war by attacking China and his Secretary of State, John Foster Dulles, passed China a message through Indian Prime Minister Nehru that the US might resort to nuclear weapons. Josef Stalin died on 5 March 1953, but it remains unclear what impact, if any, this had on negotiations. On 27 July 1953, near the small village of Panumjom, an armistice agreement was finally signed by representatives of the United Nations, the People's Republic of China and the DPRK. There was no South Korean signature as Rhee Syngman wanted the war to continue until the whole of Korea was liberated. The agreement established a demilitarized zone (DMZ) two-and-a-half miles wide along a border that left the North and South more or less where they were before the war (although part of the town of Gaesong was now in the North) (Hastings 1988).

The human cost of the Korean War was enormous. An estimated two million Koreans died, including soldiers and civilians north and south. According to US official data, 54,246 Americans died, 103,284 were wounded and 8,177 were missing in action. No official Chinese data have been published, but some estimates put the number of Chinese deaths at 900,000 (Quinones and Tragert 2003, p. 131).

The Korean War was a disaster for Kim Il-sung. Not only did it completely fail to achieve its objectives and resulted in enormous casualties, but the fighting and large-scale American bombing had destroyed the country completely. Without the Chinese intervention Kim would have lost everything and would have had to flee the country. The official version of the Korean War that Kim promulgated in North Korea and that remains the unshakeable dogma in the DPRK is that the war was started by the South at the instigation of the Americans. Under the leadership of Kim Il-sung, the KPA gloriously defended the country and vanquished the aggressor. After the war, the United States formally agreed a defence pact with the Republic of Korea and continued to station forces on its territory. Similar agreements were made with China,

Russia and the DPRK (although Chinese forces were eventually withdrawn). A stable deterrence relationship was established on the Korean peninsula that ruled out another full-scale war, establishing the division of Korea for an indefinite period of time.

North Korea after the Korean War: The Long March to Ruin

The emergence of Stalinism, Korean style

The Korean War was a devastating setback for the North Korean leader Kim Il-sung's ambitions for the reunification of Korea as a socialist state. Moreover, his having led the country into a catastrophic and unsuccessful war created some degree of political vulnerability for Kim Il-sung himself. North Korea suffered about 300,000 military and 400,000 civilian casualties; its cities and factories had been virtually destroyed by UN bombing and agriculture had suffered to such an extent that only food aid from China and the Soviet Union prevented large-scale starvation. The war precipitated an internal power struggle between the various communist factions in Korea. The South Korean communists ceased to be a factor as the predicted uprising of the South Korean people against the right-wing government based in Seoul had failed to materialize. The leader of the Southern communists in North Korea, Park Heon-young, was executed in 1955. Another group that might have threatened Kim's authority was the Soviet group that had spent most of World War II in the Soviet Union and was close to the Soviet leadership. Its most prominent figure, Ho Ka-i, committed suicide in the course of a campaign instigated against him in the Korean Workers' Party. A prominent military leader of the Yanan group, Mu Chong, the commander of the 2nd corps of the Korean People's Army, was dismissed and accused of various crimes so he might shoulder the blame for the military defeats following the Incheon landing. But the threat to Kim did not only come from the political and military elite. The American advance into North Korea had painfully revealed how fickle the loyalty of the ordinary people to the regime really was. This was also indicated by the fact that more than three million North Koreans fled to the South before the war ended. Kim tried to mobilize the masses and shore up his support by recruiting large numbers of people, mostly from a poor peasant background, into the KWP.

The political struggle was reflected in an ideological conflict that gripped the North Korean leadership in the years 1953–5 and which resembled that taking place in the Soviet Union. Kim Il-sung advocated large investment in heavy industry, whereas his opponents from the Soviet-Korean group led by Park Chang-ok and the Yanan group headed by Choi Chang-ik supported greater investment in light industry, consumer goods and agriculture, along the lines of the reformers under Malenkov in the post-Stalin USSR (Buzo 1999, p. 23). Kim attacked his opponents for uncritically following new policies in the Soviet Union and began to stress the need to apply Marxism-Leninism to the political, economic and cultural circumstances of the Korean situation. Under Kim's inspiration and guidance, North Korea developed its own ideology that was an indigenous, nationalistic form of communism. The central concept that would govern it is called *juche*. It was first introduced with a new ideological meaning by Kim Il-sung when he addressed a meeting of Korean Workers' Party propaganda and agitation workers on 28 December 1955, although it was not fully developed until the 1960s. The word *juche* is often translated as self-reliance, but it has a subtle variety of meanings. The many North Korean (and some Western) writings on the subject have not clarified its definition. It is best understood as symbol of the essence of the North Korean ideal for its own society. The Korean Central News Agency explained it in the following way:

Juche is [a] Korean word. It means the subject in English . . .
'The revolution in each country should be carried out

responsibly by its own people, the masters, in an independent manner, and in a creative way suitable [to] its specific conditions.' It raised the fundamental question of philosophy by regarding man as the main factor, and elucidated the philosophical principle that man is the master of everything and decides everything. (Oh and Hassig 2000, p. 16)

In his 1955 speech, Kim Il-sung stressed that patriotism and internationalism were intrinsically linked to each other. 'We are not engaged in any other country's revolution, but solely in the Korean revolution (Kim 1982, pp. 395–6). This meant adapting the principles of Marxism-Leninism rather than blindly following the example of other countries. The speech was clearly part of a process of legitimizing his own rule and the elimination of his opponents. Moreover, Kim did not want the DPRK to remain a puppet of the Soviet Union like the central European states. In some respects this was a difficult proposition. It was hard to speak about 'self-reliance' when the Soviet Union and China were pouring aid in to rebuild North Korea's industries after the devastation of the Korean War. It was also a delicate issue, given that the Soviets had put Kim Il-sung in power in the first place, and, even though Soviet forces had by now been withdrawn from the DPRK, the intention had clearly been to create a state loyal to the leadership in Moscow. The relationship with China had to be treated with even greater care because China essentially saved the DPRK by its intervention in the war and Chinese troops were still in the country (not being withdrawn until 1958).

Under the direction of Kim Il-sung, the DPRK developed a political and economic command system along Stalinist lines. Resources were concentrated to mobilize the workforce for rapid industrialization based on targets set in a central plan. At the same time, agriculture was collectivized, thus concentrating all the means of production in the hands of the state. By the time of the Third Congress of the KWP in April 1956, Kim had established considerable control over the party, as key members of the early elite of the DPRK had disappeared from view (Nam 1974; Lankov 2002; Buzo 1999).

Ironically, these developments occurred at the same time as the Soviet Union underwent the process of de-Stalinization under the leadership of Nikita Khrushchev. Khrushchev's denunciation of Stalin in the so-called 'secret speech' provoked a wave of liberalization in eastern Europe that threatened Moscow's control and resulted in retrenchment whose worst manifestation was the intervention in Hungary. The situation in North Korea was in many respects the opposite of that in eastern Europe. What troubled the Soviet leadership was the failure of the DPRK leadership to adopt Soviet reforms and the purge of the pro-Soviet elements of the political elite. Consequently, Moscow and Beijing forced Kim to reinstate some of them in September 1956. But this did not last long and by the First Party Conference of the KWP in 1958, the Soviet-Koreans had been expelled from the party. Kim Il-sung had taken a decisive step towards the consolidation of his own personal authority which was to become the dominant feature of the political system of the DPRK.

The political institutions of the DPRK were modelled on the Stalinist system of the Soviet Union. The Korean Workers' Party (Choson Rodong-dang), similar to the communist parties in China and the Soviet Union during the heyday of communism, controls the government and the army. There are two other parties: the Korean Social Democratic Party (called the Democratic Party of the Koreas before the 1980s) formed by businessmen, merchants, craftsmen and Christians in 1945; and the Chondist Chongu Party, a nationalist party of followers of the Chondogyo religion founded by Kim Tarhyon. The latter was purged in 1958 and its leadership arrested and probably executed. It retains a nominal existence but its activities are directed by the government.

The supreme party organ is the Party Congress which is supposed to be convened every five years. In practice, the Party Congress ceased to be a forum for debate on policy after Kim purged all the other factions of the KWP and eventually it seems Kim no longer felt any need to convene the Party Congress (the sixth and last one was held in 1980). Although the latter was supposed to elect the members of the Central Committee, in reality the members were chosen by Kim

Il-sung (now by his son Kim Jong-il). The Central Committee has 160 full members and 143 alternate (candidate) members (Lankov 2002). It has in practice become the most powerful party organ. It elects the general secretary of the party, the Standing Committee, the Politburo and nominates candidates for the leading positions in government. The Politburo (called the Political Committee until 1980) does not seem to have the significance of the equivalent committee in the USSR, where after Stalin it essentially was the ruling committee of the country. Although made up of high-ranking members of the political elite, it seems to have functioned purely as a support and advisory group to Kim Il-sung and Kim Jong-il after him.

The Supreme People's Assembly (SPA) is North Korea's parliament with 687 members elected for five-year terms (although these elections are strictly controlled by the party with only one candidate for each seat). Its main task is to approve the state budget. The head of the Presidium of the SPA (currently Kim Yong-nam) carries out many of the functions of a head of state and is given the appropriate diplomatic recognition. The government consists (in principle) of a cabinet of ministers called the Central People's Committee headed by Kim Jong-il (and his father before him) who nominates all its members. The work of the cabinet is led by the prime minister who essentially carries out the policies of the leader. Under the constitution adopted in 1972, Kim Il-sung became president of the DPRK.

The structure of political institutions in the DPRK is of secondary relevance because during the 1960s Kim Il-sung consolidated his power position to the point where he could no longer be challenged. He shaped the political elite by ruthlessly purging his opponents, often to the point of executing the leading figures, until all other factions of the KWP had been for all intents and purposes eliminated. He controlled the economy through the central planning mechanisms and the state budget. He combined a unifying ideology that stressed the unique political path of the DPRK in combination with an indigenous version of socialism supposed to produce a militarily strong, economically prosperous and socially egalitarian society with a personality cult that painted him as the father of the nation ('the Great Leader') whose deep wisdom was not open to challenge. The party developed sophisticated methods of social control that extended to the lowest level of housing neighbourhoods. Any deviations from the social norms or political loyalty to Kim were subject to very severe sanctions, which could include lengthy sentences in prison camps under appalling, life-threatening conditions, or even execution. The only institution that in principle might have been able to challenge Kim Il-sung was the military, but even there Kim relentlessly applied the principles of patronage and purging to ensure that the top and the middle-ranking military leaders were completely loyal. Any sign of disloyalty was dealt with ruthlessly.

In the early 1970s, Kim Il-sung chose his son Kim Jong-il to be his successor. This in itself shows how tightly all power had been concentrated in one person, clearly a substantial deviation from socialist principles as enunciated by North Korea's Academy of Social Sciences which until 1970 denounced hereditary succession as a reactionary custom of exploitative societies (Oh and Hassig 2000, p. 87). Although Kim Il-sung is said to have begun grooming his son for leadership in the 1960s, the first clear indications came in 1971 and 1972. In 1973, Kim Jong-il was appointed party secretary in charge of the Organization and Guidance Department, as well as the Politburo. He also received the designation 'leader of the party and the people'. These appointments put Kim right at the centre of power in the DPRK. He began his activities with a campaign of ideological mobilization centred around the *juche* ideology and loyalty to the Great Leader. Officials from his department went around the country to promote this campaign and make it clear that Kim Jong-il would be the next leader. A central purpose of his activity was to begin with the consolidation of his power. Many in the party were seeking his favour, and the younger Kim sought the allegiance and support of powerful figures in the elite. A large number of officials were replaced as younger people under the patronage of the younger Kim were promoted. A purge of those who might oppose him began. A prominent example is the mysterious death of Nam Il in 1976, who died when his car was destroyed by a truck (an unlikely accident given the scarcity of automobiles in North Korea). Another example is that of Vice Prime Minister Kim Dong-kyu who dared to criticize Kim Jong-il in1976 and was sent to a prison camp where he eventually died (Oh and Hassig 2000, p. 82).

Recent research has confirmed that Kim Jong-il began largely to run the North Korean government in the 1980s as his father, 'the Great Leader', retreated into semi-retirement and representational duties. The significance of the son's role remained obscure to some extent because Kim Jong-il eschewed public appearances and did his work behind the scenes. While initially this might have been explained by the fact that his father was still the 'Great Leader' and president of the country, this style of governance has persisted beyond Kim Il-sung's death to the present day. Kim Jong-il was designated as the successor at the Sixth KWP Party Congress in October 1980 where he was elected to various high party posts. From then on a personality cult began to form around Kim Jong-il, and he followed his father's practice of 'on-the-spot' inspections where he would dispense guidance to farmers, workers, members of the armed forces (his favourite) and anyone else he came across. Any hopes that with a new generation led by Kim Jong-il there would be a shift towards more modern policies and practices were soon dispelled. Making himself the authoritative voice of *juche* through the publication of standard works and articles on his behalf, the younger Kim reaffirmed the ideology and governance developed by his father. If anything, he seemed to be even more hardline in his attitudes towards both the West and the other Korea. Thus various terrorist actions were operations sanctioned by Kim Jong-il, possibly without his father's knowledge. These included the attempt to assassinate South Korean president Chun Doo-hwan in Burma in 1983. North Korean agents detonated a previously planted bomb prematurely by mistake and ended up killing four members of the South Korean cabinet (including Foreign Minister Lee Bum-suk), two presidential advisors and the South Korean ambassador to Burma. South Korean government officials later expressed the belief that North Korea had prepared to send commandos into the South in the aftermath of Chun's anticipated death in order to stir up unrest. Then there was the bombing of KAL Flight 858 in 1987 which killed 115 South Koreans.

In 1991, Kim Jong-il was appointed Supreme Commander of the armed forces, even though he did not have any military experience. There was some dissatisfaction in the ranks; according to Lim Yong-son, a military officer who defected in 1993, there was a belief among officers that if Kim was to lead the army into a war his inexperience would mean defeat. The propaganda machine was used to create a fictional military career to give this appointment some credibility. The constitution stipulated that Kim Il-sung was the supreme commander, so an adjustment of the constitution became necessary. It was one of the many ways in which power was passing from father to son. In April 1992, Kim Jong-il was awarded the highest military rank in the DPRK, that of Marshal. There was only one other soldier with that status, Defence Minister O Jin-u who made a significant effort to persuade the military to accept the younger Kim's leadership before his death in 1995. In 1993, Kim was appointed head of the KWP Military Commission.

According to Hwang Jang-yop, a member of the inner circle of the North Korean leadership who was the chief theoretician developing the concepts of the *juche* philosophy and who defected to South Korea in 1997, the appointment of Kim Jong-il to the supreme command of the armed forces marked the transition of power from father to son (Oh and Hassig 2000).

Kim Il-sung seemed to become increasingly withdrawn from the affairs of state. He briefly returned to the centre stage in 1994 in the course of the crisis with the United States that arose over North Korea's nuclear programme when he accepted the conditions for a deal with the United States during a meeting with former US president, Jimmy Carter. This matter is discussed in more detail in chapter 5.

On 8 July 1994, Kim Il-sung died of a heart attack at the age of 82. The circumstances of his death in his mansion at Mount Myohyang remain somewhat mysterious, but testimony from defectors (such as Chong Il-shim who assisted him with his memoirs) seems to indicate that this was a time when the Great Leader became very enthusiastic about improving relations with the South, leading possibly to unification, and expressed serious dissatisfaction with the way in which his son was running the country's affairs. He was preparing for a breakthrough summit meeting with South Korean president Kim Young-sam that had been agreed in the course of negotiations about the nuclear issue. The elder Kim expressed his desire to abandon the emphasis on military affairs and improve the living standards of ordinary people. Having been cut off from detailed information for some time, he now had become aware of the dire state of the national economy. There was a telephone conversation with his son when Kim Jong-il told his father to enjoy his retirement and he would take care of everything. Kim Il-sung was so angry that he asked to be left alone for one hour. When the Great Leader was discovered after his heart attack, it turned out that his full medical team was not present at the resort. Two helicopters rushed towards the presidential residence, but the one with the medical equipment on board crashed. Nothing could be done and the Great Leader died. More recently, on the basis of testimony of people who were present at the time, suspicions have been raised that Kim Jong-il deliberately contrived to prevent medical support for his ailing father (Martin 2004, p. 507; also based on extensive interviews in Seoul in 2005).

Kim Il-sung's death was followed by a three-year period of mourning. Kim Jong-il did not immediately take up the formal positions of leadership occupied by his father, such as president and general secretary of the KWP. Moreover, there was a notable emphasis in public propaganda on the role of the armed forces. This led to speculation in the West that Kim Jong-il, who came to be referred to as the 'Dear Leader', had not convinced the military leadership yet that he should succeed his father and that he was not in full control of the country. Although we have many indications that there was widespread contempt for Kim Jong-il, there was no power struggle and the transition of power had already largely taken place. Indeed, promotion of the personality cult around the 'Dear Leader' continued apace. Hwang Jang-yop has rejected the notion of alternative centres of power in North Korea:

> Who is in charge? No one has real power. You should know that clearly. Suppose a person comes to the fore in the diplomatic field. This does not mean he has real power. As for the *chuche* idea, I had given guidance to the overall work for the *chuche* idea for almost 20 years. However, I did not have real power. We should know the North Korean structure. Only Kim Chong-il has real power. (Cited in Oh and Hassig 2000, p. 91)

On 8 October 1997, Kim Jong-il was confirmed as general secretary of the KWP and the Chairman of the National Defence Commission. In 1998 it was confirmed that the latter was the highest office of state. The chairman is elected by the SPA every five years, and Kim has occupied the position ever since. The position of president was practically abolished by a constitutional change that proclaimed Kim Il-sung to be the 'eternal president'.

As will be discussed in more detail below, in the 1990s the DPRK suffered a severe economic decline and a catastrophic shortage of food. But the expected collapse of the country did not materialize as Kim managed to maintain control over the country. In recent years there have been some indications of disagreements among the political elite and some loosening of social controls. On 22 April 2004, there was a major explosion in Rongjon near the Chinese border involving a train carrying explosives for construction just nine hours after a train had passed through, taking Kim Jong-il back from a visit to China. There has been some speculation that this was an assassination attempt, possibly masterminded by Chang Song-taek, Kim's brother-in-law and a feared and powerful figure in the DPRK. Chang apparently fell from grace in late 2004 and was under house arrest for a while, but there is no clear evidence to prove that this event was anything more than an accident. In early 2005 there was a lot of speculation about a possible coup as Kim Jong-il's portraits disappeared from public view and there were indications of serious discontent among sections of the military. Whatever the truth behind these rumours, Kim appears to have strengthened his position by promoting younger cadres to official positions in the government and the military. Any challenge to Kim's absolute rule seems to have been defeated for now.

North Korea's economy: from industrial miracle to terminal decline

When Korea was divided after the Japanese occupation, most of Korea's industry was located in the North (e.g. 80 per cent of heavy industry, 92 per cent of electricity generating capacity), whereas most of the agricultural production was in the South. This was partly the result of Japanese policies and the geography of the peninsula. Under Kim Il-sung's leadership, the economy of the DPRK was developed on the basis of the Stalinist example. In 1947 the first economic plan was put in place whose main target was to increase industrial production by 54 per cent over the period 1946–7. The general premise was that the state would control all means of production and the first plan involved the nationalization of major industries. According to official statistics, in the second year production increased by 38 per cent. Starting from a very low level, the DPRK was able to achieve truly impressive increases in output, which bolstered Kim Il-sung's confidence as he was planning to unite the country by force. The war had a devastating impact on the economy as the United States used more ordnance in bombing North Korea than it had during the whole of World War II. Practically the entire economy was destroyed. Although this was a huge setback in many respects, it was also an advantage as it gave Kim Il-sung the opportunity to rebuild North Korea's economic infrastructure from scratch. Massive aid to prevent starvation and help rebuild the country flowed in from the Soviet Union and China. The Chinese army was an important source of manpower during the early years as Kim Il-sung sought to mobilize the population as best as possible for the task. By the end of 1956, industrial production was greater than before the war. In 1956, Kim Il-sung declared the principle of *juche* as the guiding principle of the economy. Although the DPRK was still heavily reliant on external support from China and the USSR, Kim was planning to create a base for heavy industry that would enable the country to become as self-sufficient as possible. Just as the DPRK was maintaining a close relationship with both China and the Soviet Union in order to maintain as much political independence as possible, it also declined to join the Council for Mutual Economic Assistance (CMEA) that governed the economic relations between the Soviet Union and other countries loyal to Moscow.

By 1959, North Korean industry had been fully nationalized. Kim also proceeded with the rapid collectivization of agriculture. In 1946 land had been taken away from Japanese and Korean landlords and redistributed; from 1954, the state took the land away from individual farmers and, by August 1958, the North Korean government announced the completion of privatization. Individual families were allowed to keep very small plots but spent their time mostly working on the collective farm for a wage. But external support for the North Korean economy was reducing and the Chinese soldier-workers returned home in 1959. This situation confronted Kim Il-sung with the problem of how to keep the rapid development of the economy of the DPRK on track as the state had taken over all means of production. Kim responded with a nationwide mobilization of the working population. This campaign was called the Chollima movement, named after a mythical Korean horse that could leap about 250 kilometres and rapidly cover great distances. In a manner reminiscent of Mao's Great Leap Forward, it sought to organize the workers and push them towards great feats of productivity. The results looked impressive. The goals of the Five-Year Plan starting in 1957 were reached after four years. Annual production growth rate during this period was 41 per cent (Oh and Hassig 2000, p. 49). But just as in the Soviet economy, ambitious quantitative targets were achieved at the expense of quality, and resulted in sectoral imbalances. The final year was designated a buffer year to correct the imbalances in the economy that had arisen through the misallocation of resources and serious production bottlenecks. The advantages of nationalization and mobilization were to reach their limits soon. To increase the productivity of the workforce further, Kim Il-sung introduced the Chongsan-ri method, so named after a village near Pyongyang where Kim first developed these ideas when he inspected agricultural work practices. According to the Chongsan-ri method, party officials must closely supervise all local activities to ensure that production targets are achieved. The Chongsan-ri method was first applied to agriculture and eventually to all sectors of the economy. In 1972 it was enshrined in the constitution of the DPRK (Buzo 1999, p. 63). Another new practice which served to further consolidate political control over the economy was called the 'Tae-an work system' after a power plant Kim visited in 1961. It gave all power of decision to the party secretaries who in turn were to implement the will of Kim himself.

The first Seven-Year Plan (1961–7) was an effort to continue the development of the rest of the economy along similar lines. The emphasis on heavy industry continued, with priority given to military industry. The average growth rate of industrial output was still an impressive 13 per cent but, although the plan was pronounced to be a success, it was clear that growth was slowing towards the end and not all targets had been fulfilled, requiring the plan to be extended by two years. Moreover, the government stopped publishing economic statistics except for growth rates.

Despite the systemic problems affecting the North Korean economy, which would manifest themselves more clearly in the future, on the surface at least North Korea looked like a relative success story. Its gross domestic product was greater than that of the South which had been in a rather poor state of development after the Korean War. Ordinary citizens could have a reasonable lifestyle in urban North Korea in the 1960s. Moreover, under the leadership of Kim Il-sung the armed forces of the DPRK, the bulk of which were stationed close to the DMZ, were a formidable fighting force that posed a serious threat to the South, although it was deterred by the presence of US forces equipped with nuclear weapons.

But the North Korean economic miracle, such as it was, could not last. The Six-Year Plan that started in 1971 sought to rebalance the distorted economic structure somewhat by dealing with the bottlenecks in the supply of raw materials, electric power and fuel and giving more emphasis to technical modernization and light industry. In 1972–4, the DPRK invested heavily in foreign industrial equipment, such as a cement plant, textile factories and steel-making equipment from Japan, a French petrochemical plant, a large fertilizer plant, etc., to the tune of $500 million. This meant incurring significant external debt which was to be paid back by increased exports. The assumptions on which this strategy was based turned out to be unrealistic. North Korea's industry had serious difficulties in absorbing Western equipment and making proper use of it. Some of the plants never became operable. Thus the increased export earnings were hard to realize (Buzo 1999, p. 90). In addition, there was the oil crisis of 1973 which caused a huge increase in the international price of oil. Although the DPRK was shielded from the direct effects due to oil subsidies granted by the Soviet Union and China, it suffered indirectly as the prices of commodities and hence the raw materials (minerals and non-ferrous metals) that it exported fell. North Korea was unable to service the debts and began to default in 1974. As a result, the DPRK was virtually cut off from access to Western technology. Foreign debt payments were stretched out and almost completely halted in 1985 when they amounted to $5.2 billion (Oh and Hassig 2000, p. 53). The government had practically no hard currency reserves. This fact, along with the limited export potential of North Korean industry and the inadequacies of its transport infrastructure (especially shipping), severely restricted the DPRK's capacity to trade. But Kim Il-sung seemed to be unaware of the nature of the problems the economy was facing and their causes. He considered the trade deficit to be a temporary phenomenon and the previous orientation of the economy, with the priority given to heavy industry and military spending, continued.

Faced with the problem of stagnation in the economy, the North Korean leadership resorted to its familiar method of an ideological campaign to motivate and mobilize the workforce. The idea that material incentives might be used to increase productivity was rejected. In response to the inadequate production of tractors and other agricultural equipment, Kim Jong-il launched a massive propaganda and agitation campaign at the Kumsong Tractor Works and the Sungri General Motor works which was eventually declared an enormous success. Soon Kim Il-sung decided to launch a nationwide campaign to be orchestrated by his son called 'The Three Revolutions'. Tens of thousands of young people in teams of about 25 were sent out to visit farms and factories, instil enthusiasm for the regime, shake up bureaucratic structures and raise production with so-called 'speed battles'. Another function of these teams was probably to prepare the country for the eventual succession of Kim Jong-il. Whatever the political effect of this ideological campaign, it does not seem to have done much to improve economic performance. The Six-Year Plan was completed a year early, according to the government, but failed to achieve its targets and the next plan did not start until 1978, suggesting the need for another adjustment period. Total growth in output was declared to be 16.3 per cent on average.

By 1978, the GDP of the Republic of Korea was 3.9 times that of the DPRK (Buzo 1999, p. 91). North Korea's external economic relations and the overall performance of its economy were in a state of crisis, hampered by persistent resource bottlenecks, technological backwardness and poor efficiency. The Kims did not seem to recognize that the problem was in the very structure of the economy and the central planning system. Instead of analysing the economic roots of the malaise, they persisted in the belief that it was a problem of motivation and ideology. They tried to deal with it by a reassertion of the principles of *juche*, making a virtue out of frugality. The Seven-Year Plan for 1978–84 was again constructed around increasing the production of heavy industry but also emphasized the conservation of resources. In 1980, Kim Il-sung announced Ten Long-Range Goals of Socialist Economic Construction for the 1980s. These did not involve specific quantitative targets, but rather exhorted the party and the country to improve its performance in various sectors of the economy, in particular electricity generation, coal, steel, cement, non-ferrous metals, chemical fertilizer, grain production, textiles and the reclamation of tideland. Although economic data about North Korea remained sparse because of the refusal of the DPRK government to publish them, indications of the stagnation of the economy were mounting. For example, the country was facing a mounting deficit ($355 million for 1980–3 compared to $106.1 million for 1976–9). Foreign trade fluctuated in the early 1980s but the general trend was clearly downward in overall trade volume with an increasing trade deficit. This reflected the fact that the range of commodities the DPRK could export was shrinking and the difficulties of supplying its main trading partners (the Soviet Union, China and Japan) were increasing. At the same time, the problems of meeting international debt obligations were mounting. This did not stop Kim from spending what for such a relatively poor country were significant amounts of money on huge construction projects, such as the West Sea Barrage that was designed to reclaim tidal land or prestige projects such as the facilities for the Thirteenth World Festival of Youth and Students in 1989, the cost of which has been estimated at $4.5 billion, including the 105-storey Ryugyong Hotel which was never completed due to structural flaws and which remains a curious monument that symbolizes Kim's ambitions and their failure. The various projects that were under way in Pyongyang under the control of Kim Jong-il, who was put in charge of construction in the country, were so enormous in scope that they required almost all of the construction capacity in the DPRK. But the most important area of misallocation of resources was the continuing concentration on the military, which consumed 25 per cent of GDP annually. Towards the end of the planning period, efforts were announced to improve living standards by increasing the production of consumer goods. The introduction of the so-called Independent Accounting System devolved some responsibility to state enterprises, an adjustment that was to improve the running of enterprises and their overall efficiency.

The ten major long-term goals announced by Kim Il-sung became the focus of the next Seven-Year Plan (1987–93). This was a critical time period because of the collapse of communist rule in eastern Europe which brought about a major change in the economic relations between the DPRK, Russia and China. Despite numerous indications of the economic crisis affecting the country, the plan indicated a continuing commitment to previous economic policy. The consumer goods movement was continued, but priority was still given to heavy industry. The targets set were completely unrealistic. An increase of 4 million tons of steel per annum would have required substantial investment to improve obsolete plants. The target for grain production, 15 million tons, would have amounted to a 50 per cent increase over the declared 1984 level of production. The projection of an increase of 10 per cent per annum in total industrial output likewise seemed wildly optimistic. The foreign trade section continued to give priority to trade with the socialist countries (Buzo 1999, p. 170). The already tenuous assumptions underlying North Korean economic planning were fatally undermined by the changes in the Soviet Union and eastern Europe. Trade with the Soviet Union had already declined substantially in 1989, but in September 1990 Soviet Foreign Minister Eduard Shevardnadze delivered a huge blow when he informed the DPRK that Soviet investments in North Korea would be suspended, military aid would be sharply reduced and all trade had to be conducted in hard currency in future. China also notified the DPRK in 1992 that trade would in future be conducted on a hard currency basis, although some of the trade continued to be conducted at 'friendship prices'. This meant that support for the modernization of North Korea's industry would not be forthcoming as expected and oil imports from the Soviet Union had to be sharply reduced, given the lack of foreign reserves held by the DPRK. In 1991 trade with the Soviet Union was down by 47.7 per cent. By contrast, trade with the Republic of Korea which previously had been practically non-existent (amounting to just $1 million in 1988) rose dramatically, amounting to $111.27 million in 1991. This reflected the increasing commitment in the South to a policy of political and economic engagement.

It is clear that the end of the 1980s marked a significant transition point for the North Korean economy. The subsidies and investments from the Soviet Union had mitigated to some extent the failure of economic management in the DPRK. After 1990 the economy began to shrink. The contrast with the Republic of Korea was striking: in 1990 South Korea's GDP was tenfold that of the DPRK, and its annual increase in GDP exceeded the total of the North. There was an unprecedented admission in December 1993 in a communiqué released during a KWP Central Committee plenary meeting that, due to the international situation, major targets of industrial production had not been met.

In light of the deteriorating economic situation, the third Seven-Year Plan lost all relevance and was practically discarded after the death of Kim Il-sung in 1994. A three-year economic adjustment plan announced that year also came to nothing. In 1994 the output of heavy industry fell by 5.2 per cent and that of light industry by 4.2 per cent. In the period from 1990–97, the economy as a whole decreased by 42.2 per cent, a decline of catastrophic proportions (Moltz and Mansourov 2000, p. 63).

The dismal situation in agriculture had a range of systemic causes. Some of these were a consequence of the general state of the economy. There was a shortage of electricity for irrigation, agricultural machinery and various other required supplies. Dense planting and continuous cropping had resulted in soil depletion, and the overuse of chemical fertilizers caused soil erosion, which was exacerbated as more and more marginal lands were brought into use. At the same time, the lack of fertilizer and poor storage and transportation practices contributed to the problems that were dramatically aggravated by natural disasters in the mid-1990s. Torrential flooding alternating with severe droughts intensified the agricultural crisis that reached literally catastrophic proportions. About 16 per cent of arable land became unusable. Between 1990 and 2000, grain production fell from 9.1 million tons to 3.2 million tons. Between 1994 and 1996, there was a precipitous drop in production, from 7 million tons to 2.5 million tons according to official North Korean statistics (Lee 2006). The precise dimension of the agricultural disaster and the resulting food crisis in the DPRK remains subject to intense academic debate (Noland 2000; Noland 2003; Natsios 2001). Nevertheless, estimates that in 1995 the availability of grain was around 3 million tons short of minimum requirements seem to be of the right order of magnitude. Already in 1994, North Korean radio had admitted the existence of a famine. There is no doubt that the famine of the 1990s resulted in widespread malnutrition and a large number of premature deaths from hunger (estimates range from 250,000 to 3.5 million: Noland 2003: 11). Marcus Noland conducted a thorough analysis of the various studies of the North Korean famine and the statistics used to measure the overall toll, and concludes that the most sophisticated analyses put the death toll between 660,000 and 1 million (3–5 per cent of the population: Noland 2003: 13). In 1996, foreign donors provided about 900,000 tons of food. These included the Republic of Korea, the United States, China, the European Union and Japan. In 1997, foreign food aid amounted to 1.2 million tons and, in 1998, 1.3 million tons (Oh and Hassig 2000). It certainly saved many lives, but did not bridge the total shortfall. Moreover, the North Korean government interfered with the distribution and monitoring of food aid and placed serious restrictions on donor agencies. Some parts of the DPRK were completely inaccessible to foreign aid workers. There was also the suspicion that significant amounts of donated food supplies were diverted to feed the armed forces. Some donor agencies had to leave and Japan and the United States terminated their food aid in 2001 and 2002 respectively. In 1999, various measures were introduced to strengthen agriculture, such as growing more potatoes (the 'potato revolution'), developing improved seed strains ('the seed revolution') expanding rice farming land and so on. Agricultural production recovered to some extent, but every year there is still an annual shortfall that is not wholly met by food aid or commercial food imports. While the threat of famine has receded, whole sections of the population, especially outside Pyongyang, still do not have adequate access to food, resulting in a lower than sufficient intake of calories on a daily basis.

The relentless decline of the North Korean economy in the 1990s has convinced at least some elements of the North Korean leadership that economic reform is necessary. According to Robert Carlin and Joel Wit, a debate has begun in the North Korean political elite between a group of reformers, who argue that North Korea is now a militarily strong state in which a reallocation of resources can take place, and conservatives, who continue to emphasize the 'military first' policy and the external threat (Carlin and Wit 2006). In 1998, Kim Jong-il began to signal the need for economic reform through changes in the constitution and the reorganization of government. In the year 2000, Vice Premier Cho Chang-dok made a statement that in political, ideological and military terms the DPRK could be considered to have become a powerful state. There was also considerable diplomatic activity that seemed to promise a more benign international environment, including a visit by Kim Jong-il to China and Secretary of State Madeleine Albright to Pyongyang. The most important event, however, was the summit with South Korean leader Kim Dae-jung in Pyongyang, which involved not only a major cash handout but also marked the beginning of major economic engagement with the North.

The question, however, is the extent to which the regime would be willing to go along the path of reform. In July 2002, some initial steps towards economic reform were taken that gave an indication of its possible future direction. One important element of the reform is that state-owned enterprises now have to cover their own costs. They also have the right to trade some of their production and materials between themselves and invest capital out of their earnings. The enterprises are also permitted to engage in international trade. Enterprises have an incentive to cut the number of workers, and apparently there is a practice of creating subsidiary firms to reduce the number of workers that enterprise is responsible for (Noland 2004: 47). Wages were increased substantially (in part to compensate for the higher cost of rice), but at the same time the cost of housing, utilities and food (in particular rice) also increased. Although land remains in public ownership, farmers are allocated a certain amount of land that they have the right to cultivate and they can sell any surplus produce on the market. The government drastically increased prices paid to farmers, partly because the low prices had caused farmers to change to cash crops like tobacco. Farmers are entitled to sell the produce on the open market for prices within 15 per cent of the official price. Food is distributed through the public distribution system (PDS) whereby everybody receives a ration card. Any allocations not purchased in any given month are carried over to the next month. Those who can afford it can buy outside the PDS in the market.

The possession of foreign currency was legalized. In December 1992 the euro became the official currency for all foreign transactions and since then the government has adjusted the exchange rate to bring it more or less in line with the black market rate. This devaluation was inevitable, given the enormous increases in prices and wages. In March 2004 the official exchange rate was 1400 won to the euro, compared to a black market rate of 1600 (*The Economist*, 24 March 2004). The reforms have resulted in markets sprouting up everywhere and a greater availability of goods and services (including restaurants for example) for those who have the funds to pay for them. Two years after the reforms were introduced, *The Economist* noted:

> Reform, such as it is, has plainly made life easier for many. But rescuing the North would take large amounts of foreign money, as well as measures more far-reaching than have yet been attempted. At present, there is no way for the government to get what it needs from international financial institutions like the World Bank. Such aid as comes will be strictly humanitarian, and investment in so opaque a country will never be more than tentative. Domestic reform on its own cannot fix an economy wrecked by decades of mismanagement and the collapse of communism almost everywhere else. (*The Economist*, 11 March 2004)

Marcus Noland has noted some of the obvious structural problems that render the reforms unsustainable. The most important is that, although enterprises have to cover their costs, there is no mechanism such as bankruptcy to deal with enterprises that fail. Noland suspects that a hidden system of subsidies will operate to deal with enterprises that cannot cover their costs. Another obvious problem is inflation – adjusting wages to meet price rises obviously cannot work because this measure does not fix the problem of shortage.

The deliberate introduction of inflation has had the effect of confiscating savings held by the general population and has enabled the government to yet further privilege the elite (Noland 2004: 48).

Finally, the establishment of free economic and trading zones is another strand of economic reform. The first of these was created in the Rajin/Sobong area in the north-east corner of the country in 1991. It failed to attract investment due to its remote location, poor infrastructure, bureaucratic administration and interference in its running by party officials. The only major investment was a hotel casino that became the focus for illicit activities. Another creation of a special economic zone in the north-western city of Sinuiji, also near the Chinese border. This project was given remarkable autonomy, with the power to issue its own passports and its own legal system. It was supposed to be run by Yang Bin, a Chinese businessman with Dutch citizenship. This plan was scotched when Yang Bin was arrested in China on tax evasion charges. It still remains to be seen whether the Sinuiji project will generate much investment. More promising is the industrial park at Gaesong near the DMZ as the South Korean government is committed to support major investments.

It is evident that there is some recognition in Pyongyang that the economy is in a disastrous state and that, besides procuring external aid, some economic reforms are necessary. The rationale behind all the reforms introduced in 2002 is not entirely clear, and they involve profound contradictions. Indeed it may be the case, as Marcus Noland has suggested, that groups of officials (such as the advocates of reform identified by Carlin and Wits) have devised reforms without actually understanding their implications (such as the obvious illogic of raising prices and wages simultaneously). But it is fair to conclude that Kim Jong-il is looking for benefits from reforms without having to give up central control over the economy, even though there is no longer a working economic plan. There is no intention as yet to reduce substantially the military share of GDP, or introduce property rights as they are understood in advanced economies. In 1998, when the worst of the food shortages appeared to be over, new slogans were propagated such as *Kangsung Taeguk* ('rich and powerful country') advocating a strong military and a strong economy, and *Songun jongchi* ('military first') which re-emphasizes the priority given to military spending. There is no clear vision of any path of reform yet that could lead North Korea out of its predicament.

North Korea's unification policy

The unification of the two Koreas into one state on the basis of socialism and under the rule of the Korea Workers' Party has been a central goal of the DPRK from the time of its founding. Indeed, the constitution states that the capital of the DPRK is Seoul and the KWP's supreme goal is to liberate the entire peninsula under socialism. Kim Il-sung did not wait long to demonstrate his seriousness about unification when he launched the Korean War in 1950, and he very nearly succeeded. North Korea's unification policy was based on the following assumptions:

- The DPRK was the only legitimate Korea state;
- The ROK was a military dictatorship, a fascist regime supported by imperialists oppressing its people;
- The people of South Korea were ready to rise up against their rulers;
- The leaders of the ROK were essentially puppets of the imperialist USA.

The Korean War proved some of Kim's thinking to be illusory. Not only did a large-scale uprising by the people of South Korea fail to materialize during the Korean War but, when the allied forces pushed into the North, the level of support they found in the local population was disconcerting. Moreover, the experience of the Northern occupation, which brought a taste of ruthless totalitarian techniques including executions, widespread internment, confiscation of property, the forcible movement of people to the North and the drafting of young men into the North Korean army, did not exactly endear the regime to the people of the South.

When the Korean War ended in ignominious failure, this did not alter the basic objectives of the Kim regime. The formal commitment of the United States to the security of South Korea which included the stationing there of American troops deterred the North from a repeat of the invasion of 1950. Moreover, the resources and energies of the North Korean leaders needed to focus on rebuilding their devastated country and increasing its economic strength. There was some degree of military demobilization as manpower was needed in the civilian economy, and the military budget dropped from 15.2 per cent of the state budget in 1953 to 4.8 per cent in 1958 (Martin 2004, pp. 99). The strength of the civilian economy and the life that North Korea could create for its citizens were to demonstrate to the people of the South the superiority of the social system of the North. Despite this emphasis on building up state resources, Kim began to develop his new strategy for forceful unification based on subversion and infiltration which would bring guerrilla warfare to the South. Sending agents to the South was part of a strategy to promote communism and eventually produce an uprising that would eliminate the Southern government and bring about unification. This strategy was pursued with some persistence over decades, but with limited effect. The regime clung stubbornly to assumptions which had no basis in reality: one was the idea that there was significant revolutionary potential in the South that just needed to be given a chance to gather momentum. It was true that the authoritarian character of the military regime did produce widespread discontent and there were times of serious social unrest in the Republic of Korea. When Rhee Syngman was driven from office in April 1960, the North perceived a chance to intervene but failed to do so due to the state of its armed forces. It is likely that Kim overestimated the 'lost opportunity' as US forces were present on the peninsula and the South Korean armed forces would have rallied behind the caretaker presidency that followed. Moreover, the student and union protests were not aimed at bringing about communism, but rather greater democracy and improvement in living conditions, and this political conflict sharpened after the military coup led by Park Chung-hee. Kim failed to understand the depth of anti-communism in large sectors of South Korean society, and concomitantly misunderstood the nature of the US–ROK alliance. The South Korean governments could not be described as puppets of the United States by any stretch of the imagination. Quite the reverse; their nationalism and opposition to the North reflected the view of the majority of the people and was perhaps restrained somewhat by their reliance on US support. But the US–ROK alliance was one based on consent. Finally, although the DPRK sought to develop various means of striking at the South through terrorist activities and found ways of infiltrating their agents by sea, air and through various tunnels below the DMZ, the scale of such infiltrations never seems to have been sufficient to permit the implementation of this strategy. In 1968 North Korean commandos infiltrated the South and reached the grounds of the presidential compound (Chong Wa Dae – the Blue House), intending to kill President Park Chung-hee but were captured by security forces guarding the president. Then came the incident of the *USS Pueblo*. Its crew was captured by the North Koreans for a year and only released after an official US apology for spying (which was rescinded as soon as the crew was free). In 1974, there was another attempt to assassinate President Park by an ethnic Korean from Japan. The assassin shot at him in the National Theatre in Seoul but missed and killed his wife, the First Lady, instead. In October 1983, there was an operation to kill South Korean President Chun Doo-hwan and his cabinet during a state visit to Rangoon, Burma. Once again, North Korean operatives missed their main target but killed a number of officials and ministers. The most spectacular act of terrorism was the bombing of a Korean Airlines civilian airliner that exploded over the Gulf of Thailand with 115 people aboard in November 1987. Two of the bombers were apprehended. One managed to commit suicide, the other one, a woman called Kim Hyon-hui, was extradited to the Republic of Korea. This action was probably designed to create an atmosphere of fear to disrupt the 1988 Seoul Olympics.

The last of these incidents resulted in North Korea being put on the US list of 'terrorist countries'. This list is based on legislation that empowers the US government to impose sanctions on specific countries deemed to be involved in terrorism. In the 1970s, North Korea kidnapped a number of Japanese citizens (perhaps up to fifty) to train as spies, a fact that was finally admitted by Kim Jong-il. However, North Korea has not been involved in international terrorism (except for giving a safe haven to members of the Japanese Red Army who hijacked an airliner in 1970 to seek refuge in Pyongyang). The attempts to assassinate the president of the Republic of Korea were aimed at creating social unrest and the conditions for an uprising against the South Korean government assisted by agents from the North. Not only did these missions fail in their immediate objective but, had they succeeded, it seems highly unlikely that they would have produced the desired outcome.

In the early 1960s, the armed forces of the DPRK numbered just over 300,000 but over the next two decades Pyongyang embarked on an aggressive build-up of its military power. The size of the forces (mostly deployed near the DMZ) exceeded 1 million by the late 1970s. At that time, the forces of the DPRK might have overwhelmed those of the South except for the presence of US troops with nuclear weapons. (Tactical nuclear weapons were first deployed in South Korea in 1958.) But the enormous burden the military was placing on the North Korean economy, which in any case was experiencing difficulties, was changing the balance of power as the South Korean economy was being transformed under the leadership of President Park. The external environment also began to change. The alliance between the People's Republic of China led by Mao Zedong and the Soviet Union came under strain after Stalin's death and relations between the two countries became adversarial in the late 1950s (the so-called 'Sino-Soviet split'). The consequence for North Korea was that China was no longer prepared, despite its treaty commitments, to support the DPRK if it provoked another war. In the late 1970s, President Carter wanted to withdraw US forces from Korea but, once this plan was defeated, the US commitment to the defence of the Republic of Korea was reaffirmed.

The end of communism in Europe and the dissolution of the Warsaw Pact and later the Soviet Union itself once again changed the external environment of the DPRK quite dramatically. The correlation of forces was now moving decisively against North Korea as Moscow no longer provided economic or military support. China likewise reduced its support and Pyongyang's erstwhile sponsors now developed closer relationships with its rival in the South. As discussed, the economy of the DPRK declined dramatically and the country also had to cope with consequences of major natural disasters. The Republic of Korea, on the other hand, completed a transition to a stable democracy and an advanced industrial economy. The balance of power had changed to such an extent that an aggressive unification policy seemed no longer plausible; the best the regime could hope for was survival. This does not mean that the Kim regime has given up the objective of unification on its own terms.

The first steps towards an intra-Korean dialogue were taken after President Nixon's visit to China in 1971. ROK President Park Chung-hee initiated a secret contact with Kim Il-sung, and on 4 July 1972, the first South–North joint communiqué was signed. It stated that 'unification shall be achieved through independent efforts without being subject to external imposition or interference' (a reference to the Soviet Union and the United States). The promise of this early dialogue soon faded. The newly established South–North Coordinating Committee met several times but talks soon stalled and were broken off by the North in 1973. For the rest of the decade, South Korea became preoccupied with internal political unrest and no progress in relations with the North was made until Chun Doo-hwan promoted dialogue with Pyongyang after Seoul was awarded the 1988 Olympics. A rare moment of North–South unity came in September 1984 when North Korea sent emergency supplies to the South after severe flooding. The rice, cement and cloth sent in large trucks across the DMZ were of poor quality (the rice was hardly usable), but it was perceived as a remarkable gesture. Talks resulted in the first reunion of separated families as well as a flurry of cultural exchanges. Again the dialogue fizzled out until in 1988 when the elected President of South Korea, Roh Tae-woo, promoted a dialogue to achieve an interim stage towards unification by establishing a so-called 'Korean Community'. This so-called *Nordpolitik* (an adaptation of a German word describing the dialogue between the two Germanies called *Ostpolitik*) elicited a more positive reaction in North Korea as the international environment was changing fast and Kim Il-sung seemed more eager for progress in relations with the South. The North Korean proposal for an intermediate stage that was first put forward in 1960 was a confederation of the two Koreas where the two political systems would exist side by side. There was some degree of similarity between the two approaches, although none of these proposals have yet been put into practice. Nevertheless, after a delay due to North Korean protests against the joint US–ROK military exercises called 'Team Spirit', there was a breakthrough in the intra-Korean talks that resulted in two major agreements: the Agreement on Reconciliation, Non-Aggression, and Exchanges and Cooperation, plus the Joint Declaration on the Denuclearization of the Korean Peninsula. Once again expectations were raised for a new dawn in intra-Korean relations, and once again they were dashed quickly. In August 1992, North Korea became embroiled in an international crisis about its failure to report accurately its inventory of plutonium produced by its nuclear reactor. This was the beginning of the first North Korean nuclear crisis which is discussed in chapter 5. A new beginning was made in the year 2000 as South Korea under President Kim Dae-jung embarked on a policy of engaging North Korea called the 'sunshine policy', resulting in a historic summit between Kim Jong-il and Kim Dae-jung in Pyongyang. The impact of these events and the prospects for the future of inter-Korean relations will be the subject of chapter 7.

4 South Korea after the Korean War: From Struggling Dictatorship to Vibrant Democracy

The path taken by South Korea after the Korean War could not have been more different to that of the North. In the early decades, the Republic of Korea was subject to an authoritarian government and suffered from political factionalism and uneven economic growth, misallocation of resources and corruption. Politically, militarily and to an extent economically, it was dependent on the United States. Now it is an advanced industrialized state, fully integrated into the world economy and one of the shining examples of modern democracy in Asia.

The government of the first president of the Republic of Korea, Rhee Syngman, was based on autocratic rule and fierce anti-communism. Suspected communists and North Korean agents were detained without recourse to the legal system and subject to torture. There were also a number of massacres, most notably one on Jeju island to put down an uprising by leftist forces. In 1951, Rhee Syngman founded the Liberal Party to serve as his political platform. Knowing that the National Assembly would not re-elect him as president, he sought an amendment to the constitution according to which the president would be directly elected by the people. This was defeated and in 1952, during the Korean War when the South Korean government was based in Busan, he declared martial law and pushed through his constitutional amendments. Opponents were jailed to ensure the changes would be implemented. Rhee won the elections that followed by a wide margin and also gained control over the National Assembly at the subsequent parliamentary elections in 1954. He used his power to get the National Assembly to adopt an amendment that exempted him personally from the presidential term limit. In 1956, the opposition candidate, Shin Ik-hee, enjoyed immense popularity as there was much disenchantment with Rhee's rule but, after Shin suddenly died of a heart attack on the campaign trail ten days before the election, Rhee was re-elected with 55 per cent of the vote. Cho Bong-am of the Progressive Party who was runner-up was charged with espionage in 1959 and executed.

The dissatisfaction with Rhee's government finally came to a head as a result of the presidential elections in 1960. Rhee's main opponent Cho Byeong-ok died just before it was held, giving the election to Rhee by default. There was a separate election for the position of vice-president in which Rhee's candidate, Yi Gi-bung, who was largely confined to his sick bed, was declared the winner, but there was widespread suspicion that this election was rigged. Student protests in April 1960, which prompted a violent response by the police that led to the death of 142 students, forced Rhee to resign and he was spirited out of the country by the CIA. After his departure it was revealed that he had embezzled $20 million of state funds. Nevertheless, the Rhee period was one of great social change, partly due to the Korean War, but also due to various actions taken by the government, such as increasing opportunities for education, the land reform of 1949 which made about 40 per cent of farm households into small landowners, the rehabilitation of the economy after the destruction of the war on the basis of US economic aid and the rapid urbanization that resulted from the government's economic policies aimed at increasing industrial production.

When Rhee resigned, Ho Chong, who had been appointed foreign minister the day before, took over the reins of government and maintained a transitional government as prime minister until elections for a National Assembly in July 1960. In June, the National Assembly changed the constitution to create a parliamentary form of government with a bicameral legislature. The Democratic Party won 175 out of 233 seats in the Lower House and 31 out of 58 seats in the Upper House.

The Liberal Party won only two seats and thus no longer played any role on the political scene. The National Assembly elected Yun Bo-seon to be the fourth president of the Republic of Korea (after Rhee had held the position three times). Chang Myon became premier and led the cabinet through a period in which the government struggled to maintain political control as the divisions in the ruling party became manifest. As student protests continued, the government found it hard to maintain law and order. The government was also facing serious economic challenges.

In May 1961, General Park Chung-hee led a coup in which he seized power from Chang Myon. Park was determined to overcome the cycle of poverty and economic depression in the South and embarked on a course to maintain societal stability and develop and modernize the economy. He had no time for democracy which he considered to be inefficient. His authoritarian style of government was focused on industrialization and rapid economic growth. His goal was to use economic growth to mobilize popular support for his regime. The threat from North Korea was used as a justification for his methods. In response to very severe pressure from US President Kennedy, Park held presidential elections and the Republic of Korea returned to at least nominal civilian government. Park was elected in 1963 and 1967, and narrowly in 1971 against opposition leader Kim Dae-jung after changing the constitution to permit a third term. He pledged not to run again, a promise he fulfilled in an unexpected manner by changing the constitution again. The Yushin constitution ('revitalization') was intended to eliminate inefficiency in production and promote national wealth and power by the creation of national unity. This meant that almost all political power was vested in the office of the president. The existing constitution of the country was abandoned, martial law was declared and the National Assembly was disbanded. Direct presidential elections were abolished and through indirect elections by a national convention Park was designated president for life.

Park developed close ties with Japan, then the economic powerhouse of Asia, and in 1965 the two countries signed a Normalization Treaty. From 1970, Japan was the largest source of foreign direct investment and the principal provider of advanced technology. Resistance to the communist threat from the North was another central plank of Park's rule. In his view, that required the continuation of a close alliance with the United States which continued to maintain sizeable forces on the territory of the Republic of Korea. The commitment to close alliance with the United States was symbolized by the dispatch of 25,000 troops to support the US war effort in Vietnam.

Despite the fact that South Korea's security and to some extent its economic development depended on the United States, there was a certain degree of mistrust between the two allies. For Park, it was a fundamental objective to reduce the dependence on the US as much as possible. This became more important as the US commitment to South Korea seemed to weaken. The withdrawal of the Seventh Division of the Eighth Army from Korea in 1971 as the US began to reduce its commitment in Indochina, along with the opening of US relations with the People's Republic of China in 1972, cast doubt about the reliability of the US security guarantee. President Park was informed that the deployment of the remaining US forces could not be guaranteed beyond 1980.

The repression by the authoritarian government in South Korea sparked a serious opposition movement. Park used the Korean Central Intelligence Agency (KCIA), the Army Security Command and his personal bodyguards to deal with his opponents. This would involve arbitrary arrest, detention and torture. The United States opposed Park's actions, but decided not to attempt to seriously dissuade him. Instead, the Nixon administration followed a policy of 'disassociation'. This meant that the United States declared that it had not been consulted about the steps taken by the Korean government and it would not play any role in the reorganization of the Korean political system. This had the consequence of furthering the trend of US disengagement from South Korea.

The most prominent opposition leader was Kim Dae-jung. It so happened that Kim was in Japan when martial law was imposed in October 1972 and as long as he was abroad he remained free to comment on developments in his home country. He strongly condemned Park and remained in Japan until he was kidnapped by South Korean agents in Tokyo on 8 August 1973. It is likely that he survived only due to rapid action and serious pressure by the US government, and he was released in Seoul and put under house arrest.

The main objectives of the opposition were the creation of a constitutional democracy in the Republic of Korea along the lines of the United States and a gradual move towards unification with North Korea through a process of engagement and negotiation. Although there were people in South Korea sympathetic to the North Korean regime, by and large the opposition perceived the United States as a friendly power, although the perceived failure of the United States to put greater pressure on the government in the face of its repressive measures was criticized. In 1965, 1972 and 1975, the Park government declared martial law. The opposition understood that the United States did not support these actions by their government, but that the weakening of US support for the defence of South Korea, as evidenced by the exit from Vietnam and the opening of relations with China, prompted actions to increase internal security. The opposition therefore favoured strong American support for South Korea to prevent aggression from the North or increased repression by the government in Seoul. This manifested itself for example in the opposition's stance on President Carter's plans in 1976 to withdraw the Second Army Division from Korea.

By 1979, the level of general dissatisfaction with President Park's oppressive rule had reached a point where widespread unrest was sweeping the country. In this climate the political opposition gained momentum, as Kim Young-sam was elected chairman of the New Democratic Party in May 1979 on a platform of democratic reform. At the same time, labour unrest came to a head with a police raid on the headquarters of the NDP where 180 women employees of the YH Industrial Company and 30 members of the NDP were staging a sit-in to protest against the closure of the company. This was a massive raid involving 1,000 riot police and many were badly beaten. A young woman who was an executive member of the union died. Park then tightened his control further by expelling Kim Young-sam from the National Assembly on the grounds that he had appealed to the United States to withdraw its support for the dictatorial Park regime. This action sparked large demonstrations by students and workers in the port city of Busan where Kim's political base was, and the unrest spread to the Masan Free Export zone. A few days later, in a bizarre incident at Cheong Wa Dae (the 'Blue House' presidential compound), President Park was assassinated by the Director of the Korean Central Intelligence Agency (KCIA), Kim Jae-kyu. His motive was, according to his statement in court, that he wanted to end the *Yushin* system and restore democracy. But Kim had not planned for a transition to a new government to take over after Park's death. He tried to persuade the Army Chief of Staff, Jung Seung-hwa, to declare martial war, but was subsequently arrested as his role in the death of Park was revealed. Prime Minister Choi Kyu-ha became acting president according to the *Yushin* constitution. At least partly in response to American influence, Choi abolished the emergency law that forbade criticism of the constitution and released prominent opposition leaders that had been imprisoned or put under house arrest. A new atmosphere of freedom and hope was evident as much of the population was glad of the end of the Park regime and expected a transition to democracy (Shorrock 1986).

However, at the insistence of political and military leaders the *Yushin* constitution was not abolished and on the basis of its principles President Choi was easily elected president on 6 December 1979. Only six days later, just before Choi could name his cabinet, there was a military coup led by Lieutenant Chun Doo-hwan, commander of the Korean Defence Security Command. Chun immediately purged the army leadership and placed trusted comrades in key positions. Although the United States made known its disapproval of Chun's actions, it did not attempt to reverse them and later even discouraged a counter-coup against Chun. As the military consolidated its position under Chun's leadership, President Choi increasingly became merely a figurehead.

The Gwangju uprising

Chun's dominant position in South Korea became increasingly evident as he told Choi to appoint him acting director of the Korean Central Intelligence Agency (KCIA), a move which the US Embassy in Seoul interpreted as a first move towards the presidency itself. The early months of 1980 saw increasing unrest as labour and student unrest swept the country. In large demonstrations, hundreds of thousands of students in the second week of May 1980 demanded an end to martial law and democratic government. The demonstrations were halted when the government indicated it would consider the demands, and student leaders set a date of 17 May for an announcement of a schedule for a move towards democratic government. At first Chun signalled to the American ambassador, William Gleysteen, that the student demonstrations would be dealt with calmly, but on 13 May he invoked the threat of a North Korean attack. It turned out later the evidence for this threat was entirely fabricated. On 17 May, instead of the introduction of democracy, there was a full extension of martial law. This was followed by widespread arrests of student leaders and politicians, including possible contenders in a presidential election, Kim Dae-jung, Kim Young-sam and ex-Prime Minister Kim Jong-pil. The National Assembly was closed down, press censorship was imposed and all political activity banned (Oberdorfer 2001, pp. 124–7). This was the end of the 'Seoul Spring' as troops and tanks were deployed in cities and paratroopers occupied the universities.

The arrest of the hero of the opposition, Kim Dae-jung, provoked a sharp reaction in Gwangju, the capital of South Jeolla province, Kim's home region. Special forces began to attack demonstrators and local people in general indiscriminately, beating and killing many. The response of the local people was a growing and increasingly violent opposition to the security forces. Arms dumps were raided and various kinds of firearms and ammunition were seized. With the use of these weapons, including a machine gun mounted on top of a hospital, the security forces were beaten back and were forced to withdraw to the outskirts of the city. The following day 30,000 people gathered in the centre of the city, demanding that the special forces should stay out of Gwangju and all people detained under martial law should be released.

The stand-off continued for a number of days, but the government did not use this time to negotiate a solution. On the contrary, they ordered the Twentieth Division of the army and some special forces to mount an assault on Gwangju which began on 27 May. The armed forces swiftly took control of the city, killing 240 people in the process (according to a review of the evidence in 1995), although local people claim the toll was much higher.

Many South Koreans had been hoping for American support to defend them against the forces of martial law, but no such help was forthcoming. In point of fact, the US was widely perceived as backing Chun. This perception was encouraged by the government. A government-controlled radio station reported falsely that the United States had approved the sending of special forces to Gwangju. It was also believed that the United States had given permission for the twentieth Infantry Division to be released from the joint command. In reality, Chun had simply notified the removal of two elements of the Twentieth Division from the Combined Forces Command on 16 May, just before the extension of martial law was declared. US policy was discussed at a National Security Meeting in the White House on 22 May (in the absence of President Carter). The previously classified report of the meeting concluded:

> There was general agreement that the first priority is the restoration of order in Gwangju by the Korean authorities with the minimum use of force necessary without laying the seeds for wide disorders later. Once order is restored, it was agreed that we must press the Korean Government, and the military in particular, to allow a greater degree of political freedom to evolve. (Cited in Oberdorfer 2001, p. 129)

The US commander in Korea, John Wickham, was asked for permission to use the Twentieth Division even though Chun did not require any permission. Wickham and Gleysteen indicated their approval after consultation with Washington because it was felt that the army would cause less resentment than the hated special police. This was falsely interpreted as a carte blanche; the Americans did not anticipate the massacre of the demonstrators that subsequently occurred. The US government did not disguise its disapproval of Chun and his actions. Diplomatic contacts were kept at a minimal level and plans for a US economic mission in Korea were shelved. The 'cold and aloof' policy was accompanied by the recognition that South Korea might not yet be ready for democracy. Soon Choi resigned the presidency, making room for the ascent of Chun to the highest political office. US relations with Seoul became hostage to the fate of Kim Dae-jung. Kim was charged with plotting the uprising in Gwangju and was sentenced to death by a court martial. Saving the life of Kim Dae-jung became a matter of the highest priority for Washington. Chun demanded the normalization of US–Korean relations as the price of Kim's life. Despite the direct involvement of US Deputy Secretary of State Warren Christopher, the issue remained unresolved until the Reagan administration came into office. President Reagan reversed US policy, invited President Chun to the White House and publicly disavowed any plans for troop withdrawals (in fact troops were increased to a level of 43,000). Moreover, he agreed to the sale of F-16 fighter planes which had initially been negotiated during the Carter presidency but had not been completed.

Relations between Seoul and Washington were further strengthened by two major incidents. The first was the shooting down of the Korean Airliner KAL 007 by Soviet air defence forces in September 1983. This became a major incident in US–Soviet relations that were at a very low ebb at the time of what came to be known as the 'Second Cold War'. For President Reagan, who had characterized the Soviet Union as the 'evil empire', the KAL 007 incident was further proof of the malicious nature of the Soviet regime. However, the fact that the Korean airliner had mysteriously strayed deep into Soviet airspace gave rise to myriad conspiracy theories. It was alleged that there was no way the pilots could not have known they were in Soviet airspace, that the airliner was on a spying mission, such as investigating the ballistic missile defence radar in Krasnoyarsk. In 1993 the Russian government released the black box and the recordings of air defence personnel which made it clear that the pilots had no inkling that they were so far off course. The Soviet air defence controller assumed the plane was a spy plane and obtained authorization to shoot it down. This incident postponed the development of relations between the Soviet Union and South Korea.

One month later, in October 1983, the Republic of Korea suffered another shock when North Korean agents attempted to kill President Chun during a state visit to Burma. President Chun reacted with extraordinary restraint; despite severe pressure from the surviving members of his government and especially the military, he refrained from any reprisal attacks on the North.

One of the enduring puzzles of the history of inter-Korean relations is that the bombing in Burma coincided with a North Korean initiative to open three-way talks with the United States and South Korea, in a complete departure from previous policy. Some South Koreans and Americans suspected the initiative, which came through Chinese diplomatic channels, was a ploy to avoid recriminations for the assassination (on the mistaken assumption that the assassins would not be apprehended). Korea expert Don Oberdorfer dismisses the possibility that Kim Il-sung or Kim Jong-il were unaware of both the diplomatic track and the assassination plot (Oberdorfer 2001, p. 145). However, given what we have since learnt about relations between Kim Il-sung and his son, the possibility the Kim Jong-il ran his own operation cannot be excluded.

The Reagan administration initially opposed the idea of three-way talks, but in a speech to the National Assembly in Seoul one month after the Burma bombing, President Reagan himself endorsed the idea, only for Washington to renounce it again once North Korea agreed. The United States subsequently suggested two-way talks between the two Koreas, to be expanded into four-way talks including China if necessary. While Seoul rejected any direct talks with North Korea until there was an apology for the Rangoon bombing, the DPRK did not want to involve China in any discussions. The sincerity of all parties remains in doubt. Neither Washington nor Seoul wanted to get involved in direct talks with Pyongyang, whereas Kim Il-sung was looking for propaganda returns, such as preventing an increase in US forces in the South while talks were in progress.

North–South relations received an unexpected boost as the result of a natural disaster. The South experienced torrential rains and landslides in the vicinity of Seoul that resulted in local devastation, 200,000 homeless and 190 deaths. Despite its economic backwardness, North Korea offered to send relief to the South. Hundreds of North Korean trucks delivered cement, textiles, medical supplies and rice. Although much of the supplies were of extremely poor quality, they were gratefully received in the South as a political gesture that resulted in the opening of North–South economic talks.

Despite the initially negative attitude of the Chun administration to North–South talks, there was an intensive, albeit secret dialogue that began in the mid-1980s. The secret diplomacy began with a visit to Pyongyang and a meeting with Kim Il-sung by Channing Liem. Liem had been the ROK delegate to the UN in the government that was toppled in 1961 and had since then lived in the US where he was a political science professor. This meeting resulted in a direct channel between Pyongyang and Seoul in the persons of Park Chul-un in the Blue House and Han Se-hae in the DPRK Ministry of Foreign Affairs. Efforts to bring about what would have been a historic meeting between Chun Doo-hwan and Kim Il-sung foundered eventually, largely due to disagreements over the details of the arrangements and a non-aggression pact proposed by the North. The final nail in the coffin was the holding of joint exercises between the United States and the Republic of Korea called 'Team Spirit', involving a total of 200,000 troops, that was considered very threatening by the North.

Even though Chun came to power in the wake of the assassination of Park by suppressing any movement towards democracy, his presidency proved to be the beginning of a path to political transition in South Korea. In June 1980, before he assumed the presidency, Chun said that he wanted to be 'the first one in Korea to turn over power in a legitimate and constitutional manner' (Oberdorfer 2001, p. 162). Soon after he assumed office, he announced that he would only serve one term of seven years.

In 1986, political life in Korea was consumed by the future of the constitutional arrangements. President Chun proposed a parliamentary system as the solution. The opposition focused on the reinstatement of direct elections of the president. This ironically constituted a complete reversal of the positions held by government and opposition political groupings. There was renewed impetus for constitutional change with the rebirth of the labour movement and the emergence of the student movement as a political force. The National Alliance for Constitutional Reform was founded on 17 March 1986. Its council included leading opposition politicians Kim Dae-jung, Kim Young-sam and Lee Min-woo.

Against the background of continuing social unrest (in particular student protests) and the nomination of Roh Tae-woo as the presidential candidate for the ruling Democratic Justice Party (DJP), the government was forced to climb down. On 29 June, Roh announced a set of reform measures under the heading 'Grand National Harmony and Progress toward a Great Nation'. Among the key concessions to the opposition demands were direct presidential elections and the release of political prisoners (Kihl 2005, p. 83). The government and opposition groups eventually hammered out an agreement on constitutional change which, due to the extent of public pressure, had become inevitable. On 12 October 1987, the National Assembly approved the new constitution by 254 votes to 4. On 27 October a referendum was held that approved the new constitution by 93.1 of the recorded vote (Kihl 2005, p. 84). The new constitution represented a significant step towards democratic reform by improving the rights of ordinary citizens and giving more power to the National Assembly.

The presidential elections in December 1987 resulted in a clear victory for Chun's chosen successor, Roh Tae-woo, primarily because the opposition was split with both Kim

Young-sam and Kim Dae-jung running. On the basis of the new constitution, Roh was elected to serve a single term (1988–1993).

Despite the reforms, the political struggles in South Korea continued. While the limitations on presidential executive power were significant, the new constitution was based on a clear separation between executive and legislative, resulting in the phenomenon of *yoso yadae* where the government party has a minority in the unicameral National Assembly. The DJP failed to achieve an overall majority in the National Assembly elections on 26 April 1988. It won 125 out of 299 seats, with 70 going to Kim Dae-jung's Party for Peace of Democracy, 59 to Kim Young-sam's Reunification Democratic Party, 35 to Kim Jong-pil's New Democratic Republican Party and 10 seats to independents (Kihl 2005). This result revealed a pattern of political support according to regional interests which has persisted to this day.

This situation made it difficult to govern the country and consequently Roh Tae-woo, Kim Young-sam and Kim Jong-pil agreed to merge their parties in 1990 to form the Democratic Liberal Party. This was not a very natural alliance and internal disagreements persisted, partly because Kim Young-sam's supporters felt betrayed. It solved the problem of governance only temporarily, because the DLP lost its majority in the National Assembly elections in 1992. But it enabled Kim Young-sam to set himself up as the presidential candidate of the DLP. On 18 December 1992, Kim Young-sam was democratically elected as the first civilian president of the Republic of Korea. The new era of South Korean democracy had begun.

US–North Korean Relations and the First Nuclear Crisis —

Until the end of the 1980s, the dividing line between the two Koreas was also perceived as part of the Cold War boundary between communism and the free world. Of course the DPRK did not remain a Soviet client state for long and tried to maintain an equal distance between China and the Soviet Union. But its relationship with both the large communist powers meant it had allies of sorts that provided crucial support, especially in the supply of cheap energy. But the world changed as communism collapsed in the Soviet Union and eastern Europe while the People's Republic of China embarked on a process of modernization and economic reform. Both Russia and China began to develop closer relations with the Republic of Korea and reduced their support for North Korea. Eventually it became clear that in the event of war North Korea would no longer be able to rely on the support of its erstwhile allies, previous agreements notwithstanding. As the Cold War came to a close, the foreign policy of the DPRK was modified to adapt to the newly emerging international environment. A key element of this was North Korea's opening to the United States, which began in the late 1980s. In the 1990s it became very clear that for the DPRK the relationship with the United States was viewed as the central path to regime survival. The main instrument that North Korea had with which to engage US interest was its nuclear programme. The history of North Korea's nuclear programme, which is discussed in more detail in chapter 8, began with agreements with the Soviet Union to cooperate in the field of atomic energy and establish the Yongbyon Nuclear Scientific Research Centre, which contained a range of facilities. In 1980, US intelligence concluded that a new research reactor which was being constructed at Yongbyon could be used to produce plutonium for nuclear weapons. (This reactor became known as the 5 MW(e) reactor on the basis of its energy output.) The US and the Soviet Union agreed that North Korea should join the Nuclear Non-Proliferation Treaty (NPT), which the DPRK did in 1985 as a result of Soviet pressure.

The various elements of the nuclear research complex at Yongbyon were designed to produce fissile materials (plutonium). Kim Il-sung had already embarked on the development of nuclear weapons. The main purpose of joining the NPT was to be able to acquire nuclear technology legitimately, while the pursuit of a nuclear weapons option continued. Apparently oblivious of the contradiction, the North Korean government argued for a nuclear weapons-free zone on the Korean peninsula, which would require the withdrawal of US tactical nuclear forces.

For most of the decades since the Korean War, the United States had no direct contact with the DPRK except through the armistice commission. US diplomats were even barred from entering into conversations with North Korean officials. However, the Reagan administration adopted a new approach designed to explore some degree of engagement with North Korea to make progress on various issues, an approach that was continued by the Bush Sr administration. Informal contacts between North Korean and American officials were permitted. Sanctions were eased to permit humanitarian trade. More substantial improvements in relations between the DPRK and the United States would be possible if there was progress on a range of issues, including relations between Seoul and Pyongyang, human rights, the recovery of American soldiers missing in action from the Korean War and North Korea's renunciation of terrorism.

The United States had closely observed the development of nuclear facilities in Yongbyon and elsewhere in North Korea, especially since 1980 when the construction of the nuclear reactor began. Washington wanted to bring North Korean nuclear facilities under IAEA safeguards. The nuclear issue thus became central to efforts to improve US–DPRK relations, because the prospect of a North Korean nuclear weapon was of such serious concern to the United States. Consequently it was also the most significant asset that North Korea had in any negotiations. Former North Korean Foreign Minister Kim Yong-nam openly deployed the threat to develop nuclear weapons in discussions with Soviet Foreign Minister Eduard Shevardnadze during his visit to Pyongyang in January 1991 when the latter was explaining the new basis of relations with the DPRK which would include the diplomatic recognition of South Korea. (Mansourov and Moltz 2000, pp. 93–100). However, the notion that the nuclear programme might become a bargaining counter in the game of ensuring the survival of the state was probably not yet clearly developed as Pyongyang did not yet realize the kind of crisis that its programme was about to provoke.

The manner in which the crisis unfolded was initially not politically driven, but rather a result of the process of implementing IAEA safeguards. According to the NPT, the DPRK was obliged to ratify and implement an agreement with the IAEA that would involve a declaration of all nuclear materials and installations and permit the IAEA to conduct inspections to verify the declaration and that all the facilities were used for peaceful purposes within 18 months.

Despite joining the NPT, the DPRK was reluctant to submit to IAEA inspections. After the 18 months expired, it transpired that the IAEA had sent the wrong form of agreement to North Korea, a fact that had gone unnoticed by officials at the IAEA, the United States and the DPRK. Consequently another 18 months passed without North Korea's acceptance of a safeguards agreement.

In the meantime, North Korea continued to develop its nuclear programme considerably. The new reactor, now known as the 5 MW(e) graphite-moderated reactor, came online in 1986. Construction of an even larger reactor, the 50 MW(e) graphite-moderated reactor, began a few years later. It became evident that North Korea was engaged in developing a major

capacity for the production of plutonium, including a reprocessing facility that would permit the separation of plutonium
from spent fuel rods.

The administration of President Bush Sr, building on an initiative developed during the Reagan presidency, adopted a
policy of 'comprehensive engagement'. Based on a review of US
policy towards Korea entitled 'National Security Review 28',
it was founded on the concept of normalizing relations with
North Korea once the DPRK had abandoned its nuclear
weapons programme. It listed a comprehensive range of objectives, from getting Pyongyang to accept its non-proliferation
obligations to restraining the sale of missiles, giving up terrorism and promoting North–South dialogue. The administration
also put legislation in place permitting the export of $1.2
billion worth of US goods to the DPRK, such as food or humanitarian supplies, without any progress on the nuclear issue
(Galluci et al. 2004, p. 7).

An opening for this policy of engagement came as a consequence of a development which was largely unrelated to the
Korean situation, namely the end of the Cold War and the dissolution of the Warsaw Pact. As part of a mutual series of unilateral steps taken by the United States and the Soviet Union
(which was to soon be dissolved as well), President Bush
ordered the removal of all land- and sea-based US tactical
nuclear weapons from overseas locations, including South
Korea. Free-fall weapons on aircraft in Europe were excluded
from this initiative, but Bush secretly ordered all nuclear
weapons to be removed from aircraft based in Korea. The
purpose of this initiative was to enable Soviet President
Gorbachev to reciprocate, but it also addressed a long-standing
North Korean concern that US nuclear weapons based in
the Republic of Korea constituted a threat to the DPRK.
Consequently, South Korea President Roh Tae-woo publicly
declared the Republic of Korea to be nuclear free and suggested
talks to make the Korean peninsula a nuclear-free zone.
Negotiations between the prime ministers of the two Koreas
resulted in a non-aggression pact and an agreement not to inter-
fere in each other's internal affairs. By the end of 1991, intensive diplomacy produced the North–South Denuclearization

Declaration (NSDD). At the urging of the United States, the declaration included a prohibition on the production of plutonium and uranium enrichment, thus cutting off all avenues to nuclear weapons production as long as the declaration was adhered to.

The declaration was followed by a similar breakthrough on the issue of IAEA safeguards. Before the end of 1991, Pyongyang declared its intention to sign a safeguards agreement provided the United States declared that there were no nuclear weapons on the Korean peninsula. In support of the improvement in relations, the US and South Korea agreed to cancel the annual 'Team Spirit' joint military exercise for 1992 if the DPRK made good on its declaration. At a meeting between US Under-Secretary of State Arnold Kanter and his North Korean opposite number, Kim Young-sun, the US further offered to improve relations between the two countries if North Korea fulfilled its obligations with respect to non-proliferation. The North Korean government initialled the safeguards agreement at the end of January and ratified it in April in the same year.

IAEA Director General Hans Blix visited North Korea and toured the facilities that would be subject to inspection. In May 1992, Pyongyang submitted a declaration to the IAEA that confirmed the existence of a reprocessing facility at Yongbyon and the separation of 90 grams of plutonium in 1990 from damaged fuel rods that had been removed from the 5 MW(e) reactor. Scientific data gathered during inspections in July and September showed that there were discrepancies in the declaration. The inspectors concluded that more plutonium had been recovered than had been declared, and that reprocessing took place over a longer time period than indicated by the North Koreans. Indeed, laboratory analysis showed that three different batches of plutonium had been produced over a time period of three years, as opposed to the one batch declared by North Korea. US intelligence also suspected that North Korea was concealing two underground sites from the inspectors that might contain waste from additional reprocessing. US specialists estimated that enough additional spent fuel might have been reprocessed to yield sufficient plutonium for one or two nuclear weapons.

The diplomatic gains made during 1991 quickly evaporated. Tension mounted between North and South Korea over the implementation of the NSDD, i.e. the frequency and scope of mutual inspections. Relations between the DPRK and the IAEA deteriorated as the IAEA sought access to the suspect sites, demands that were rejected by Pyongyang. The US and the ROK announced that preparations for the 1993 'Team Spirit' exercise would continue, given the lack of progress in the bilateral inspection regime. Moreover, the US rebuffed North Korean requests for another high-level meeting with Kim Young-sun. Thus all the gains that Pyongyang had achieved were draining away.

In February 1993, the first democratically elected president of the Republic of Korea who was not a military officer, Kim Young-sam, took office. The election was a momentous event, completing the Republic of Korea's path to full democracy. Kim and the newly elected US president, Bill Clinton, took office as relations with North Korea were moving towards a serious crisis. Paradoxically, the incomimg South Korean administration was considering radical changes to its policy vis-à-vis the North. The newly appointed unification minister, Han Wan-sang, supported the idea of a grand gesture towards the North. Consequently various statements about a summit between Kim Young-sam and Kim Il-sung were made that could take place once the nuclear issue was resolved. The IAEA, which had to prove itself after the failure to discover the Iraqi nuclear programmes, decided to invoke for the first time its right to request 'special inspections' of any site it deemed necessary to verify safeguards. This was rejected by North Korea, and consequently a special meeting of the IAEA Board of Governors was convened in late February, at which IAEA officials displayed satellite photographs of the suspect sites that had been provided by US intelligence. Although Russia and China were reluctant to confront North Korea, the Board adopted a unanimous resolution on 25 February 1993 giving the DPRK one month to comply with its safeguard obligations. In order to ensure Russian and Chinese support, the resolution did not insist on 'special inspections', but merely that the IAEA be granted access to the suspect sites.

The North Koreans were confronted with the evidence but conceded nothing.

The atmosphere of an impending crisis was heightened further by the 'Team Spirit' exercise which began in February. North Korean forces were put on a semi-war footing. On 12 March 1993, Kim Il-sung landed his bombshell: it was announced that the DPRK would withdraw from the Nuclear Non-Proliferation Treaty. Pyongyang invoked a clause that permits a country to withdraw if its 'supreme interests' are threatened, giving 90 days notice. It cited US military threats (it considered 'Team Spirit' as a preparation for nuclear war against the DPRK) and the manipulation of the IAEA to get access to secret military sites in North Korea. Pyongyang stated it might reconsider its withdrawal if 'the United States stops its nuclear threats against our country' (IISS 2004, p. 8). This statement caused the Republic of Korea to place its forces on high alert (Watch Con 3) but both Koreas quickly stepped back from the brink once the 'Team Spirit' exercise ended.

The internal deliberations that prompted these moves in Pyongyang remain shrouded in secrecy. One factor that became clear in the course of later discussions was that the North Koreans would not contemplate a finding from the IAEA that would essentially convict the DPRK of submitting a false declaration. This was a matter of saving face. At the same time, however, it had also become clear that the policy of continuing a nuclear weapons programme while at the same time being a signatory to the NPT as a non-nuclear state had become difficult to maintain. The crisis came at an inopportune time as Kim Jong-il was named chairman of the National Defence Commission to replace his father. The regime was in the process of leadership transition and Kim Jong-il was facing a foreign policy crisis at a time when the political elite and especially the military leadership had to be convinced that he was capable of leading the country. The confrontation between Iraq and the United States was a salutary example for North Korea. Although the Hussein regime survived the Gulf War, it ended up in a situation where it was defeated and essentially under perpetual siege. This was a fate that the DPRK needed to avoid.

The Clinton administration adopted a policy of gradually escalating diplomatic pressure on the DPRK, while at the same time engaging in direct talks with Pyongyang. The dual-track strategy was intended to put the maximum pressure on North Korea, while gathering as much international support as possible and, most importantly, keeping China and Russia on board. On 11 May, the United Nations Security Council adopted Resolution 825 which called on North Korea to retract its withdrawal from the NPT and implement the safeguard agreement and asked 'interested states' to assist with a solution to the issue.

In the United States there was considerable debate about North Korea's objectives. Some took the view that North Korea was irrevocably committed to the development of nuclear weapons. Another possibility was that Pyongyang was playing a game of brinkmanship to reach some accommodation that would alleviate its perceived security risks and the economic problems it was facing.

North Korea was keen to enter into direct talks with the United States. After North Korea acceded to a US demand to allow IAEA inspectors back to continue their work on the facilities where they had already worked on a temporary basis (the inspectors were not to be given access to the 'suspect sites' that had been declared off-limits), the Clinton administration agreed to direct talks which began at the end of May. The North Korean delegation was led by Vice Foreign Minister Kang Sok-ju; relations with the United States had become the purview of the Ministry of Foreign Affairs after Kim Young-sok lost his place in the Politburo. Ambassador Robert Gallucci, a non-proliferation expert who had served at the Arms Control and Disarmament Agency for a long time and had been involved in inspecting the Iraqi nuclear programme after the Gulf War, headed the American team that was made up of representatives from the Departments of State and Defense, the National Security Council and the Joint Chiefs of Staff.

The first round of talks held in New York in June 1993 proved extremely difficult. Nevertheless, it became apparent that North Korea was interested in progress. Initially Kang insisted that a 'suspension' of North Korea's withdrawal from the NPT was impossible. Although Gallucci failed to persuade the DPRK delegation to consider remaining in the NPT on a permanent basis, the talks ended with an agreement to 'suspend' the withdrawal. The joint document issued at the end listed a number of agreed principles, such as an assurance not to use force or the threat of force (including nuclear weapons), respect for national sovereignty and non-interference in the internal affairs of other countries. The most important statement was that North Korea 'decided unilaterally to suspend for as long as it considers necessary the effectuation of its withdrawal' from the NPT (Gallucci et al. 2004, p. 59). This meant that the IAEA inspectors would be able to resume inspections, although the details still had to be agreed. The statement did not reveal the fact that Kang had discussed at least the possibility of a more far-reaching arrangement to end the production of plutonium in North Korea.

At the second round held in Geneva in July 1993, the North Korean delegation made an ambitious proposal to resolve the nuclear crisis. It would abandon its moderated graphite reactors that produced plutonium if the United States were to provide light water reactors (LWR) to provide for North Korea's energy needs. In principle this was an attractive idea for the United States because it would stop the production of plutonium in North Korea and prevent the accumulation of a stockpile of plutonium under IAEA safeguards which could be used to manufacture nuclear weapons if North Korea were to 'break out' from the NPT (assuming that it remained within the treaty in the first place). Although in principle plutonium could be extracted from LWRs, nevertheless there was confidence that this could be prevented by safeguards and measures to remove the spent fuel from North Korea on a continuous basis. There remained the question of discrepancies in the North Korean declaration, in particular with regard to plutonium produced prior to 1992, possibly enough for two weapons. The North Korean delegation expressed concerns about such discrepancies being revealed by IAEA inspections. The meeting ended without any formal agreement as the US delegation was unwilling to provide any assurances regarding the provision of LWRs until the non-proliferation concerns were dealt with, beyond 'considering' such a proposal. The US delegation procured Pyongyang's agreement to talk to the IAEA about safeguards and to South Korea about the implementation of the NSDD.

Relations between the IAEA and Pyongyang proved difficult as North Korea considered that the extent of inspections was a political issue to be settled by negotiation, whereas the IAEA considered it a matter of the technical verification of safeguards that simply required North Korea to fulfil its obligations under the treaty. In particular the organization was exercised about the continuity of safeguards, i.e. accounting for the history of the plutonium. Relations with Seoul were also difficult, as President Kim Young-sam had to avoid being seen to be making too many concessions and, in order to placate the more conservative elements, adopted a hardline stance that incensed Pyongyang. The NSDD was subject to the same problems as the safeguards, namely that verification and inspections were considered by North Korea to be a political issue, to be settled by political negotiations, and not a technical matter that required all possible sites of concern to be inspected in order to give confidence that the declaration was being adhered to. North Korea was not really interested in negotiating with three different partners, but saw the entire issue as something to be settled in bilateral discussions with the United States.

The third round of bilateral talks, scheduled for September 1993, had to be postponed as a result of these difficulties which meant that the agreements of the Geneva meeting were not being met. Hectic diplomacy between US and North Korean representatives resulted in the agreement on a package of four steps to be taken simultaneously on 1 March 1994, dubbed 'Super Tuesday'. The most important one from the US perspective was that North Korea would permit the IAEA to complete its inspection. Then working-level meetings between Pyongyang and Seoul would begin to arrange the exchange of special envoys. The Republic of Korea would announce the cancellation of the 'Team Spirit' exercise and the US would support it. North Korea and the United States would announce the date of the next round of bilateral talks.

The 'Super Tuesday' deal failed to materialize because North Korea refused to permit the completion of IAEA inspections so long as the Republic of Korea made the cancellation of 'Team Spirit' conditional on the *completion* of the inspections. Thus the IAEA team that visited the DPRK in March could not complete all of the intended activities. At the North–South working-level meeting in Pamunjom on 19 March, the North Korean representative, Pak Yong-su, said to his South Korean counterpart: 'Mr Song, your side has to deeply consider the dear price of war. Seoul is not far from here. If war breaks out, it will be a sea of fire' (Gallucci et al. 2004, p. 149). (This remark was later disavowed by North Korean leader, Kim Il-sung). The key dispute between the IAEA and Pyongyang centred on inspections designed to ascertain the history of the plutonium, to ensure there had been no diversions and to reconcile the facts with the declaration submitted by the DPRK. This issue divided the US government; the non-proliferation experts at State stressed the importance of ensuring that the history of the plutonium was preserved, whereas at Defense the more pragmatic view of preventing the accumulation of plutonium for weapons in the future was seen to take priority. The problem was that the insistence on the former could render the latter objective unachievable. The US response to the breakdown of the 'Super Tuesday' deal was to renew planning for 'Team Spirit' and to cancel the next round of talks. Tension also escalated as the United States began to deploy *Patriot* air defence missiles in South Korea. In May 1994, North Korea, raised tension further by warning that it would unload the approximately 8,000 spent fuel rods from the 5 MW(e) reactor at Yongbyon for 'safety reasons'. It began implementing its plan in June. By refusing to allow the IAEA to record the location of individual fuel rods, it began to destroy the operational history of the reactor that the IAEA had fought so hard to preserve.

With the fuel rods out of the reactor, North Korea was moving one step closer to reprocessing to extract plutonium for weapons production. The IAEA estimated that the 8,000 fuel rods would yield approximately 25–30 kg of plutonium, enough for perhaps up to six nuclear warheads.

The crisis was escalating dangerously. By unloading the reactor North Korea had crossed 'a red line'. As Gallucci et al. have commented: 'Whether North Korea's defueling was the product of delusion or desperation, in crossing that line it essentially dared the United States to cut off dialogue and to refer the nuclear issue to the Security Council for punitive action' (Gallucci et al. 2004, p. 193).

Conservative commentators in the United States such as Charles Krauthammer were openly calling for an end to discussions with North Korea and for more coercive measures. The United States prepared to seek United Nations Security Council sanctions. Efforts to build an international consensus to impose sanctions began to bear fruit. Japan was considering measures to cut off the remittances of North Korean residents in Japan to the DPRK which amounted to about $600 million per annum. China was indicating its impatience with Pyongyang's behaviour and hinted that unless it came into line it would not oppose sanctions. South Korea was in favour of a firm stance and was prepared to participate in sanctions against the North.

North Korea issued threats of its own, declaring that sanctions would amount to an 'act of war'. The possibility of a strike on North Korea's nuclear facilities (in particular the reprocessing plant at Yongbyon) came under active consideration. President Clinton considered plans of how to rapidly reinforce American forces in South Korea. After briefings on the likely casualties of a war on the Korean peninsula, Clinton actively discouraged any 'war talk'. Still, as North Korea announced its intention to withdraw from the IAEA and a draft resolution for sanctions against the DPRK was circulated, the drift towards confrontation seemed inexorable.

At this point former President Jimmy Carter proposed that he should visit North Korea for a personal visit with Kim Il-sung. He followed the suggestion of the US Ambassador to the Republic of Korea, Jim Laney. Carter's involvement was a reflection of the seriousness with which the risk of escalation to armed conflict in this crisis was being viewed. The idea was that Carter might be able to reach the one person in North Korea who would be able to pull back from the brink and take the decisions necessary to avoid war. The administration was divided on the proposed trip (it was opposed by Secretary of State Warren Christopher) but it was approved by President Clinton after Vice-President Gore persuaded National Security Advisor Tony Lake to support it. The South Korean government privately opposed the Carter trip. President Kim thought that support for sanctions was growing and Carter would have a different agenda.

On 13 June 1994, Jimmy Carter arrived in Seoul. The plan was to travel to North Korea by car through the DMZ. There was an extraordinary sense of crisis. Private citizens were stockpiling supplies and the South Korean government reviewed the mobilization status of over six million reservists. Two days later, a previously planned nationwide civil defence exercise was held, which added to the sense of crisis. According to the National Ministry of Defence, the armed forces of the DPRK were at their highest state of readiness since 1990. Later it was reported by a defector that Kim Jong-il spent most of the period of the nuclear crisis in a bunker. Embassies in Seoul reviewed evacuation plans and some foreign companies ordered dependants of their employees to leave the country. US Ambassador Laney himself told his daughter and grandchildren to leave Korea. The South Korean government feared that the United States was preparing to evacuate its citizens and take steps towards a conflict in North Korea without prior consultation with Seoul. This impression was mistaken, but discussions about increasing US forces and a possible strike on the nuclear facilities were getting under way in Washington as Carter began his visit.

At the initial meeting with Foreign Minister Kim Yong-nam, Carter was confronted with a hard line. The basic message was that IAEA inspectors would be asked to leave until an agreement was reached. However, a meeting with Kim Il-sung produced a breakthrough. The 'great leader' stressed that his country could not and need not develop nuclear weapons. He also emphasized the need to be able to generate sufficient electricity.

He also made it clear that North Korea would give up its graphite-moderated reactors if it were to receive LWRs. When

Jimmy Carter sought a commitment that the IAEA inspectors should be able to complete their work without hindrance, it became clear that Kim Il-sung was not fully aware of the current state of the confrontation. The chief negotiator Kang Sok-ju advised the North Korean leader that he could make the commitment to full transparency, including remaining in the NPT, and said that a decision had already been made to permit the inspectors to stay. It transpired later that the opposite had been the case but now, with the commitment from Kim Il-sung, the immediate crisis was resolved. Kim Il-sung also supported a proposal by Carter to hold the first ever North–South inter-Korean summit. Controversially, Carter suggested to Kang that reprocessing of the fuel rods from the reactor might be permissible, provided it occurred under IAEA safeguards. Although Carter was correct in terms of his interpretation of the NPT, reprocessing had been anathema to the Clinton administration, given that it would give North Korea sufficient plutonium for perhaps five nuclear weapons. Moreover, it was expressly prohibited by the North–South Declaration on Denuclearization.

Despite the unofficial nature of Carter's visit, the ex-president made a statement on CNN that criticized the move towards sanctions and made it difficult for the US government to back away from the kind of 'deal' that seemed to be on offer. President Clinton decided to put the best face on it and interpret it in a way that satisfied US requirements, putting the burden on North Korea to challenge the 'interpretation'. Thus the US understood the commitment to mean that the 5 MW(e) reactor would not be loaded with fresh fuel and that there would be no reprocessing of spent fuel rods. This became the basis of the negotiations from there on.

Three weeks after the meeting with former President Carter, Kim Il-sung died of a heart attack on 8 July 1994. These events interrupted the talks briefly but negotiations resumed, resulting in what came to be known as the Agreed Framework on 21 October 1994.

The core of the Agreed Framework was that North Korea would abandon its nuclear programme in stages, according to progress of the LWR project that involved two 1000 MW(e) reactors that were to be completed by the target date 2003. The first step would be the freezing of additional plutonium production, but full compliance with safeguards, which would include whatever plutonium North Korea had produced prior to 1992, would not be required until a 'significant portion' of the LWR project had been completed in four or five years' time. US and IAEA officials were to supervise the freezing of the Yongbyon 5 MW(e) reactor and the storage of the fuel rods. The second phase of implementation involved the supply of 500,000 tons of heavy fuel oil annually (funded by the United States). Other elements included the reduction of barriers to trade and investment, and improvements in political relations, ultimately leading to full diplomatic relations.

Before the key nuclear components of the LWR could be delivered and the first reactor could come online, the IAEA safeguards agreement would have to be implemented, 'including all steps deemed necessary by the IAEA' (Agreed Framework, cited in Gallucci et al. 2004, p. 423).

In the third phase, after the first unit of the LWR project was completed, the 8,000 spent fuel rods would be removed from North Korea. The entire dismantlement of the graphite-moderated reactors and all elements of plutonium production in the DPRK would take place after completion of the LWR project. Once North Korea had complied with its IAEA safeguards agreement and had been accepted as a non-nuclear weapons state in the NPT, the United States would provide formal assurances to the DPRK against the threat or the use of nuclear weapons.

It is fair to say the Agreed Framework was controversial both in the United States and in South Korea, and political disagreements resulted in significant problems in its implementation which are discussed in the next chapter.

The signing of the Agreed Framework was not the end but rather the continuation of complicated bargaining between the various parties. The Agreed Framework was a sole executive agreement and, unlike treaties, was based on presidential executive authority without any formal assent from Congress. Moreover, it was a 'non-binding political agreement' that was not legally enforceable. While this meant that there were no obstacles to the adoption of the Agreed Framework, it contributed to some of the problems of implementation.

These began before the ink was even dry. The predominant mood among the American political elite and commentators was negative (Sigal 1998, pp. 192–5). The Agreed Framework was perceived to be a form of appeasement and most of the Republican leadership, including for example Senator John McCain, believed that the North Korean leadership should have simply been faced down. Senator Robert Dole, the Senate majority leader, said about the Agreed Framework that it 'shows it is always possible to get an agreement when you give enough away' (Gallucci et al. 2004, p. 336). Democrats were not exactly enthusiastic either. The obvious criticism of the Agreed Framework was that it could be viewed as a form of 'extortion'. From this perspective it could be argued that North Korea was being rewarded for breaking its international treaty commitments, and was using the threat to develop nuclear weapons to extort large-scale economic support and various political concessions. The critics, however, ignored the realities of dealing with North Korea. They did not have any workable alternative options to deal with the plutonium programme and failed to appreciate the extraordinary feat of diplomacy that was required to obtain the Agreed Framework. They may also have not fully understood the risks of military conflict on the Korean peninsula.

In view of the sceptical attitude in the media and Congress, the administration capped funding to implement the Agreed Framework at $30 million, assuming that HFO shipments could be funded with foreign contributions and that the Department of Energy would submit a separate funding request for the storage of fuel rods from the North Korean reactor.

To the surprise of the Clinton administration, the Agreed Framework was not only a hard sell in Congress, but also to some of its allies abroad. The French criticized the fact that there would be some delay before North Korea would be obliged to comply with safeguards and, on the other hand, in order to verify the freezing of nuclear facilities in the DPRK, the IAEA would conduct inspections beyond its mandate. Somehow the accord was seen as compromising the NPT, even though it achieved the much greater damage that would arise if North Korea were to finally leave the NPT. The Russians grumbled that the Agreed Framework set a bad example for countries like Ukraine that had inherited nuclear weapons from the Soviet period and after some political struggle had been persuaded to denuclearize. The Americans, however, believed that the Russians were nursing a grudge because they had reneged on their own light water reactor deal with North Korea at the behest of the Americans, only to find that another country was going to get a similar contract (Gallucci et al. 2004, p. 343). China declared that they would support any action by the UN only if it was acceptable to the DPRK. In the end the United States managed to obtain agreement for a UN Security Council statement on 4 November 1994 that supported the Agreed Framework and sanctioned the IAEA to monitor the nuclear freeze (United Nations 1994).

After that, the first phase of implementation went smoothly – the IAEA and US officials were allowed to enter North Korea to supervise the freezing of the reactor at Yongbyon and the storage of the fuel rods. The canning of fuel rods was completed by September 1999.

One of the peculiar features of the Agreed Framework was that it had been negotiated between the governments of the United States and the DPRK, but its implementation involved primarily other parties who had not been directly involved in the negotiations or were officially bound by them. The role of the Republic of Korea was particularly crucial. There was a perception in the US government that the support of the South Korean government would be critical to shore up enough support at home. Despite his misgivings and the opposition of conservatives in South Korea, President Kim Young-sam did endorse the deal (*Chosun Ilbo*, 20 October 1994; *Joongang Ilbo*, 21 October 1994). The reactors would be built by South Korea, using Korean technology (albeit derived from an American design). The Republic of Korea would also provide most of the financing (about 70 per cent of the original $4.5 billion dollars estimate), with the remainder to be provided by Japan. Kim did little to promote the Agreed Framework and most of the PR work in South Korea was done by Foreign

Minister Han Sung-joo, yet another sign that like many in the Republic of Korea Kim was rather conflicted about the Agreed Framework and the degree of financial support North Korea was to receive. While the problem of the nuclear weapons programme was recognized to be serious, Cheong Wa Dae (the Blue House – the seat of the presidential office in Seoul) thought it was witnessing the gradual collapse of the North. The economic situation had become so dire that, on the basis of the example of German unification, it was thought that the Pyongyang regime could not last much longer. This mood was quite pervasive in the Blue House; interviewees told me at the time that they thought they had another two or three years before they would have to start coping with a mass of refugees from the North. Indeed, there was a degree of recklessness in the air, a feeling that the South was finally triumphant and that it could provoke the collapse of the DPRK. The Agreed Framework was shoring up the regime in Pyongyang, and might serve to postpone unification. Some commentators in the South Korean press interpreted the Agreed Framework as part of US strategy to keep the Korean peninsula divided in perpetuity. In response, senior members of the US administration such as Defence Secretary Bill Perry and Secretary of State Warren Christopher engaged in efforts to assure South Koreans of the unwavering commitment of the United States to the alliance with the Republic of Korea.

As the US administration struggled to win support for the Geneva accord at home and abroad, it faced some unexpected obstacles. First of all there was an incident when a US helicopter strayed outside the DMZ and was shot down over North Korea. One of the two pilots (David Hilemon) was killed, the other one (Bobby Hall) captured by the North Koreans. This incident seriously threatened to derail the agreement whose implementation had just begun to work rather smoothly. Bill Richardson, a Democratic Representative visiting Pyongyang just after the incident, managed to secure the release of Hilemon's body. The North Koreans attempted to obtain various concessions in order to secure Hall's release, but Ambassador Thomas Hubbard who came to Pyongyang at the request of Kang could not agree to anything of the sort. In the end Hall was released in return for a US statement of regret and the willingness to hold military-to-military talks in the appropriate forum.

In January 1995, the first shipment of heavy fuel oil took place to the Sonbong Thermoelectric Power Generation Station. The Agreed Framework specified that these deliveries were to provide for heating and electricity generation, and not for military-related activities such as fuel tanks or aircraft. It transpired that some of the oil had been diverted to steel plants, in violation of the Agreed Framework. The Clinton administration realized that the tenuous acceptance of the Agreed Framework by congressional leaders would collapse unless the cheating was stopped. Robert Gallucci and Kang engaged in discussions by correspondence to deal with this thorny issue. Kang admitted that there had been some diversion but agreed to the principle of monitoring the disposition of heavy oil delivered by the United States. The details were worked out with Lee Tae-gun, the managing director of Pyongyang's oil import agency. Eventually it was agreed to monitor the fuel flows at various power plants. Lee pushed hard for a specific schedule for HFO delivery, but the United States was not willing to go beyond what was stated in the Agreed Framework.

In order to implement the agreement, the United States, Japan and South Korea formed an international consortium called the Korean Peninsula Energy Development Organization (KEDO) in March 1995. Its task was to provide 500,000 tons of heavy fuel oil per annum to North Korea and manage the LWR project. Initially, KEDO was a trilateral organization involving the United States, the Republic of Korea and Japan. Later the European Union played a more significant role and various other states became members of KEDO. The executive director has always been an American, and KEDO has been described as 'an extension of the US administration in dealings with North Korea to implement the agreement' (Strohmaier 2003, p. 161).

The United States accepted the South Korean demand that a Korean company should supply the reactors in return for Seoul's acceptance that the executive director of KEDO would

be an American. Seoul insisted that the phrase 'Korean standard reactor' was included in the charter of KEDO. The source
of financing excluded the possibility of using third-party (e.g.
Russian) technology. The offer was made by Kim Young-sam
to ensure that the ROK would have a central role in the
Agreed Framework and in order to provide the basis for
broader North–South cooperation, but Pyongyang initially
rejected the idea of South Korean reactors. During expert
talks in Berlin when the US delegation was led by Gary
Samore and the DPRK delegation by Kim Jong-woo (the self-
styled leader of the North Korea's LWR task force), the DPRK
delegation rejected both South Korean and Russian reactor
models (the latter due to safety concerns). Later the North
Koreans modified their stance, accepting South Korean reactors so long as Seoul's involvement would not be formally
acknowledged and Pyongyang would not have to deal directly
with the South Koreans. The Americans finally imposed a
compromise using a generic description of the reactors that
infuriated ROK President Kim but saved the LWR project
(Gallucci et al. 2004: chapter 11).

A joint statement outlining the implementation of the
Agreed Framework was issued in June 1995 after a harrow-
ing set of negotiations between the US and the DPRK in Kuala
Lumpur. Negotiations regarding the supply contract between
KEDO and the DPRK were hampered by disagreements over
logistical details (e.g. transport links between the construction
site at Sinpo in North Korea and the Republic of Korea, the
wages of North Korean workers employed on the project,
etc.). For example, the DPRK negotiators initially demanded
that KEDO should fund all costs associated with the LWR,
including construction of the LWR infrastructure, assembly of
the LWR and the remuneration of North Korean staff. In addition they demanded compensation for the full value of the
investment the DPRK had made in the development of nuclear
power until then. This amounted to a sum exceeding $10
billion that was naturally rejected by KEDO. Indeed, KEDO
was only prepared to cover the LWR assembly and some of
the costs of the site survey and preparation. KEDO also
rejected the objections of the DPRK delegation to the fact that

the Republic of Korea was to provide the LWR. The disagreements resulted in the temporary suspension of the talks and threats from the DPRK delegation to threaten 'other options' (i.e. restarting the plutonium reactor). However, eventually the delegations met again and by 5 December 1995 the supply agreement was signed, based on the general principles of the Agreed Framework.

The DPRK agreed to two important compromises. The first was the acceptance that a South Korean contractor would build Model 3 and Model 4 of the Ulchim-type reactor at the site in Sinpo. This was to be done under supervision of a US representative. The Korea Electric Power Corporation (KEPCO) became the prime contractor for the LWR. The supervision and technical coordination of the project was to be carried out by Duke Engineering & Services under the direction of the Project Operation Division of KEDO. The second compromise was that North Korea had to be in full compliance with all IAEA requirements (including special inspections to verify the amount of processed plutonium and any issues relating to the history of North Korean reprocessing) before the reactors would be completed and go online. KEDO assumed responsibility for the delivery (including assembly and transportation) of the two LWRs and for a certain amount of infrastructure at the site (roads, water supply, facilities for unloading construction supplies). KEDO was granted what amounted to an extra-judicial status in North Korea, freedom from any duties, taxes, local regulations or any interference by local authorities, free to engage in any financial transactions, including converting currency and could freely import and export any goods related to the LWRs project. It is important to emphasize that North Korea was not to get the reactors for free; the costs were to be repaid (without interest) over a 20-year period (including an initial period of three years when no payments were due). Given North Korea's difficult financial position and the poor record of honouring such commitments in the past, it is unclear whether the United States or the other partners in KEDO seriously believed that the repayments would ever be made.

Negotiations between KEDO and the DPRK on draft protocols for the details of the project made good progress and it was anticipated that all outstanding issues would be resolved by the end of 1996, so that work on the assembly of the reactors could begin. But significant delays resulted from an incident on 18 September 1996 when a North Korean submarine was scuttled off the South Korean coast near Kangnung. A two-month-long manhunt ensued in pursuit of 26 North Korean soldiers who tried to reach North Korea by land and of whom only two survived.

Both work on the LWR project and the storage of spent fuel rods was suspended for a number of months at the insistence of South Korea. The incident nearly brought about the collapse of the Agreed Framework and military retaliation by ROK armed forces. It set the schedule of the LWR project back, making it impossible to achieve the target date of 2003. The head of the DPRK delegation to the fourth and fifth protocol negotiations, Choe In-hwa, corroborated the suspicion that this incident had been instigated by those in Pyongyang opposed to the Agreed Framework (although he later recanted) (Moltz and Mansourov 2000, p. 159). The submarine incident was finally settled in December 1996 through a package deal involving an apology from North Korea, a US pledge to provide $6 million in food aid, a promise by North Korea to assist in finding American MIAs from the Korean War, and the setting up of four-party talks between the United States, China and the two Korean states.

Negotiations soon resumed and two protocols were signed on 8 January and 8 February 1997 respectively. The first of these concerned various aspects of the takeover of the site, and the second related to labour, goods, facilities and other services. Subsequently KEDO signed a preliminary works contract (PWC) with KEPCO. There were also intense negotiations resulting in a protocol relating to 'actions in the event of non-payment'. In August 1997, a ceremony of groundbreaking took place and, despite all the delays, the LWR project was moving forward.

The purpose of the four-party talks was to further reduction of tension on the Korean peninsula and replacing the armistice by the achievement of a permanent peace treaty that would bring an official end to the Korean War. From the US position, the reason for starting these talks was to unfreeze the inter-Korean dialogue by changing the political atmosphere. Six meetings took place between 1997 and 1999, without any progress. The position adopted by North Korea was that the withdrawal of US forces from South Korea was a precondition for peace negotiations. Moreover, North Korea wanted a bilateral treaty with the United States, but leaving out the Republic of Korea was a non-starter. As North Korea was receiving substantial food aid by 1999, it no longer had any incentive to pursue the four-party talks. Relations between the North and South remained prickly during the presidency of Kim Young-Sam and the hoped for North–South summit did not materialize.

Clearly the implementation of the Agreed Framework was a very complex project, both in terms of management and politics. It involved cooperation between three national governments, who in turn had to secure domestic political support, and North Korea which proved to be capable of throwing a spanner in the works at the most inopportune moment, although it proved willing to compromise when the agreement threatened to fail.

The United States was obligated to provide funds for the running of KEDO and the supply of HFO to North Korea. This meant that although Congress did not have to approve the Agreed Framework and associated agreements, it had to approve the funding. Thus the vicissitudes of US domestic politics impacted on the implementation of the Agreed Framework, as Congress placed restrictions and preconditions on the use of funds. In the first year of the Agreed Framework, there was a separate agreement with North Korea to supply 150,000 metric tons of HFO. The United States supplied one third, at a cost of $5.5 million, and the remainder (at $10,293,000) was funded by several other countries and by financing from commercial banks. From 21 October 1995, the US had to provide 500,000 tons of HFO annually, to be delivered in monthly shipments of about 42,000 metric tons each.

Funds for KEDO were appropriated through the 'Nonproliferation and Disarmament Fund'. In February 1996, Congress agreed to $22 million for KEDO to fund HFO and administrative costs. The legislation required the administration to certify that North Korea was in compliance with its obligations under the Agreed Framework, that the 1992 Joint Declaration on Denuclearization was being implemented and that the dialogue between North and South, including efforts to reduce barriers to trade and investment, was improving. Further conditions were added in 1997 – the president had to certify that the DPRK was fully cooperating in the safe storage of the spent fuel rods from the 5 MW(e) reactor, and that this process would be completed by the end of 1997. In addition, Congress required that the House Committee on Appropriations would receive a report on North Korea's military activities, including any violations of the armistice agreement and North Korea's dealings with other countries with regard to the support or development of a ballistic missile capability. The president had to certify that HFO was not used for military purposes (including industry that might produce military goods). However, the president was given the authority to waive certification requirements if the administration considered it vital to national security interests (Strohmaier, p. 184). In 1998 the allocated funding was inadequate. Consequently the US fell behind with its deliveries and the administration had to negotiate with North Korea to extend the 1999 deadline. The inability of the US to keep up with the schedule of HFO deliveries became one of the reasons why North Korea repeatedly threatened to withdraw from the Agreed Framework.

In the summer of 1998, there were two issues that fuelled congressional criticism of the Agreed Framework. The first resulted from concerns raised by US intelligence about an underground facility at Kumchang-ri in North Korea. It was resolved in 1999 when the North Koreans permitted the Americans to inspect the Kumchang-ri underground complex, evidently to save the Agreed Framework and because they had nothing to hide.

The other issue was North Korea's missile programme. On 31 August, North Korea launched a *Taepodong-2* missile, ignoring US attempts to persuade them not to launch. It was described as a space launch to celebrate Kim Jong-il's ascension to power. There were two aspects of the launch that were considered to be alarming. The first was that it demonstrated North Korea's technical capability to add a third stage to their missiles, thus raising the spectre of the development of an intercontinental ballistic missile (ICBM) in the future that could hit American cities. The other was the trajectory of the missile that brought it hurtling over Japan, exposing that country's vulnerability to missile attack from North Korea and eliciting a very strong political reaction. Japan temporarily suspended funding for KEDO and the United States warned the DPRK that further missile tests would endanger US support for the Agreed Framework and everything that it involved, including humanitarian support.

Despite the failure of these initiatives, there was a momentum towards improvement in US–DPRK relations. Vice Marshal Jo Myong-rok, the first vice-chairman of North Korea's National Defence Commission and one of Kim Jong-il's closest military advisors, came to Washington for talks with President Clinton, Secretary of State Albright and Defence Secretary Cohen, which were followed by a visit by Albright to Pyongyang where she met with Kim Jong-il. American and North Korean negotiators made progress on a deal to terminate the DPRK's missile exports. As a first step, the DPRK agreed in 1999 to a moratorium on testing of its long-range missiles. A summit meeting between Kim Jong-il and President Clinton in Pyongyang was mooted to sign a deal on missiles and promote bilateral cooperation. However, time ran out on the agreement as the negotiations became more protracted and after the election, the incoming Bush team signalled that it would not support the agreement.

The lessons of the Agreed Framework

The Agreed Framework was widely criticized in the United States. Conservatives were opposed to it because they saw it as a reward for bad behaviour. In other words, North Korea was in violation of its obligations under the Nuclear Non-Proliferation Treaty. The only way forward was for North Korea to cooperate with the IAEA to remedy this situation. For North Korea to obtain political and economic benefits as a result of its treaty violations would only encourage other would-be proliferators to likewise extort concessions by developing nuclear weapons. According to this view, US policy should be designed to force North Korea by means of sanctions or, if need be, military action, to comply with its obligations. Even the very fact of negotiations with the DPRK was seen as a sign of weakness. In the view of its critics, the Clinton administration lacked the will to confront North Korea and the Agreed Framework amounted to an unacceptable form of appeasement.

In many respects, the logic of these criticisms was very compelling. However, they ignored the reality that the IAEA was principally equipped to verify declared activities, but the mechanisms to enforce the NPT with respect to undeclared activities were and remain deficient. Even worse, given that the NPT guaranteed its adherents access to civilian nuclear technology, countries could acquire all the technology necessary to assemble fissile materials for weapons programmes without technically violating the NPT. The 'special inspections' demanded by the IAEA appeared to the DPRK to be unfair treatment. Moreover, there was nothing in international law to prevent the DPRK's withdrawal from the NPT.

The brutal fact of the matter was that the international community lacked the instruments to compel North Korea to give up its nuclear programme which by that time had become self-sufficient. In principle there was a military option to destroy the Yongbyon reactor and associated facilities. But such action would have caused widespread environmental contamination. More importantly, it was extremely risky as it might have provoked an escalation to a general military conflict on the Korean peninsula which would have resulted in an unacceptable level of civilian casualties. Finally, it was unclear what the impact of such an attack on North Korea's nuclear programme would be. Ultimately the DPRK would be able to reconstitute its facilities at secret underground locations and was unlikely to pay any attention to the international community from then on. Moreover, if it was true that the North Koreans had already separated enough plutonium for two nuclear devices, such an attack might still not prevent a residual nuclear capability. Critics of the Clinton administration's approach did not seem to properly appreciate the limits of US options or the dangers of an overly aggressive approach.

The Clinton administration was in two minds about its objectives. The maximalist goal was to compel North Korea to reveal the full history of its nuclear programme as well as curtailing future progress towards a weapons capability. But the priority of the non-proliferation absolutists led by Ashton Carter was to stop the programme, even if it meant sacrificing the verification of past activities. This approach prevailed, and indeed there would not have been an agreement without it.

The attempts to reach a solution to the North Korean nuclear programme problem were hampered by divisions in the United States and a lack of willingness on the North Korean side to make concessions. Profound opposition in Congress to any direct contact with North Korea, not to mention concession of any kind, restrained the US administration to a significant extent. Although it became apparent fairly early on that Pyongyang was after a light water reactor to replace its plutonium programme, this was not picked up and incorporated into the American negotiation strategy. At the same time the opposition to any concessions and especially to the acceptance of special inspections had become so deeply ingrained in the minds of North Korean officials who were ultimately directed by Kim Jong-il that there was not enough room for compromise.

The situation changed dramatically because of former President Jimmy Carter's visit to Pyongyang. Despite its unofficial nature, it transformed the American stance because it put the provision of LWRs and other economic concessions firmly on the agenda. At the same time Carter's visit brought Kim Il-sung into the process who apparently had been aloof and to some extent uninformed until that point. Once Kim Il-sung had agreed to the deal in principle, the North Korean bureaucracy had little choice but to find a way to implement it.

What can we learn about North Korean intentions from the process? It seems clear that there was some level of uncertainty about how best to use the leverage of the nuclear programme either in security or political and economic terms. It seems reasonable to conclude, however, that in view of the very severe economic difficulties which in themselves threatened North Korea's security, Pyongyang was serious about making a deal, i.e. trading its nuclear capability for security insurances and economic support. Indeed, this is what the Agreed Framework represents. At times the desire to trade military technology for cash became quite overt, as was demonstrated in the shameless effort to negotiate an end to North Korea's missile programme and proliferation for a specific sum of money.

The corollary is that the North Korean leadership had no clear concept about how to use nuclear weapons in a military role. By developing nuclear warheads and placing them on top of missiles, Pyongyang could have created an effective deterrent force that would hold the whole of South Korea as well as Japan and US forces based in Korea and Okinawa at risk. This raises the question of why they did not do so. One possible answer is that there are still technical problems that prevent this. But it is also clear that the primary purpose of these non-conventional weapons is political. For the North Korean leadership, its nuclear and missile capabilities clearly represent an asset that could be exploited to create leverage with the United States and compel the United States to deal with North Korea. The obvious problem is that such a card can ultimately only be played once, and that the deal must be such that it is worthwhile to give it up. In other words, it must solve North Korea's problem once and for all. Such a deal might not be possible even in principle. The Agreed Framework came as close as could be expected at the time. Moreover, it seems that North Korea was quite serious about giving up its plutonium programme and that this could have become permanent if it had been fully implemented. Nevertheless, it became apparent towards the end of the Clinton administration that North Korea was cheating. At the very least it was trying to develop a reserve capability that would allow it to develop nuclear capabilities via a different route if considered necessary. Evidence had emerged that North Korea had a programme to enrich uranium to weapons grade. Ultimately this problem would cause the Agreed Framework to unravel.

6 The 'Sunshine Policy': South Korean National Security in a New Era

In 1997, the veteran opponent of South Korea's military rule, Kim Dae-jung, was elected president of the Republic of Korea. This icon of the student protest movement and the nemesis of military rule had also opposed his predecessors' hard-line policies towards North Korea. Instead he had advocated a policy of relaxing tensions on the Korean peninsula and engaging North Korea.

When he was inaugurated as president in February 1998, he announced what became known as South Korea's 'sunshine policy' towards North Korea. The term 'sunshine policy' was derived from one of Aesop's fables in which the Sun and the North Wind compete to see which one of them would be able to strip the clothes off a traveller.

> The North Wind tried first. He blew violently. As the man clung to his clothes, the North Wind attacked him with greater force. But the man, uncomfortable from the cold, put on more clothes . . .
> The Sun now shone moderately, and the man removed his extra outer cloak. Then the sun darted beams which were more scorching until the man, not being able to withstand the heat, took off his clothes and went to take a dip in a nearby river. (Aesop 1998)

This was a complete departure from the unification policy of the previous South Korean government. The heart of the policy was the separation of politics and economics to permit the development of economic and business relations with North Korea. Instead of expecting the imminent collapse of the DPRK, the North Korean regime could adapt to the changing circumstances gradually. After a longer period of time, the increasing economic dependency on the South would result in unification on the South's terms (although this particular point was hinted at and not fully articulated). A North–South confederation was perceived as an intermediate stage some time in the future. The 'sunshine policy' was based on the principles of opposition to North Korea's military provocation, the rejection of unification through the absorption of one state by another, and the active support for reconciliation and cooperation. The underlying intention was to promote a resolution of the intractable conflict on the Korean peninsula by creating what Kim Dae-jung called 'a new benign dynamic of change'.

The assumptions underlying the 'sunshine policy' can be summarized as follows:

- the underlying dynamic of North Korean foreign policy is driven by the need for regime survival. This explains its often bellicose and aggressive behaviour;
- instead of challenging North Korea, a sustained process that provides political reassurances and economic stability through engagement will induce changes in North Korea and increase North Korea's dependence on the South and the outside world generally;
- greater dependence of North Korea on the South will restrain North Korea's behaviour and give the South greater control over inter-Korean relations;
- engaging North Korea is the only alternative. A continuing policy of confrontation is dangerous and will not yield any progress towards unification. (Han and Levin 2002, p. 31)

There were problems with the implementation of this approach from the beginning of Kim Dae-jung's presidency. Kim Dae-jung's election victory required the formation of an alliance with the conservative Kim Jong-pil, a known hardliner on North Korea, who occupied the post of prime minister in

1998 and 1999. The new unification minister was Kang In-duk, who as a senior member of the KCIA had supported the previous policy towards the North. Kim Dae-jung was aware that his policy could not fully develop until there was greater support in the country. Secondly, during the mid-90s the Republic of Korea was experiencing major economic problems as a result of a financial crisis which was exacerbated by the financial crisis in South-east Asia in 1997 and resulted in a major devaluation of the South Korean currency. This damaged the international reputation of the South Korean economy, at least temporarily, constrained the financial resources available to the Seoul government significantly and meant that the government was preoccupied and weakened by the domestic problems engendered by the crisis.

Most important, however, was the North Korean reaction. North Korea recognized the intention to gradually subvert the Northern regime. The presence of previous hardliners in the government made North Korea suspicious, as did the failure by Kim Dae-jung to reaffirm his previous commitment to a confederation. Foreign Minister Kim Yong-nam considered Kim Dae-jung to be controlled by the same group in the South Korean elite as his predecessors (Harrison 2002, p. 85). Their attitude changed to some extent when Kim Dae-jung called for the end of sanctions on North Korea during his visit to the US for a summit with President Clinton in June 1998. President Kim considered the lifting of sanctions to be imperative, because sanctions prevented North Korea's opening to the outside world. Moreover, sanctions strengthened the hand of the hardliners in Pyongyang as evidence of the hostility of the outside world and justified the continued maintenance of North Korea's isolation. However, this was a hard sell in Washington. On 6–7 August 1998, US and South Korean officials met to discuss what sanctions might be lifted. It became clear that the Republican Congress would represent a significant obstacle; many of the administration's opponents in Congress were keen to adopt a much harder line towards North Korea and were looking for ways to frustrate the implementation of the Agreed Framework and perhaps scuttle it altogether. Kim Dae-jung's new approach to North Korea was sorely tested in the first year when there was another North Korean submarine incursion and the discovery of the body of a North Korean commando off the coast three weeks later. The recalcitrance of Congress with regard to funding the Agreed Framework manifested itself in delayed shipments of heavy fuel oil. Pyongyang then issued threats in advance of a meeting with the US on 21 August to the effect that the nuclear programme would be restarted if the heavy fuel oil deliveries did not resume according to the agreed schedule.

Another issue that came to the fore in August 1998 was the discovery of a large underground complex at Kumchang-ri near the Chinese border by US reconnaissance satellites. It was believed to contain a secret plutonium reactor and a reprocessing plant, but there was not enough evidence to be certain about the purpose of the underground facility. The issue acquired considerable political salience as a consequence of a story in the *New York Times*. Pentagon spokesman Kenneth Bacon said that the intelligence was inconclusive and there was no evidence that North Korea was in breach of the Agreed Framework. The Defence Intelligence Agency (DIA) had issued a 'finding' in July 1998 that there was 'probably' an underground nuclear facility at Kumchang-ri. Although the Clinton administration tried to dampen the speculation, it contributed to the opposition to engagement with North Korea. Even the South Korean government expressed the belief, through a statement by the Minister for Foreign Affairs and Trade Hong Sun-yong, that the underground complex was connected with the nuclear programme.

By the autumn of 1998, there was mounting concern in the Clinton administration that political support for the Agreed Framework and for the policy of engagement with North Korea was crumbling. With a congressional mandate, former Secretary of Defence William Perry was appointed coordinator for US policy towards North Korea and asked to undertake a comprehensive policy review. Perry visited Seoul, Tokyo and Pyongyang as part of the review process. The timing of his visit to Pyongyang was propitious because just prior to his visit, after six months of negotiation, Pyongyang had permitted an inspection of Kumchang-ri in return for

600,000 tons of food and a new potato-production programme (although the United States denied any link between
the supply of food and the inspections). Nothing was found
and it became clear that the underground caverns were unsuitable for nuclear facilities (Oberdorfer 2001, pp. 413–14).
Perry's report advocated a 'two-path strategy':

> The first path involves a new, comprehensive and integrated
> approach to our negotiations with the DPRK. We would seek
> complete and verifiable assurances that the DPRK does not
> have a nuclear weapons program. We would also seek the com-
> plete and verifiable cessation of testing, production and deploy-
> ment of missiles exceeding the parameters of the Missile
> Technology Control Regime, and the complete cessation of
> export sales of such missiles and the equipment and technology
> associated with them. By negotiating the complete cessation of
> the DPRK's destabilizing nuclear weapons and long-range
> missile programs, this path would lead to a stable security sit-
> uation on the Korean Peninsula, creating the conditions for a
> more durable and lasting peace in the long run and ending the
> Cold War in East Asia. (Perry 1999)

The first path obviously depended on North Korea's cooper-
ation. The second path, in the absence of such cooperation,
would consist in containment of the North Korean threat.
Even then the Perry report recommended that the Agreed
Framework should be implemented and direct conflict with
North Korea should be avoided, if possible.

The Perry report was successful in building a new consensus to move forward with the Agreed Framework and with the
engagement of North Korea in arms control. The Clinton
administration began to focus in particular on the problem of
North Korea's development and proliferation of ballistic
missile technology. It also became concerned about reports
indicating North Korean interest in technology related to the
production of highly enriched uranium which might provide
Pyongyang with an alternative route to the development of
nuclear weapons. To deal with these concerns, the US proposed so-called 'nuclear transparency talks' with the purpose
of developing a bilateral inspection regime. Moreover, given

the concerns about uranium, the administration proposed to modify the Agreed Framework to replace the proposed light water reactors with conventional power stations. Since the non-nuclear power stations could be delivered more quickly, North Korean acceptance of IAEA safeguards obligations and inspections could be brought forward, allaying fears about nuclear activities. The first of these initiatives led to preliminary talks with North Korea but went no further; the latter faced opposition from the government in Seoul which did not want to abandon the investment it had made in light water reactors or risk any setback in relations with North Korea.

Whereas the threat of Kumchang-ri was manufactured, the same cannot be said for that of the *Taepodong-2* missile, later confirmed as a failed attempt to launch a satellite, on 31 August 1998. The fact that the two first stages of the missile came down in the Sea of Japan created near panic in Japan and brought a sharp reaction from the Japanese government. It threatened to withdraw from its commitments to support the Agreed Framework, suspended humanitarian aid to North Korea, put on hold the restoration of diplomatic relations (which would have been accompanied with substantial reparations) and initiated military counter-measures, including a satellite reconnaissance programme and the development, jointly with the US, of a regional tactical missile defence system.

Although without doubt North Korea aspired to a capability to hold at risk Japan and US forces in Okinawa, nevertheless it does not appear to have been the intention of Pyongyang to present such a direct threat to Japan as the main object of the exercise was to launch a satellite. There were many indications that North Korea wanted to preserve the Agreed Framework and sought to maximize its bargaining power in order to alleviate its economic problems and improve relations with Washington and Seoul.

Kim Dae-jung remained undeterred from his course despite the various crises during the first year of his presidency. He supported the project of the president of the Hyundai Corporation, Jung Ju-young, to develop a tourist resort in North Korea at Mount Kumgang, a project that had been blocked by his predecessors. It involved a payment of $942 million over six years for the exclusive right to operate tours for thirty years, thus providing a welcome source of cash for Pyongyang while encouraging South Korean tourists to visit the North. The tours proved very popular, with more than 190,000 South Koreans participating by April 2000, but they were run at a loss amounting to $206 million by June 2001, compelling Hyundai to seek assistance from the government in Seoul (Harrison 2002, p. 86; Oberdorfer 2001, p. 416). The ROK government considered it crucial that it was consistent and reliable in delivering on its economic commitments to the North and therefore ensured that payments were made, aided by loans from the Bank of Korea and other means. Of course the most significant form of expenditure in financial support for the North consisted of the heavy investment in KEDO for the construction of the LWR which was largely funded by the Republic of Korea.

Indeed the year 2000 was the time when North Korea seemed to be ready to resume a more cooperative relationship with the South and the United States. Kim Dae-jung for his part decided early in 2000 that his efforts should be concentrated on achieving a summit meeting with Kim Jong-il. He first publicly proposed such a meeting on 20 January. In March, during a tour of European capitals, Kim proposed a wide-ranging programme of assistance for North Korea, aimed at improving the country's infrastructure including transport, electricity and communications as well as structural support for agriculture to help avert future famines. The effort to induce North Korea to accept his bold invitation had the desired effect. A series of secret meetings were held in China involving the ROK Culture and Tourism Minister Park Jie-won and North Korean diplomat Song Ho-gyong, and on 10 April 2000 the agreement to hold a North–South summit was announced. The details were worked out during a trip to Pyongyang by Lim Dong-won, the director of the ROK National Intelligence Service and previously President Kim's advisor on inter-Korean affairs.

On 13 June 2000, President Kim Dae-jung and his entourage arrived in Pyongyang to a reception on a scale typical of North Korean public events. For three days the two leaders discussed a large range of issues in relations between the two Koreas, including the Agreed Framework, South Korean assistance, the reunion of divided families, cultural exchanges and regular meetings between officials. Kim Jong-il and Kim Dae-jung spent much time debating the notion of a confederation between the two states that was to constitute the first concrete state in the process of unification. The North Korean concept involved a very loose 'confederation' that would amount to little more than political declaration, called a 'federation of lower stage', but Kim Jong-il in the end accepted that the South's proposal for more formal structure involving a council of ministers and a council of representatives along the lines of a 'Korean commonwealth' previously proposed by Roh Tae-woo could be a possible solution (Harrison 2002, p. 89). The summit ended with the following joint declaration:

1 The South and the North have agreed to resolve the question of reunification on their own initiative and through the joint efforts of the Korean people, who are the masters of the country.
2 Acknowledging that there are common elements in the South's proposal for a confederation and the North's proposal for a federation of lower stage as the formulae for achieving reunification, the South and the North agreed to promote reunification in that direction.
3 The South and the North have agreed to promptly resolve humanitarian issues such as exchange visits by separated family members and relatives on the occasion of the August 15 National Liberation Day and the question of former long-term prisoners who had refused to renounce communism.
4 The South and the North have agreed to consolidate mutual trust by promoting balanced development of the national economy through economic cooperation and by stimulating cooperation and exchanges in civic, cultural, sports, public health, environmental and all other fields.
5 The South and the North have agreed to hold a dialogue between relevant authorities in the near future to implement the above agreement expeditiously. President Kim

Dae-jung cordially invited National Defense Commission chairman Kim Jong-il to visit Seoul, and Kim Jong-il decided to visit Seoul at an appropriate time. (Cited in Oberdorfer 2001, p. 431)

The statement in the communiqué in which the two Koreas agreed to establish a confederation of two states was breathtaking in its implications. Unfortunately neither Kim Jong-il nor Kim Dae-jung seriously believed that it would come about in anything like the near future. Kim Dae-jung doubted that concrete talks would take place during his time in office and that unification would probably not occur in his lifetime (Harrison 2002, p. 91). Instead of representing a great step forward towards national reconciliation and eventual unification, the summit can be more correctly interpreted as marking the mutual acceptance of peaceful co-existence. (It should be mentioned that any achievements of the summit were marred by the revelation that $450 million were transferred to North Korea through the Hyundai Corporation just before the summit.)

As soon as the summit ended, President Clinton moved to relax sanctions on North Korea which, according to the analysis by the veteran North Korea observer Selig Harrison, was one of the most important results Pyongyang expected (Harrison 2002, p. 89). As mentioned in the previous chapter, in the autumn of 2000 there was a sustained effort to improve relations between Washington and Pyongyang. Vice Marshal Jo Myong-rok, one of Kim Jong-il's closest advisors and director general of the General Political Bureau of the Korean People's Army, visited Washington in early October, and Secretary of State Madeleine Albright travelled to Pyongyang for a summit with Kim Jong-il later in the same month. Kim Jong-il mooted the possibility of stopping the international sale of missiles and limiting future production and deployment of missiles to those with a range of not more than 500 km, which would eliminate the long-range missiles such as the *Rodong* and the *Taepodong-2*. In return, Kim was expecting compensation in various forms (including launches of North Korean satellites) and a summit meeting with the

US president. Although the prospect of such an agreement addressed major US national security concerns, it proved impossible to finalize before the end of Clinton's presidential term and the incoming Bush administration had no interest in pursuing the matter.

The reception Kim Dae-jung received on his return from Pyongyang was rather mixed and the event sparked off a national debate on the future of relations with the North. The leader of the opposition Grand National Party (GNP), Lee-Hoi-chang, congratulated Kim but issued some important reservations. These fell into three categories:

1 The problem of security. The Joint Declaration did not deal with the reduction of the political and military tension.
2 The issue of reciprocity in economic relations. The GNP demanded that economic support for the North needed to be transparent and result in reciprocal economic and political concessions from the North.
3 The need for a national consensus and political transparency regarding relations with the North. The National Assembly needed to be involved in the formulation and implementation of policy towards the North, especially as such drastic steps as a Korean confederation were being considered. (Lee 2000).

Conservative voices as expressed in the national press echoed the criticism that too many one-sided concessions had been made and that rapprochement with the North was moving too fast. Other issues that should have been addressed were the South Korean prisoners in the North from the time of the Korean War (concessions had been made regarding long-term Northern prisoners in the South), apologies from the North for starting the Korean War and for its various terrorist attacks on the South since. The opposition said that Kim Jong-il should not be invited to a summit in Seoul before these issues were dealt with.

Despite all the criticism, there was a great deal of support for Kim Dae-jung and the 'sunshine policy' in the immediate aftermath of the summit. The nomination in 2000 of

Kim Dae-jung to receive the Nobel Peace Prize for his efforts to secure peace on the Korean peninsula further strengthened this especially among the younger generation who favoured the new approach to relations with the North.

North Korea considerably reduced its attacks on the South in the aftermath of the summit and focused its attention on 'rightist' critics of the summit who were branded as being opposed to unification. It also tried to encourage those at the other end of the political spectrum through various actions designed to invoke the emotional desire for unification, such as inviting leftist South Korean workers to North Korea for debates, arranging other cultural exchanges and having its athletes join its South Korean colleagues to march under a single flag at the opening ceremony of the Sidney Olympics. Two emotional family reunion meetings were organized for 100 families separated as a result of the Korean War (Han and Levin 2002, p. 104).

Paradoxically, the family reunions and cultural exchanges afforded South Koreans a glimpse into the reality of North Korean life that revealed its stark difference to that of the South and the rest of the world. But enthusiasm for the new relationship with the North began to decline as it became clear that, when it came to the implementation of the other agreements reached at the summit, Pyongyang was dragging its feet and concentrating on its relations with Washington, seemingly seeking to bypass Seoul. For example, the North did not begin rebuilding the North–South railroad link and did not send a delegation to the groundbreaking ceremony for this project in the South. Meetings were often cancelled at short notice. The first North–South defence ministerial meeting did take place, but no substantial talks on military matters took place. More importantly, no date was set for Kim Jong-il's visit to the South and eventually the postponement of the return summit seemed to be indefinite.The implementation of the 'sunshine policy' became more difficult after the Bush administration came into office in 2001. Essentially Bush considered any effort to engage North Korea pointless. During a summit meeting between Bush and Kim Dae-jung in 2001, the two presidents were unable to disguise their sharp disagreement on policy towards the DPRK. This in turn deepened the division in South Korean society about the wisdom of the 'sunshine policy'. In 2001, the conservative ULD led by Kim Jong-pil, who in 1961 had helped Park Chung-hee to mount his military coup, withdrew from coalition with Kim Dae-jung in protest against the 'sunshine policy' which Kim Jong-pil constantly tried to undermine from within. They withdrew from the government and supported a non-confidence vote against the Director of the National Intelligence Service, Lim Dong-won, in the National Assembly. The cabinet had to resign and the president lost his majority in the National Assembly, thus constraining his ability to govern effectively.

Engaging North Korea: the prospects for the future

The foundation of the national security policy of the Republic of Korea during the presidency of Kim Dae-jung was the 'removal of the cold war system on the Korean peninsula' (MND 2000). This policy had three elements. The first was the maintenance of a strong defence posture. The second element of the national security policy of the Kim Dae-jung government was the creation of a 'combined North–South economic system'. The third element was the removal of the Cold War system from the Korean peninsula, including the elimination of North Korean WMD (MND 2000).

The 'sunshine policy' proved very controversial in South Korea and the debate about policy towards the North revealed deep fissures in South Korean society, based to an extent on a generation gap. Younger people who had no memory of the Korean War, but had grown up in the time of the struggle for democracy and against the military dictatorship tended to have a less critical attitude towards the North and a less positive attitude towards the alliance with the United States. Paradoxically, their image of the North was more benign than that of the anti-communist conservatives, and yet they had less interest in the idea of Korean unification. But as Yong-sup Han and Norman Levin have pointed out, these divisions have deeper roots in Korean history, but were to some extent suppressed during the period of the military dictatorship (Han and Levin 2002: chapter 4). As the Republic of Korea has become an open democracy, many on the left have articulated the view that the United States is to a significant extent responsible for the division on the Korean peninsula and its perpetuation. In this view, that presence of US forces is unnecessary and a hindrance in inter-Korean relations. The conservatives on the other hand continue to see North Korea as the enemy, bent on subverting the South and see the presence of US forces as essential for the security of the Republic of Korea and are suspicious of the 'sunshine policy' which is believed to be used as a propaganda instrument by the North.

Kim Dae-jung and the Millennium Democratic Party, which was formed in 2000 from the National Congress for New Politics that Kim formed in 1995 as a platform for his presidential bid, represented the student protest generation. Conservative opinion is represented mainly in the Grand National Party, which emerged in 1997 from a variety of predecessors including Roh Tae-woo's Democratic Justice Party (DJP) and Kim Young-sam's Reunification Democratic Party (RDP). Further to the right were the United Liberal Democrats led by Kim Jong-pil and supported by businesses and anti-communist organizations.

Critics questioned its underlying assumption. While there was no doubt that North Korea was facing serious economic problems, to the point where the survival of the country was in jeopardy, there was no evidence to suggest that it had abandoned its ambition to undermine and eventually incorporate the South to unify the country under its own regime. Moreover, there is little evidence that the expectation that North Korea would moderate its behaviour has been fulfilled. Indeed, severe political and military provocations continued since the inauguration of the policy virtually unabated, and despite the summit the promise of a new era in inter-Korean relations remained largely unfulfilled. Critics charge that 'one-sided' concessions do not persuade North Korea that the South is 'sincere', but rather encourage the DPRK to seek even further concessions. The point was made in the *Chosun Ilbo*:

What conservatives oppose is the sunshine only policy. As clearly demonstrated in several surveys, people want a careful balance of sunshine and wind, carrot and stick. They want to be consulted and not have the president determine North Korean policy on his own without aides, ministers or the National Assembly. On this issue, he should not disregard the people's wishes, as it is important for the future of the country. To argue over the policy for too long a time is also not beneficial, particularly when North Korea is slowly watching. (*Chosun Ilbo*, 11 September 1999)

From the critics' point of view, this problem became considerably worse during the presidency of Roh Moo-hyun who defeated Lee Hoi-chang in the presidential elections in 2002. Policy towards the North was largely defined by Roh's national security specialist Lee Jong-seok (initially deputy national security advisor and later unification minister until he resigned in the aftermath of North Korea's nuclear test in 2006). Lee, who previously worked at the Sejong Institute, promoted a perspective based on the assumptions of the 'sunshine policy' and an unswerving belief in constructive engagement. The Roh government seemed to want to go out of its way to accommodate North Korea, but consistently refused to support sanctions against the DPRK when Pyongyang showed recalcitrance, especially with regard to its nuclear weapons programme. The policy of the Roh administration with regard to the nuclear weapons programme was to denounce it and declare that the nuclear problem had to be solved, but oppose sanctions or any other form of pressure on Pyongyang. Seoul even did its level best to discourage defections from North Korea, and remained ambivalent in its criticism of the humanitarian situation in the DPRK. Eventually, as the talks about the nuclear programme stalled, the Roh government behaved as a quasi-spokesperson for the Pyongyang regime, representing its viewpoint abroad. This behaviour persisted until North Korea broke its missile-testing moratorium in July 2006 and engaged in a number of provocative missile launches which resulted in Seoul stopping promised deliveries of food and fertilizer.

Much of the criticism has focused on the tactics, i.e. the policy of the Kim Dae-jung and the Roh Moo-hyun governments was simply ineffective in countering the tactics of the North Korea regime. But conservatives in South Korea were concerned about a much deeper underlying problem, namely that the 'sunshine policy' was based on a false understanding about the nature of the North Korea regime and its ultimate objectives. It was not just that the regime was based on a different philosophy of social organization, or that the current situation was the result of a bitter civil war that had divided the country for over half a century. At the core of the continuing division of the two Koreas was the fact that the DPRK was a society organized around the rule of the Kim dynasty which would be unwilling to relinquish power under any circumstances. While it was true that the regime was under very severe pressure due to its failing economy, the very fact that it survived even the consequences of a severe famine in which over a million people died demonstrated the extreme measures it was prepared to undertake to ensure its survival. It showed how tight its grip was on the population and that as long as the livelihood of the political elite and the army was guaranteed (although even soldiers were not entirely immune from the problems of food scarcity), there was no hope of an indigenous uprising. But this understanding of the nature of the North Korean regime has important implications for the prospects for alternative arrangements on the Korean peninsula, such as a confederation offered by Kim Jong-il or even unification. It implies that from the Northern perspective any arrangement that brings the Koreas closer means greater influence for the North over the South (while keeping the North closed to influence from the South) and unification means extending the rule of the Kim dynasty over the entire Korean peninsula. This means there can be no real rapprochement between North and South without regime change.

Even if this analysis of the situation on the Korean peninsula is accepted, this does not negate the rationale for a policy of engagement entirely. First of all there is a general consensus in the Republic of Korea that a sudden collapse of North Korea is not desirable. Indeed, the possibility of such an event is the most serious threat that South Korea faces. The expected flood of refugees would create massive instability in both North and South, threatening both the economic and societal cohesion of the South. The costs of unification are hard to quantify and depend on the manner in which it occurs, but have been variously put at somewhere between $500 billion to $2 trillion (Harrison 2002: chapter 8; Noland 2004). Moreover, the movement of refugees could occur in both directions, prompting a possible intervention by China. Finally, given the size of the armed forces and their enormous conventional military arsenals, there would be plenty of scope for uncontrolled violence. A sudden unification along the lines of the example of Germany is not viable because the Republic of Korea does not dispose of the resources that West Germany had, and the level of the North Korean economy is very much lower than that of the German Democratic Republic in its final years. The only viable alternative therefore is a 'soft landing', a gradual regime change and a long period of economic and political reform in the North that will make unification possible to achieve some time in the future. The prospects for a 'soft landing', however, are also hampered by the persistence of the Kim regime. There is no doubt that the regime is resisting any efforts by the South to promote political change in the North. This is why the situation on the Korean peninsula remains so intractable.

Despite its inherent difficulties and the recalcitrance of the North Korean regime, the logic of the policy of engagement remains compelling. At the very least this policy will prevent a catastrophic collapse of the North. There is also no doubt that North Korea is gradually becoming economically more dependent on the South. Trade between the two Koreas has grown steadily to the point where the Republic of Korea has become the DPRK's most important trading partner ahead of China and Japan (the share was 27 per cent, 26.9 per cent and 23.3 per cent respectively in 2002) (Samuel Kim 2004: chapter 4). During the term of Kim Dae-jung's presidency alone the volume of trade increased from $221 million in 1998 to $641 million in 2002. South Korea is an important source of critical aid for the North, both in terms of cash and the provision of rice, fertilizer and other essential goods. The Republic of Korea is also providing investment for various projects in the North, the most significant of which is the Gaesong Industrial

Complex. The GIC is located forty miles north of Seoul and was designed to attract South Korean business with cheap North Korean labour and government loan guarantees of up to $10.5 million per loan. Over 1,300 companies applied to set up production facilities in Gaesong. Businesses have to provide for infrastructure (electricity, transport communications). Yoon Young-kwan, South Korea's foreign and trade minister from 2003–4 and one of Korea's leading experts on the International Political Economy (now at Seoul National University) told the author that he envisaged the Kaesong Industrial Complex would become economically united with the northern region of South Korea. It is better positioned than the Rajin-Sonbong Free Economic Zone that has a hotel and a casino as its main attractions. The attempt to develop the Sinuiju Special Administrative Region near the Chinese border has stalled as Yang Bin, the Chinese businessman who was appointed to run it, was arrested in China and deported on charges of corruption (Samuel Kim 2004).

The theory then is that an increase in the density of North–South interactions and greater involvement of the South in the North's economy drive forward a process of economic change which ultimately will translate into social change. One version of this argument is that North Korea's nuclear programme and other threatening activities can be ignored because essentially North Korea is deterred. Ultimately the increasing economic engagement with the South will bring about political reform and regime change whether the North Korean elite accepts it or not. However, it is unclear whether to ignore the security dimension is in the interests of either the Republic of Korea or the region. As the regime weakens, it may increase its military provocations as a means of reversing the trend. Moreover, the strategic situation will change as North Korea will be able to increasingly target Japanese forces and American forces based outside the Korean peninsula (especially if nuclear weapons are involved). Perhaps the most problematic feature of the 'sunshine policy' is the ambiguity it has generated both about the direction of the process and the status of the Republic of Korea itself. The precise nature of any 'closer association' between North and South has remained unclear. Specific steps on the road of unification have not been elaborated upon, except for the intermediate stage of 'confederation'. Conservatives have been deeply concerned by the fact that this process effectively abandons South Korea's claim to represent the true Korea, and a confederation might ostensibly give equal legitimacy to both Korean states. In other words, critics of the 'sunshine policy' have emphasized that any rapprochement between the two Koreas must avoid undermining the integrity and the status of the Republic of Korea.

The road to ending the crisis on the Korean peninsula is still long and arduous. The population of South Korea is deeply divided about the way forward. As the almost unconditional commitment to engagement with North Korea has finally reached its limits, a more balanced policy may emerge in the future. But ultimately there is no going back on a policy of engagement based on the principle of peaceful co-existence of the two Koreas until they are ready for unification.

Renewed Confrontation and the Second North Korean Nuclear Crisis

At the end of the twentieth century, it seemed that fundamental progress had been made towards transforming the crisis on the Korean peninsula into a stable form of peaceful co-existence. The threat of the North Korean nuclear programme had been contained by the Agreed Framework, while the historic summit between the two Korean leaders promised a new era of inter-Korean relations. There were signals from Pyongyang that other security issues, such as the North Korean missile programme, might be susceptible to similar solutions.

Those hopes were soon dashed. When George W. Bush assumed the presidency of the United States in 2001, he initiated a fundamental review of US national security policy. The Bush national security team took pride in its radical approach, finally abandoning the Cold War approach to international security. But its world view remained rooted in old-fashioned realism according to which states are the main actors in the international system. The Bush administration was not ready to deal with, or even recognize the importance of the 'new wars' that were emerging as the main threat to international security and stability. Bush wanted to reduce US responsibilities abroad and focus on the US national interest rather than support efforts to build global collective security. He signalled that he was not going to get involved in further attempts to resolve the Israel–Palestine conflict, Northern Ireland or any sort of nation-building in crisis regions. The initial focus of the security policy of the Bush administration was on national missile defence, even though it was uncertain whether a strategically significant system would ever materialize.

The new strategic outlook and the general tendency to eschew international regimes and depend on unilateral or bilateral arrangements, to rely on the overwhelming military power of the United States and neglect soft power, exhibited itself first of all in arms control and nuclear policy, but then extended to other areas of international security. While Bush himself was inclined to reduce US global responsibilities, a different impulse came from the so-called neo-conservatives and their supporters in the government, such as Paul Wolfowitz, Richard Perle and Donald Rumsfeld. They advocated a form of hegemonist realism, using US military power to constrain 'rogue states' and bring about either regime change or at least a fundamental change in the behaviour of those regimes which were seen as posing a threat to international security and US interests. 'Rogue states' that sponsored terrorists and sought to acquire weapons of mass destruction were described as an 'axis of evil'. The neo-conservatives believed that these states could either be coerced to move towards conformity with international norms or even be replaced by democratic governments (Daalder and Lindsay 2005; Bluth 2004; Lott 2004).

The Bush administration took some time to review its policy on North Korea that resulted in a policy vacuum in the final days of the Kim Dae-jung government. Secretary of State Colin Powell made statements in support of further diplomatic efforts, while President Bush openly voiced his doubts about attempting to engage North Korea in a difficult meeting with ROK President Kim Dae-jung where little effort was made to disguise the fundamental disagreement between the two leaders.

On 6 June 2001, a policy statement was issued by the US government that indicated support for the Agreed Framework as long as North Korea fulfilled its conditions. This was despite the fact that among conservative Republicans there was deep disapproval of the Agreed Framework. The Bush administration even secured increased funding for the heavy fuel oil deliveries to North Korea. It also promised to continue to provide humanitarian food assistance. At the same time it rejected a continuation of the previous talks on missiles and instead stated that future talks should follow a broad agenda, including 'improved implementation of the Agreed Framework relating to North Korea's nuclear activities; verifiable constraints on North Korea's missile programmes and a ban on its missile exports; and a less threatening conventional military posture' (US White House 2001). In return, the United States would ease sanctions and take other steps to help the North Korean people. Gary Samore aptly described this approach as demanding more and offering less than the previous US government (Samore 2003: 11). Efforts by the North Korean government to revive the missile talks, including attempts to enlist Russian and European support, fell on deaf ears in Washington.

The events of 11 September 2001 had a profound impact on US national security policy in general and relations with North Korea in particular. The demonstration of the willingness of international terrorists to cause mass casualties raised the fear of a confluence of 'rogue states' that pursue weapons of mass destruction and sponsor international terrorism. This was 'the axis of evil' described by President Bush in his 2002 State of the Union address. The president stated that the United States had the right to take pre-emptive action against threats, rather than wait until the US or its allies were attacked with weapons of mass destruction. North Korea reacted strongly to its inclusion in the 'axis of evil' , which it interpreted as a manifestation of Washington's desire to put pressure on North Korea in order to 'stifle' the regime.

During a visit to Pyongyang in April 2002, South Korea's national security advisor Lim Dong-won tried to persuade Kim Jong-il to receive a special envoy from the United States. North Korea decided to resume the bilateral dialogue with the US. The Assistant Secretary of State for East Asian and Pacific Affairs, James Kelly, was supposed to visit Pyongyang on 10 July but, due to clashes between North and South Korean naval forces, the visit was postponed until October.

Prior to Kelly's October trip to North Korea, US intelligence issued a secret assessment according to which North

Korea had started a clandestine programme to produce highly enriched uranium (HEU) using centrifuge technology it had acquired from Pakistan in return for *Rodong* missiles. The information on which this assessment was based had come from a variety of sources. In 1999, Seoul informed Washington that North Korean scientists had visited Pakistan, and in March 1999 the Republic of Korea and the United States jointly prevented the purchase by North Korea of components for gas centrifuges in Japan. In 2001, a North Korean defector said that North Korea had been pursuing centrifuge technology for uranium enrichment for some time. Moreover, there was evidence that North Korea was seeking components such as certain types of aluminium tubes and equipment for uranium feed-and-withdrawal systems for which no other purpose appeared plausible.

The uranium enrichment programme was interpreted as a substantial breach of trust and evidence for the strong belief of the opponents of any accommodation with North Korea that the DPRK simply could not be trusted. Although technically not a breach of the Agreement Framework which was concerned only with plutonium, it was nevertheless incompatible with commitments under the Agreed Framework which reaffirmed the North–South Declaration on denuclearization (1992) which banned uranium enrichment. It also violated North Korea's obligations under the NPT (Strohmaier 2003). However, the status of this programme and the location of any enrichment facility were unproven.

The provisional assessment of the CIA was that North Korea was constructing a uranium enrichment plant that would be able to produce HEU for two weapons annually once fully operational, possibly by mid-decade. The Republic of Korea and China were doubtful about the existence of an actual HEU programme. An analysis by experts from the International Institute of Strategic Studies in the United Kingdom, using the information that has come into the public domain, shows that, although no definite conclusions can be drawn, it seems unlikely that North Korea has an operational enrichment plan at present and may not have one for more than ten years. This tentative assessment is based on an indication that North Korea is still seeking components for an enrichment plant, the difficulties of building other elements of the infrastructure required (i.e. a UF6 feeder plant) given what is known about North Korea's nuclear facilities, and the technical difficulties of successfully operating a uranium enrichment plant based on centrifuge technology. More recent internal South Korean assessments seem to broadly concur with the judgement that North Korea is not yet very close to possessing the capacity for producing HEU (based on interviews in Seoul 2004–6). Thus Kim Tae-woo from the Korea Institute for Defense Analyses suggests that the Khan Research Laboratory may have provided North Korea with a number of P-1 and P-2 type centrifuges, 50 kg of UF6 for calibration and technical information for the construction of enrichment stages and cascades. He concluded (as of the autumn of 2004) that North Korea most likely did not yet have any full-scale enrichment facilities or weapons-grade HEU, but that it might have laboratory-scale centrifuge facilities (Kim, Tae-woo 2004: 40). Of course, these conclusions are based on estimates, given the available information, and the actual state of the uranium enrichment programme in North Korea remains unknown.

Nevertheless, after the summit meeting between Japanese Prime Minister Koizumi and Kim Jong-il on 17 September 2002, the United States decided to confront North Korea about the clandestine uranium enrichment programme at the postponed meeting in Pyongyang that finally took place on 4–5 October 2002. Kelly met with vice foreign minister Kang Sok-joo and other North Korean officials. He outlined the broad proposals, but then brought up the question of the clandestine uranium enrichment programme, stating that no progress could be made until the uranium programme was dismantled. According to the American version of events, the North Koreans initially denied the existence of the programme but the next day, to the Americans' surprise, Kang admitted that the enrichment programme existed and claimed it was justified by the belligerence of the Bush administration and its various threats. Subsequently, North Korea circulated versions of the meeting that differed substantially from that reported by Kelly. In November, the DPRK ambassador to the

United Nations stated that North Korea would be prepared to satisfy all security concerns the US might have, including those relating to the uranium enrichment programme, and the possibility of inspections of all North Korean nuclear facilities would be considered. Despite the presence of Korean speakers on the US delegation, there remains some uncertainty as to what precisely transpired (Pinkston and Saunders 2003: 81–2). Later, in December, North Korea denied it had acknowledged the existence of a uranium enrichment programme, claiming that Kang had merely asserted North Korea's right to have such a programme. At a conference at Wilton Park in the UK on North-east Asian security in October 2004, the North Korean delegation first stated that the DPRK did not have a uranium enrichment programme as such. When pressed, the North Korean ambassador to the UK, Ri Yong-ho, categorically denied again that North Korea had a uranium enrichment programme (Harrison 2005a and 2005b; Gallucci and Reiss 2005; Garwin 2005.) (In view of the controversy that later ensued in the journal *Foreign Affairs* about what transpired, it should be said that the author was present at this meeting.) North Korea accused the United States of violating the Agreed Framework because of the failure to deliver the light water reactor on time and to provide formal assurances that it would not threaten or use nuclear weapons against the DPRK.

The South Korean government was unwilling to abandon the 'sunshine policy' and make South Korean assistance to North Korea dependent on the abandonment of the enrichment programme. While Japan made normalization of relations dependent on the resolution of the nuclear issue, leading to a breakdown in the talks, both Japan and the Republic of Korea were concerned that taking actions that would lead to the 'suspension' of the activities of KEDO would induce North Korea to retaliate by resuming nuclear activities frozen by the Agreed Framework. In the end the decision was that heavy fuel oil shipments would be suspended once the shipment that was already en route was delivered.

The calculation in Washington was that North Korea was too weak to retaliate against the suspension of HFO and that pressure from the international community and the threat of sanctions would yield the desired result, i.e. dismantlement of the nuclear programmes. Moreover, the growing confrontation with Iraq over its alleged WMD was thought to put pressure on Kim Jong-il as well by signalling that a similar confrontation might be on the cards with regard to the North Korean nuclear programme (Huntley 2004: 96). This turned out to be a major tactical misjudgement. First of all, it flew in the face of past experience with North Korean negotiating behaviour that was characterized by extreme brinkmanship in apparent defiance of practical realities and what outsiders might have calculated to be in the DPRK's best interest. As Scott Snyder has demonstrated, if North Korea judges the external environment to be unfavourable to the pursuit of its agenda, then it adopts a position of *kojip* (stubbornness or unyielding attitude) until the external environment becomes more favourable (Snyder 2002). Secondly, North Korea drew precisely the opposite conclusion from the example of Iraq: 'The Iraq war teaches a lesson that in order to prevent a war and defend the security of a country and the sovereignty of a nation, it is necessary to have a powerful physical deterrent' (KCNA, 18 April 2003). North Korea may also have calculated that the United States would be preoccupied with the Iraq crisis and could not afford to mount a similar confrontation in the Far East at the same time. On 12 December 2002, the DPRK announced that it was restarting the 5 MW(e) reactor and resuming construction of the 50 MW(e) and 200 MW(e) reactors (two projects that had been started but not completed prior to the Agreed Framework).

These events occurred in the run-up to presidential elections in the Republic of Korea. During the election campaign, the GNP and its candidate Lee Hoi-chang were very critical of the 'sunshine policy'. The candidate of the Millennium Democratic Party, Roh Moo-hyun, on the other hand was prepared to expand cooperation with North Korea even further. The question of relations with the United States was very much on the agenda, especially as a result of an incident where two Korean schoolgirls were killed in a traffic accident by a US armoured vehicle. Roh refused to visit the United States prior to the election and called for the revision of the SOFA (Status of Forces Agreement) in order to put the bilateral relationship on a more equal basis. On 19 December Roh was elected by a narrow margin, partly due to the anti-American sentiment that affected parts of the electorate. Roh's success may also have been due in part to an electoral strategy that focused on the internet in order to get young people to think about politics and turn out to vote (Kim Sung-han 2003; Kihl 2005).

It is tempting to speculate that Roh's victory gave North Korea the sense that its hand had been strengthened. On 22 December, a mere three days after the election, North Korea ordered the IAEA to remove surveillance cameras and seals on the 5 MW(e) reactor, the spent fuel storage pond and the reprocessing facility, and expelled the inspectors themselves on 27 December. It also announced that preparations to resume reprocessing would be completed soon. The action was justified on the basis of safety concerns relating to the handling of spent fuels from the reactor that had been unfrozen. However, it was clear that reprocessing 8,000 spent fuel rods that had been removed from the reactor in 1994 would give North Korea about 25–30 kg of plutonium, enough fissile material for up to eight nuclear weapons.

The reaction by the United States was surprisingly muted. Secretary of State Colin Powell was almost nonchalant about the prospect of North Korea, which was believed to have acquired enough plutonium for two nuclear weapons before the Agreed Framework, building more nuclear weapons: 'What are they going to do with another two or three nuclear weapons when they're starving, when they have no energy, when they have no economy that's functioning?' (Daalder and Lindsay 2005). There was no longer any talk of pre-emptive strikes or any form of military pressure to be brought to bear. Even more surprisingly, those conservative pundits such as Charles Krauthammer and William Safire who had derided negotiations with North Korea in 1994 and called for military action now played down the North Korean threat and advocated doing nothing. Ivo Daalder and James Lindsay from the Brookings Institution noted acerbically: 'The Bush administration and its hawkish supporters have found their match in Kim Jong Il's North Korea' (Daalder and Lindsay 2003).

Pyongyang signalled its interest in entering discussions with the United States, but the Bush administration did not want to enter negotiations with North Korea 'under duress', and thus responded by initiating steps designed to gradually bring the pressure of the international community to bear through the mechanisms of the IAEA and the UN Security Council. The IAEA Board of Governors passed a resolution on 6 January 2003 that called on the DPRK to allow the return of inspectors and the restoration of monitoring equipment. This was described as the last chance for North Korea to reinstate the freeze; failing that, there was the prospect that DPRK noncompliance would be reported to the UN Security Council. The US also offered to 'talk to North Korea about how it will meet its obligations to the international community', a softening of its previous refusal to have discussions with North Korea before it abandoned its nuclear weapons programme.

North Korea seems to have perceived the US response as a further escalation of its pressure tactics. The American attitude to the nuclear issue seemed to be of one piece with its general hostility to the DPRK as symbolized by the latter's inclusion in the 'axis of evil'. Political support for the Agreed Framework was vanishing, both in Washington and Pyongyang. On 10 January, the DPRK announced that it was formally withdrawing from the NPT in order to be free from all obligations in relation to safeguards. Technically, withdrawal from the NPT is subject to a 90-day notice period. North Korea declared that the required notice had already been given in March 1993 when it stated its intention to withdraw from the NPT. At the same time it sought to reassure the international community that it would not actually build nuclear weapons: 'Though we pull out of the Treaty, we have no intention to produce nuclear weapons and our nuclear activities at this stage will be confined only to peaceful purposes such as production of electricity' (IISS 2004, p. 19).

The DPRK views the International Atomic Energy Agency (IAEA) from quite a different perspective. The role of the IAEA is, in effect, to verify compliance with the obligations under the NPT. This is viewed by the United States as a purely technical task. To require North Korea to submit to IAEA inspections is therefore simply to ask the DPRK to comply with the obligations that it has signed up to. North Korea, however, sees the IAEA as an instrument of the hostile policy of the US towards the DPRK. Adopting the position that it has not acknowledged the existence of a highly enriched uranium programme and claiming that no hard evidence has been produced that it does exist, it considers the resolution by the IAEA Board of Governors that calls for its abandonment through verifiable means as part of an American conspiracy to strangulate the North (KCNA, 10 January 2003). This is yet another example where the IAEA has been used to brand North Korea a criminal country by alleging violation of international treaty obligations. Thus the activities of the IAEA are viewed as politically motivated, the IAEA acting on instructions from Washington and using intelligence fabricated by the United States. The withdrawal from the NPT is explained as a response to the hostile policy of the US and its nuclear threats against the DPRK. It is alleged that the US has violated the negative security assurances embodied in the framework of the NPT which state that nuclear states may not threaten the use of nuclear weapons against a non-nuclear state that has ratified the NPT. The war against Iraq is cited as an example of how the United States abuses international organizations, and that the attempt to use inspections to bring about disarmament does not help to avert war, but rather brings it about (KCNA, 7 April 2003). On the basis of Article 10, section 1 of the NPT, North Korea claims it has the right to withdraw from the NPT if its national interests are severely threatened. Such a threat exists because of the nullification of the Geneva Agreed Framework as a result of KEDO's cessation of heavy fuel oil supplies, and the hostile policy of the US including the threat of pre-emptive nuclear attacks (KCNA, 10 January 2003).

Seeing the US as the source of the problems, the DPRK sought bilateral talks with the United States to deal with the nuclear issue, but Washington demurred because it did not want to be seen to have been blackmailed into negotiations.

Instead the Bush administration proposed multilateral talks, in order to increase the pressure on North Korea to accept the dismantlement of its nuclear programmes and shift the onus for dealing with North Korea onto the regional states. Thus in late January the US proposed privately a set of multilateral talks involving the five permanent members of the UN Security Council plus the EU and four regional states (the ROK, the DPRK, Japan and Australia). North Korea rejected the idea out of hand, insisting on direct bilateral talks with the United States.

Clearly Pyongyang did not want a set of talks where it was confronted by an array of countries hostile to its position. It perceived the United States as the source of external threat, and therefore a deal could only be made with Washington.

The US approach to the issue was fundamentally flawed. While it was in line with the moral absolutism of the Bush administration, it was based on false premises and would be unable to deliver any results. Not all parties in the proposed multilateral talks could be counted on to put pressure on North Korea. While China did not want a nuclear-armed DPRK, it was unclear to what extent it would use its considerable leverage as North Korea's largest trade partner and supplier of aid to achieve compliance with the demands of the international community (Hwang 2006). China did not want the North Korean regime to collapse and preferred the continued existence of two Koreas with the North acting as a buffer state. This does not mean that China was necessarily happy with the Kim regime, but it wanted the DPRK to engage in economic reform along the lines of the Chinese model (Samuel Kim 2004: 81–96). The Republic of Korea took the nuclear issue very seriously because of its direct ramifications for South Korean security, but Roh's version of the 'sunshine policy' was one of engagement with North Korea that did not really have any place for 'sticks' along with the 'carrots'. There were deep divergences between the Bush administration and the Roh government on how to approach the issue of the North's nuclear programmes. The Bush team adopted a surprisingly relaxed, approach that belied its bellicose rhetoric. While it wanted a nuclear-free DPRK, it did not see the current situation as a crisis or a development that was so alarming that everything had to be done to prevent the reprocessing of plutonium, which was the attitude that had dominated the perspective of the Clinton administration. The Roh government on the other hand saw the suspension of the Agreed Framework as a serious crisis which could result in North Korea having something of the order of eight nuclear weapons and could raise tensions between the US and the DPRK to such an extent that the United States might take military action against North Korea. There is also a profound difference with regard to strategic objectives. The Bush administration was unsure that the nuclear crisis could be resolved without regime change in the North, and therefore adopted a policy of isolating, containing and transforming the North (Paik 2005). The ROK government on the other hand was and remains convinced that the only chance of transforming the DPRK is through a policy of engagement. In this context the nuclear issue has to be resolved with some urgency, as it threatens to derail the policy of engagement (Moon 2004; Bae and Moon 2003; Lee and Moon 2003). The paradoxical result was that both countries adopted contrary policies, neither of which had any chance of achieving their objectives. There was no prospect that the Bush administration's goal of isolation and containment of North Korea could be achieved, given that its regional partners resolutely refused to implement such an approach. Moreover, multilateral talks with North Korea had no chance of success due to the divergent objectives of the participants and the unwillingness of the Republic of Korea and China to come up with the appropriate mix of sticks and carrots to induce concessions from the North Korean side. The policy of the Roh government in Seoul, on the other hand, was flawed for the same reason, namely that despite the rhetorical affirmations of the seriousness of the nuclear problem, it was neither able nor willing to devise any instruments that would have a serious chance of dealing with it.

Tensions increased once more in February 2003 when North Korea announced that it was putting its nuclear facilities for the production of electricity on a normal footing, which presumably meant it was restarting the 5 MW(e) reactor at Yongbyon. Satellite observation detected very heavy activity at the spent fuel facility, indicating that North Korea might be moving fuel rods for reprocessing. On 12 February 2003, the Board of Governors of the IAEA found North Korea in violation of its NPT safeguard obligations and referred the matter to the UN Security Council. The US deployed add-itional bombers and stealth aircraft to the region. The DPRK responded with a warning that it might launch a first strike in response to a build-up of US forces in the region, and North Korean fighter planes harassed a US RC-135 reconnaissance plane. During the 'Foal Eagle' exercises that were conducted jointly by the US and the ROK, the United States deployed a number of F-117A stealth fighter bombers to South Korea and 2 long-range bombers to Guam (IISS 2004).

The next move on the diplomatic front came from China, after Secretary of State Powell visited Beijing in February. China was concerned that tension between the DPRK and the United States was rising. On the one hand, China wanted to avoid a collapse of the DPRK under US military and economic pressure (i.e. it opposed US ambitions for regime change in North Korea). After all, China would have to deal with many of the social and economic consequences. At the same time it wanted to avoid instability or even a military conflagration in its backyard. China was under strong American pressure to use its influence with Pyongyang, which in private discussions it always claimed was minimal. China's role in the diplomacy vis-à-vis North Korea became part of a complex diplomatic game. By rejecting bilateral talks with North Korea and its general approach to the nuclear issue, Washington had con-siderably reduced the available policy instruments at its dis-posal. It was looking to Beijing to inject new momentum into the process, i.e. to get the North Koreans to see sense. Reliance on China was problematic for several reasons. First, it was unclear how much influence Beijing had in Pyongyang. Secondly, Chinese and US objectives for the outcome of the process were not wholly congruent. Thirdly, seeking favours from Beijing could have an impact on the situation with Taiwan which was the dominant issue in Sino–US relations.

Extensive shuttle diplomacy by China's vice premier Qian Qichen resulted in Kim Jong-il's agreement for North Korea to take part in the Three-Party Talks that were held on 24–25 April 2003 in Beijing. China temporarily halted oil supplies to the DPRK for 'technical reasons', putting pressure on Pyongyang to cooperate. At the same time Russia and China prevented action by the UN Security Council against North Korea in response to the IAEA report on 9 April. After consultations with Tokyo and Seoul, Washington agreed to the Three-Party Talks. The Bush administration was determined not to talk the North Koreans directly, whereas Beijing and Pyongyang saw the talks as a means of establishing a direct dialogue between the United States and North Korea.

During the Three-Party Talks, the DPRK delegation made a concrete proposal which it described as a 'bold initiative'. It was based on the concept of four stages of simultaneous steps to be taken by the United States and North Korea, resulting in the dismantlement of North Korea's nuclear weapons programme. In the first stage, North Korea would declare its intention to dismantle nuclear weapons and HFO shipments would be resumed. In the second stage, inspections of North Korea's nuclear facilities would take place, and the United States and the DPRK would sign a non-aggression pact. In the third stage, other issues would be resolved – there would be an agreement on missiles and political relations between the DPRK, the US and Japan would be normalized. In the final stage, once the light water reactor was completed, North Korea would finally dismantle its nuclear programme.

The United States rejected the North Korean proposal out of hand. The head of the US delegation, James Kelly, restated the position of the Bush administration that only after complete, irreversible and verifiable (CVID) disarmament would any political and economic agreements be possible. The North Korean delegation had come to Beijing expecting direct bilateral talks with the Americans, who were under strict instruction not to participate in such a meeting. The Chinese tricked the US delegation into an informal bilateral meeting by arranging for the two delegations to be in the same room at the same time. The Chinese were frustrated by the behaviour of both the Americans and the North Koreans. The chief delegate of the DPRK delegation, Li Keun, informally told Kelly that the DPRK already had one or two nuclear weapons and had completed reprocessing the 8,000 spent fuel rods from the 5 MW(e) reactor, even though North Korea had denied these facts to the Chinese. There was also a hint that North Korea could make more weapons or transfer them. The talks broke up in failure after one formal meeting and a day earlier than scheduled.

On 12 May 2003, the DPRK proclaimed the nullification of the North–South Declaration on Denuclearization, and there were indications that the reprocessing of spent fuel rods had begun. In July 2003, North Korea told the United States privately that it had completed the reprocessing of the 8,000 fuel rods. Intelligence assessments indicated that some reprocessing had most likely occurred, but it could not be confirmed that reprocessing had been completed.

Given the past experience with North Korea's missile proliferation and the statements at the Beijing meeting, the prospect that North Korea might be tempted to proliferate nuclear materials and technology emerged as the most serious threat posed by the nuclear programme. In June 2003, the Bush administration launched a Proliferation Security Initiative (PSI) as an international effort to interdict shipments of items related to WMD. North Korea was the immediate target of this initiative, but it was unclear how ultimately the transportation of plutonium which could be carried in a small suitcase could be prevented. This is not to say that PSI is not important and indeed it is gaining international support, but it cannot entirely mitigate the dangers of proliferation from a state like North Korea (Lehrman 2004).

In early July, Russia and China once again prevented action by the UN Security Council against the DPRK, while China was engaged in the resumption of diplomacy. Pyongyang was offered extra food and oil deliveries as an inducement to accept participation in the new talks which involved six parties, namely the United States, Russia, China, Japan, North Korea and South Korea. The various parties came to the talks with different agendas. China, Russia and South Korea intended the talks to provide a means of establishing a bilateral dialogue between the US and the DPRK. The United States had accepted the principle that there should be a bilateral meeting with North Korea on the margins of the conference, but it wanted to maintain the multilateral framework and enlist the support of the other regional states to put pressure on North Korea. Japan wanted progress on the issue of kidnapped Japanese citizens as well as the nuclear issue.

The first of the Six-Party Talks was held in Beijing on 27–29 August 2003. As expected, North Korea proposed once again a series of simultaneous steps, beginning with the exchange of a US assurance of security and a North Korean pledge to give up its nuclear weapons with a view to eventual disarmament. The DPRK delegation hinted that it might accept a freeze on its nuclear activities as a first step. The US stuck to the principle of 'dismantlement first'. Although the US delegation did not present a detailed counterproposal to the DPRK, it suggested that North Korean disarmament could take place in several phases, leaving the door open for some 'rewards' before complete, irreversible and verifiable disarmament had taken place. Nevertheless, security assurances and the resumption of heavy fuel oil deliveries could only be discussed after some disarmament had occurred. Moreover, the US also made it clear that full diplomatic normalization would require more than the dismantling of nuclear programmes; other issues such as ballistic missiles, biological and chemical weapons and conventional forces would need to be addressed (Kahn 2003).

The South Koreans proposed a three-stage process which was to be a compromise between the North Korean and the US approach. The first stage would consist in simultaneous declaration of security assurances and commitment to nuclear disarmament, followed by sequential actions that would involve the implementation of disarmament in different stages, reciprocated by inducement on the part of the US and other parties to the talks. After a resolution of all of the issues, nuclear, missiles, other WMD and conventional forces, full normalization of relations with North Korea and the US and Japan could take place. However, due to the attitude of some of the other parties, this proposal did not gain any traction.

The paradoxical feature of these talks was that there was a great deal of common ground regarding the shape of any final agreement. The disagreement was primarily about the modality of the disarmament process. North Korea was not willing to relinquish its tangible assets without some down-payment, while the United States had adopted the principle that it would not be seen to be blackmailed into negotiations and to be rewarding illicit behaviour, thereby completely restricting its freedom of manoeuvre in the discussions. In addition, however, the issue of the HEU programme remained an insurmountable obstacle as North Korea denied the US allegations about the existence of such a programme. In private conversations, the North Koreans told the Americans that Kelly had misunderstood what Kang had said in October 2002. Such a denial, however, meant that the programme was not on the table for inclusion in any disarmament deal, and without it there could be no such deal. True to form, the North Koreans again issued threats; this time they said they would declare their nuclear status and conduct a weapons test if there was no solution. This behaviour, which was quite consistent with the DPRK's previous negotiating tactics, did nothing to improve North Korea's bargaining position and only hardened the American stance.

There was no joint final communiqué but the Chinese Ministry of Foreign Affairs issued a statement as chair of the talks that summarized some general principles that all parties seemed to agree to, including the need to resolve the North Korean nuclear issue through dialogue, the denuclearization of the Korean peninsula and the need to continue the Six-Party Talks.

Despite the lack of progress, the United States was content with outcome of the talks in so far as a clear message was sent to North Korea. The North Koreans reacted negatively. The delegation issued a statement at Beijing airport prior to leaving to the effect that North Korea had no interest in future talks (Moon 2004, p. 25). The Ministry of Foreign Affairs in Pyongyang issued a statement on the talks that said: 'The six-party talk was nothing but empty discussions. We came to realize that there are no other alternatives but self-defense capability and nuclear deterrence capability unless the US changes its hostile policy' (KCNA, 30 August 2003). Nevertheless, North Korea's chief delegate, Vice Foreign Minister Kim Young-il, stated: 'The denuclearisation of the Korean peninsula is our ultimate goal, and possessing nuclear weapons is not our goal' (Moon 2004, p. 26).

As China and the Republic of Korea made efforts to achieve the resumption of the talks, North Korea indicated a lack of interest. On 2 October 2003, Pyongyang made a public announcement to the effect that it had completed the reprocessing of spent fuel rods from Yongbyon and that the plutonium would be used to enhance its nuclear deterrent force. However, these claims could not be independently confirmed.

Some progress was made at the Asia-Pacific Economic Cooperation (APEC) summit in Bangkok. In separate conversations with the Chinese President Hu Jintao and the President of the Republic of Korea, Roh Moo-hyun, President Bush expressed his willingness to join in a multilateral written security guarantee to North Korea if the DPRK agreed to dismantle its nuclear weapons programme. This indicated some movement in the US position.

On 4 November 2003, KEDO formally suspended the light water reactor project for one year, which was not unexpected given that the entire Agreed Framework was in effect in suspension. China's efforts to convene another round of the Six-Party Talks in December ran into difficulties as various public statements re-emphasized the differences between North Korea and the United States. China's initial draft was rejected and the US proposed its own text, supported by Japan and the Republic of Korea. On 6 December, the North Korean Foreign Ministry issued the following statement:

A package solution based on the principle of simultaneous action is the core issue to be agreed upon between the DPRK and the US, being the key to solving the nuclear issue. This is our consistent claim. The DPRK advanced a productive proposal to put into practice measures of the first phase if the US found it hard to accept the package solution all at once. These measures are for the US to delist the DPRK as a sponsor of terrorism, lift political, economic and military sanctions and blockade on it and for the US and neighbouring countries of the DPRK to supply heavy oil, power and other energy resources to the DPRK in return for its freeze of nuclear activities. (KCNA, 6 December 2003)

But simultaneous action was precisely what President Bush was not going to accept.

In view of the lack of progress, there was some shift of policy in Washington. This may have been the consequence of more intense lobbying on the part of Seoul, coupled with the politically risky commitment to send some South Korean troops to Iraq. It may also have been helped by the forthcoming presidential election in the US which meant that some of the potentially controversial foreign policy areas were given to Powell in order to diffuse any attacks by presidential candidate John Kerry. Whatever the reason for the shift, at the next round of the Six-Party Talks, Under-Secretary of State Kelly for the first time presented a detailed US proposal for the resolution of the nuclear crisis. It involved some concessions to the concept of simultaneous action, in that the US was willing for fuel shipments to be resumed and to give a provisional guarantee not to attack North Korea. It also offered talks on lifting US sanctions. In return, the DPRK would have to freeze its nuclear activities within three months, to be followed by complete dismantlement. This proposal involved significant elements of a proposal that had been developed by the Ministry for Foreign Affairs and Trade in Seoul previously, thereby narrowing the differences between Seoul and Washington about how to handle talks with the DPRK (based on interviews in Seoul, 2004–6).

During the two-hour bilateral meeting between the US and the DPRK, the North Korea delegation discussed the proposal, but insisted on 'freeze for compensation' and, characteristically, threatened to test a nuclear weapon if the US would not accept their proposal.

After the talks the North Korean Foreign Ministry issued a statement to the effect that some common ground had been reached at the talks in Beijing but stressed that there were still 'big differences', in particular with regard to the issue of whether North Korea had a secret uranium enrichment programme. Moreover, the time-frame was characterized as unrealistic. On 30 June, the North Korean ambassador to Russia stated that the DPRK wanted 2 million kilowatts in energy compensation before freezing its nuclear programme.

In July, the Under-Secretary of State for Arms Control and International Security, John Bolton, visited Seoul and affirmed in a lecture at Yonsei University that the US was not interested in a temporary freeze of North Korea's nuclear activities. Instead he invited North Korea to follow the example of Libya which had given up its support for international terrorism and its WMD programmes in return for lifting of sanctions and a return to the international community. It was clear that the US still required CVID as the final outcome of the process, even though this had been rejected by the DPRK.

Although the participants of the Six-Party Talks agreed to hold a fourth round in September 2004, North Korea soon began to send signals that it was backing away from holding another round so soon, even though US Secretary of State Powell and DPRK Foreign Minister Paek Nam-sun met in Jakata at the ASEAN regional forum, the highest level encounter since the crisis began. On 25 July 2004, the Foreign Ministry called the US offer a sham and, after the passage of the North Korea Human Rights Act in the US Congress on 27 July 2004, the Ministry questioned the usefulness of the Six-Party Talks. There was a widespread view that North Korea had decided to postpone the resumption of the talks until after the US presidential election in November 2004, an interpretation that North Koreans vigorously denied (based on discussions by the author with North Korean officials in October 2004). Instead they said that they would not attend the talks unless the United States abandoned its hostile stance towards North Korea.

Pyongyang did not yield many clues as to the real reason for its decision to stall the six-party process. For over a year there were conflicting messages and the participating governments appointed new representatives to the talks without any clear signal as to if and when they would resume. One school of thought suggested that North Korea had decided that, as economic relations with China and the Republic of Korea continued, whereas relations with the US remained tense, it needed to at least partially remove the ambiguity over its nuclear programme in order to deter the United States. However, in many respects Pyongyang's behaviour was similar to that in the past – by continuously ratcheting up the threat, completing the reprocessing of the fuel rods from the reactor, threatening the resumption of missile tests, claiming to have a working nuclear deterrent and stopping the 5 MW(e) reactor to extract fuel rods, it seemed to try to increase its leverage while at the same time demanding the resumption of dialogue with Washington on a bilateral basis. Reports from the US Defense Intelligence Agency that North Korea might be preparing a nuclear test and could have missiles capable of delivering nuclear weapons to the United States contributed to the growing atmosphere of crisis. The DIA has been consistently hawkish on North Korea – it was responsible for the (false) reports of nuclear facilities at Kumchang-ri, and in 2005 the director testified that North Korea had the capability to strike at the US with nuclear weapons, a judgement disputed by most experts.

By June 2005, this game seemed to have come full circle. During the meeting in Pyongyang to celebrate the 2000 unification summit involving a sizeable South Korean delegation, Kim Jong-il arranged an impromptu meeting with the ROK unification minister Chung Dong-young in which he indicated a willingness to return to the Six-Party Talks in July 2005 and even give up nuclear weapons and medium- and long-range missiles provided that US ceased its hostile attitude and respected North Korea rather than despising it (*Korea Herald*, 21 June 2005). After the meeting, it became clear that the government of the Republic of Korea had been successfully enlisted in North Korea's diplomatic campaign. Foreign Minister Ban Ki-moon (now the secretary-general of the United Nations) for example stated that assertions by US Secretary of State Rice and Under-Secretary of State Paula Dobriansky that North Korea was an 'outpost of tyranny' were 'regrettable' as they might prevent Pyongyang from rejoining the Six-Party Talks, and he questioned the intention of US diplomacy towards North Korea (*Chosun Ilbo*, 21 June 2005).

Towards stalemate

Before the Six-Party Talks resumed in September 2005, the parties nominated new delegation leaders. The leader of the North Korean was the veteran diplomat and vice foreign minister Kim Kye-gwan, while James Kelly had been replaced by Christopher Hill. Hill had previously been US ambassador to the Republic of Korea, had a deep knowledge of Korean affairs and set a completely different tone from his predecessor by projecting an aura of flexibility and a desire to achieve results. The talks concluded on 19 September in Beijing with a joint statement of principles that appeared to be a genuine breakthrough. North Korea would abandon its nuclear programmes, return to the NPT and adhere to the 1992 Joint Declaration on the Denuclearization of the Korean Peninsula. The United States gave security assurances to the DPRK to the effect that there were no US nuclear weapons based on the Korean peninsula, and that the US had no intention of attacking North Korea with either nuclear or conventional weapons. Finally, the statement included a reference to various economic benefits for North Korea in the fields of energy, trade and investment, including the proposal from South Korea to provide two million kilowatts of electric power. But the next day Kim Kye-gwan dropped a bombshell – the DPRK would return to the NPT and sign a safeguards agreement with the IAEA as soon as the United States provided light water reactors (LWR). It looked like North Korea wanted to return to the Agreed Framework. But the Bush administration had decided that it would only support conventional means of securing North Korea's energy needs. Any nuclear programme would only initiate another round of problems about safeguards. Only after a verifiable cessation of all nuclear programmes could discussions about the use of nuclear technology for civilian purposes at some point in the future be held.

The Roh administration subsequently stated that it supported North Korea's right to peaceful nuclear energy, but the United States stuck to its view that this matter could not be discussed until North Korea was in full compliance with its safeguards obligations (Pinkston 2006).

As the talks had effectively stalled again, the North Koreans and the Americans tried to get the other side to move. Pyongyang attempted to open up a direct dialogue with the United States which Washington staunchly resisted. For example, Kim Kye-gwan suggested a meeting with Hill at the North-east Asia Cooperation Dialogue held in Tokyo on 10–11 April 2006. The US delegation refused and insisted that any discussions should take place in the forum of the Six-Party Talks. The US State Department also launched the Illicit Activities Initiative aimed at curbing foreign currency earned through criminal activities such as counterfeiting currency and drug trafficking (Nanto and Pearl 2006). The freezing of North Korean assets in the Banco Delta Asia based in Macao and others cost Pyongyang in excess of $20 million. The US government also imposed sanctions on North Korean companies for engaging in activities related to proliferation, such as the Korea Mining Development Corporation and the Korea Ryonbong General Corporation. Such actions had been demanded by conservatives in the United States for a long time. Targeting North Korea's illicit foreign exchanges earnings seemed one of the few possible points of leverage against a state that was otherwise impervious to military or political pressures, and moreover it highlighted the allegedly criminal nature of the state. But if it was designed to compel North Korea to return to the Six-Party Talks and accept the joint statement of principles, it failed entirely. Instead it created yet another seemingly insuperable obstacle in the way of progress as North Korea made return to the talks conditional on the lifting of these sanctions (KCNA, 24 April 2006). The sanctions are interpreted as part of a coordinated effort to topple the North Korean government. On 5 July, North Korea broke its missile testing moratorium and launched seven missiles, including a *Taepodong-2*. Once again Pyongyang resorted to increasing the military pressure in the hope of inducing a shift in the US stance. Although the *Taepodong-2* exploded soon after lift-off, the intention was clear. As a missile of almost intercontinental range, it was meant to demonstrate that North Korea was increasing the capacity to hold US forces at risk. The launches were timed to take place shortly after the United States launched the space shuttle *Discovery* to celebrate Independence Day. The gesture, however, backfired on Pyongyang. It was interpreted universally as a hostile and provocative act. The United Nations Security Council voted unanimously on 15 July 2006 to impose sanctions on North Korea in response to the missile launches. Pyongyang's actions created a state of shock in the South Korean government. It was a deep embarrassment for unification minister Lee Jong-seok who had described North Korean leader Kim Jong-il as a man he could do business with. President Roh, faced with a provocation that undermined the whole premise of his policy towards the North, refused to make any comments. For the first time the South Korean government stopped the shipment of supplies to the North and this had an immediate effect on the entire range of inter-Korean relations, with talks reaching a dead end as South Korean tours were halted.

By September 2006 there seemed little prospect of the resumption of negotiations on North Korea's nuclear programme. Then North Korea decided to escalate even further. On 9 October 2006, the North Korean news agency KCNA announced that the DPRK had tested a nuclear device. According to the South Korean National Intelligence Service, the explosion occurred at Sangpyong-ri, North Hangyong Province, near the town of Kimchaek. The relatively modest size of the detonation (estimated at the equivalent of less than 1,000 tons of TNT and thus less than a tenth of the size of the atomic explosion over Hiroshima) initially raised some doubts as to whether a nuclear detonation had in fact occurred. After a brief investigation, the US Director of National Intelligence, John Negroponte, confirmed that radioactive debris had been detected and that a nuclear test had taken place. It is possible that the small size of the detonation means that the test was a partial failure and that nuclear fission did not quite take place according to plan. This raised speculation that North Korea would have to conduct further tests to ensure that its nuclear devices are working properly and that they can be fitted to delivery vehicles (Pinkston and Shin 2007).

It did not take long for UN Security Council Resolution 1718 to be agreed, imposing an array of sanctions targeted at North Korea's elite. These included a ban on military exports to and from the DPRK, a ban on the sale or export of nuclear- or missile-related items, a ban on the sale of luxury goods to North Korea, a freeze on North Korean financial assets and a travel ban for all persons involved in the nuclear and missile programmes and their families. For South Korea, the most controversial element was the inclusion of inspections of North Korean ships, which had the potential for producing a serious confrontation at sea. For both the United States and the Republic of Korea, North Korea's nuclear test had proven a critical turning point in relations with Pyongyang. As regards the United States, it demonstrated the complete failure of the policy of the Bush administration to counter Pyongyang's nuclear programme. North Korea has acquired precisely the capability that years of sanctions and negotiations were supposed to stop. But the Roh government likewise had to face the fact that its policy of engaging North Korea appeared to have failed. Pyongyang had responded to South Korean generosity and patience with contempt. The government in Seoul faced pressure both from the United States and from the opposition Grand National Party (GNP) to terminate the major joint North–South projects such as the Kaesong industrial complex and the Mount Kumgang tours to prevent the DPRK from using the money earned for its nuclear weapons programme. All the achievements of inter-Korean relations since the summit between Kim Dae-jung and Kim Jong-il in 2000 seemed to have come to naught. Unification minister Lee Jong-seok (President Roh's right-hand man on North Korean policy since the beginning of his term) and Defence Minister Yoon Kwang-ung resigned.

North Korea's belligerence also caused a shift in Chinese policy. By going ahead with the missile launches and the nuclear test, Pyongyang openly defied Beijing's advice, causing profound diplomatic embarrassment. For this reason China supported UN Security Council sanctions against the DPRK, something it had staunchly resisted hitherto. Beijing sent a special envoy to Pyongyang to convey a stern message to Kim Jong-il, emphasizing China's displeasure and warning against further nuclear tests. China also tightened border security and instructed Chinese banks not to deal with North Korea (Yuan 2006).

Soon after the nuclear test, North Korea signalled that it was prepared to attend another session of the Six-Party Talks without preconditions. While on the surface this appeared to be surprising, and some believed that it was due to Chinese pressure, it is consistent with North Korea's negotiating behaviour. Once it had demonstrated its nuclear status, the DPRK expected that it had greater bargaining power and that it needed to be treated with the respect due to a nuclear power. Consequently it could afford to rejoin the talks without preconditions. Another session of the Six-Party Talks was held in Beijing in December 2006. The North Korean chief delegate, Kim Kye-gwan, made it clear that the DPRK would only discuss the nuclear programme after financial sanctions were lifted. He characterized US policy as one of carrots and sticks, i.e. dialogue and pressure, and contrasted this with Pyongyang's policy of dialogue and shield. He also stated that North Korea would improve its nuclear deterrent. The North Koreans also repeated their demand that in return for giving up the plutonium programme, they needed to be compensated with light water reactors in order to provide for the energy needs of the country. After five days of talks in which no further progress was made, the meeting ended on 22 December 2006 with a statement by the Chinese delegate, Wu Dawei, which simply restated the agreement of September 2005 that the DPRK would disarm in return for security guarantees and aid (*BBC News*, 22 December 2006).

Following the December meeting, the United States began to engage in bilateral negotiations with North Korea in Berlin. These talks revealed greater flexibility on the part of the US and North Korea, both with regard to style and substance, as they resembled the kind of bilateral bargaining that occurred in the run-up to the Agreed Framework. The US chief nego-tiator, Christopher Hill, agreed that the issue of financial sanc-tions could be resolved and that the United States was willing to remove North Korea from the list of sponsors of terrorism as well as to lift trade sanctions. At a meeting in Beijing on 13 February 2007, it was announced that an agreement had been reached. It required North Korea to shut down its nuclear facilities at Yongbyon within 60 days, with the purpose of eventual abandonment. North Korea was to receive 60,000 tons of fuel oil for concluding the agreement. A package of economic, energy and humanitarian assistance was agreed (to the value of about $250,000), to be gradually implemented as the dismantlement of nuclear facilities proceeded. The agree-ment did not mention nuclear weapons or devices, the disposal of nuclear materials or the uranium enrichment programme. The latter triggered the collapse of the Agreed Framework and the second nuclear crisis in the first place. There were signals from the US administration that it may have exaggerated the significance of the uranium enrichment programme. It also does not address the missile programme. The deal clearly marked a significant about-turn in the attitude adopted by the Bush administration. But the US government clearly expects that this is the framework for a grand bargain that will induce North Korea to give up its nuclear programme and long-range missile development. To what extent it will succeed in this ambition still remains to be seen.

8 The Military Confrontation on the Korean Peninsula ——

In previous chapters we have discussed the political roots of the crisis on the Korean peninsula. A central aspect of this crisis is the military confrontation. Two massive armies, ready to go to war at short notice, are facing each other from the opposite sides of the DMZ. President Clinton, when he visited the DMZ in 1993, described it as the 'scariest place on Earth'. This chapter will discuss the nature of this military confrontation and assess the balance of forces. It will seek to draw some conclusions about the intentions and strategies of the two sides and discuss the likelihood of conflict and the stability of the deterrence relationship on the Korean peninsula.

The conventional military confrontation on the Korean peninsula

The current military confrontation across the DMZ in Korea developed as a consequence of the Korean War (1950–52) which ended in stalemate. The peninsula remained divided at the 38th parallel. North Korea began to deploy a large military force near the DMZ, seemingly preparing to invade the South once again. Numerically, in terms of troops and reservists, artillery pieces, tanks and combat aircraft, the DPRK clearly outnumbered the Republic of Korea. Until the mid-1980s, the military confrontation on the Korean peninsula was embedded in the global confrontation of the Cold War. This meant that any conflict in Korea would also involve the allies of the two Koreas: the Soviet Union and the People's Republic of China on one side and the United States on the other. While in principle China and the Soviet Union were committed to come to the aid North Korea if it were attacked, by the mid-1980s Pyongyang could not place much reliance on these commitments. In 1995, Russia notified Pyongyang that it would not renew the Treaty of Friendship, Cooperation and Mutual Assistance concluded with the Soviet Union in 1961. A new treaty, initialled in 2000, no longer contained a provision for Russia to provide military assistance to North Korea in the event of an attack. The People's Republic of China, which saved North Korea during the Korean War, is also unlikely to come to North Korea's aid in the event of conflict. The commitment of the United States was and remains more credible because US forces are stationed on the peninsula (about 37,000 in 2005), together with state-of-the-art equipment and (until 1990) nuclear weapons. Moreover, any attack from the North was going to result in very substantial military reinforcements from the United States. Consequently, North Korea was not in a position to launch an invasion and expect to complete the unification of Korea by force.

Still, North Korea maintains a military establishment that is huge given the size of the population and the country's resources. The armed forces consist of about 1.1 million active-duty personnel and Pyongyang can count on reserves of the order of 7,480,000. Under the 'military first' policy, total priority for financial and other material resources is given to the military. The official military budget is about $1.5 billion per annum, but experts estimate that the real outlays amount to approximately $5 billion, about 25 per cent of the GDP of the DPRK. Even this may still understate the degree to which the military consumes virtually all resources, as from the mid-1990s it became apparent that the only factories operating at full capacity were those producing military goods (Oh and Hassig 2000, p. 105).

North Korea's army consists of four armoured corps, four mechanized corps, an artillery corps and a front-line corps. Another five corps-sized units are based throughout the territory of North Korea. These are organized into 27 infantry divisions, 21 artillery brigades 15 armoured brigades and 14 infantry brigades (Kim 1998, p. 172; IISS 2004, p. 88). In addition, North Korea has more than 20 special forces brigades (about 100,000 troops) whose tasks will include disrupting US and South Korean military operations.

The armoured forces of the DPRK include about 3,700 main battle tanks, 3,000 armoured personnel carriers and light tanks, and in excess of 12,000 heavy-calibre artillery pieces. Most of the main battle tanks are older Soviet models (T-54, T-55, T-59); there are also about 800 T-62s manufactured by the DPRK. To many observers, North Korea's military posture appears very aggressive, designed to support an invasion of the South if circumstances changed such that it seemed opportune, or if North Korea found itself backed into a corner without any other options. According to the IISS, about 80 per cent of North Korea's firepower is deployed within 100 km from the DMZ, including about 8,000 artillery pieces, 2,000 tanks and 700,000 troops (IISS 2004, p. 85). According to the US Defence Intelligence Agency (DIA), about 65 per cent of North Korean arms is deployed within 65 km of the DMZ. Thus in principle North Korea could launch an attack at relatively short notice without major redeployment of its forces. Of particular concern are the capabilities for an attack on Seoul from the northern side of the DMZ with its self-propelled artillery, its multiple rocket launchers and short-range surface-to-surface missiles. The North Korean army also has about 7,500 mortars, 10,000 surface-to-air missiles, a range of anti-tank weapons and 500 ballistic missiles. In addition to a million tons of conventional munitions, chemical weapons are likely to play a major role in the opening phase of any war. The DPRK has a stockpile of an estimated 5,000 tons of chemical warfare agents (MND 2004; IISS 2004, p. 89; O'Hanlon and Mochizuki 2003, p. 66). In order to facilitate the infiltration of troops into South Korea in the event of conflict, North Korea has dug various tunnels under the DMZ (two of which were discovered). North Korea has a substantial air force with some 605 combat aircraft. These are mostly older MiGs, although there are some more modern MiG-23, MiG-29 and Su-25. A significant proportion of the air force is based close to the DMZ. North Korea's naval forces are mostly coastal defence vessels without the capability to foil US naval operations or move large numbers of forces to the South. They consist of 158 patrol craft, 100 torpedo craft, 43 missile craft, some 26 Soviet-designed diesel submarines, some 65 miniature submarines for sending special forces into enemy territory, 10 amphibious ships and 23 anti-mine ships. Coastal defence has been enhanced with the deployment of anti-ship cruise missiles.

The major weakness of North Korea's military capability is that its equipment is obsolete relative to that of the Republic of Korea and the United States. An assessment of the military balance is therefore not very straightforward because most of North Korea's military equipment dates from the 1950s and 1960s and is not comparable to the advanced military equipment the ROK has been able to develop and purchase. Analysis of the comparative capability of weapons technology based on observations from the Gulf War of 1991 indicate that modern western weapons systems are two to four times better than older Soviet-designed systems. In particular, North Korea lacks the target acquisition, precision guidance and space reconnaissance capabilities of its opponents.

While the manner in which North Korea has deployed its forces suggests an aggressive intent, this interpretation has to be qualified. With Pyongyang only 120 km north of the DMZ, a defensive force posture would suggest similar patterns of deployment as these forces are clearly designed to impede an advance on the capital. Moreover, Soviet military thought which to some extent informs North Korean thinking has always emphasized the counter-offensive as a central part of defence strategy. The entire country is heavily fortified to provide a deep defence to prevent it from being overrun, and the population has been conditioned with a militant, xenophobic way of thinking and equipped to defend against invaders on the basis of the slogan that, in the event of war, the whole people should become 'bullets and bombs' (Oh and Hassig 2000, p. 108). Perhaps the most disturbing aspect of the indoctrination of North Korea's military is the apocalyptic image of a future war. According to defectors, North Korea's soldiers are taught that in a war there will be a large-scale attack on the South Korean military and population, using conventional and chemical weapons. The implication is that it is lawful to kill South Korean civilians who are resistant to communist ideology and would not fit into a united Korea. It is almost expected that the majority of South Koreans and North Koreans will die in such a conflict and, that if North Korea were to lose this war, it should just take actions to destroy everyone (Martin 2004, p. 487).

Despite this apocalyptic image of a future war on the Korean peninsula, the evidence seems to suggest that the regime is not suicidal. In other words, both the emphasis on the likelihood of war and the destructiveness of war is designed to deter and influence North Korea's opponents. By portraying themselves as being capable of anything and afraid of nothing, the North Korean leaders seek to deter an attack and convert their weakness into strength while negotiating with the United States or the Republic of Korea. At the same time, they are clearly aware that a war would mean the end of the regime. While during the first three decades after the Korean War the leaders of the DPRK entertained the idea of relaunching an attack if the conditions were right, they were even then sufficiently deterred to confine themselves to various terrorist attacks and very small-scale reconnaissance incursions. Their hope was that social turmoil in the South would provide the right opportunity to eliminate the ROK government and reoccupy the entire peninsula. At the present time, their focus is more clearly on deterring an attack and preventing a collapse of the state. While as a strategy of deterrence this approach is very successful, at the same time this policy of brinkmanship is risky because it cannot be excluded that at some point events may get out of control and war break out through miscalculation.

The government of the Republic of Korea is naturally keenly aware of North Korea's force posture and the force imbalance. Indeed, North Korea's army is almost twice the numerical strength of that of the ROK: it has 3,700 main battle tanks, compared to South Korea's 2,360, and more than twice the reserve forces of South Korea (3,040,000 for the latter). However, for example, the cutting edge K-1 tanks deployed by South Korea are much faster and have superior firepower to North Korea's T-62 equipped with technology from the 1970s. North Korea's fighter jets include only 60 advanced models, whereas South Korea has 520 advanced fighters including 162 F-16. Even though the DPRK spends a substantial proportion of GDP on its armed forces, South Korea's defence expenditure is close to three times that (although this figure needs to be adjusted for the lower man-power costs in the North). The armed forces of the Republic of Korea has a personnel of about 685,000. The army consists of 11 corps, organized into 52 divisions and 20 brigades. In addition to main battle tanks, the ROK army fields 2,500 armoured personnel carriers and light tanks, about 5,000 artillery pieces, 115 attack helicopters, some 6,000 mortars, about 1,000 air defence missiles and a dozen *Hyunmoo* surface-to-surface missiles based on US technology (range 180 km, payload 500 kg).

The Republic of Korea has significantly greater naval capabilities than the DPRK. With 67,000 personnel, the navy consists of three fleets in the Korea Strait, the Yellow and the East Seas under the operations command. The navy has 18 submarines, 6 destroyers, 9 frigates, 28 corvettes and 5 missile boats. It also has ships and aircrafts for amphibious, special warfare, anti-submarine, amphibious and other types of operation (globalsecurity.org). From a small force to protect national territorial waters, the navy embarked on an ambitious modernization programme under President Kim Dae-jung to become a twenty-first century strategic blue water navy. The major procurement programmes include aegis destroyers, sub-marines and enhanced anti-submarine warfare capability.

So what can we say about the military balance between the two Koreas? A modern model developed by the Analytic Sciences Corporation in the United States, called the Technique for Assessing Comparative Force Modernization (TASCFORM), has been used by the US Department of Defence Office of Net Assessment. Using TASCFORM, analysts have concluded that the combat equipment of the DPRK and the ROK is roughly equivalent, with South Korea maintaining an edge in aggregate air capabilities. However, once superior training, logistics, equipment maintenance, reconnaissance and command control capabilities are taken into account, then the Republic of Korea appears to enjoy significant superiority over the military capabilities of the North. This is indeed the official assessment of the US Department of Defence (O'Hanlon and Mochizuki 2003, p. 70).

Of course, a critical factor is the presence of US forces in the Republic of Korea. At the beginning of 2004, the United States had 38,500 personnel stationed on the Korean peninsula (28,600 army, 9,420 air force, 300 navy and 300 special forces). Two brigades of the Army's Second Infantry Division are based in 17 camps on both sides of the two main potential attack corridors in the north-west of South Korea. There are about 300 fixed-wing aircraft in the vicinity of Korea deployable in any crisis (including aircraft based in Japan and on nearby aircraft carriers).

Currently the headquarters of US Forces Korea is based in Seoul, but it is to be moved to the Osan-Pyongtaek area and the US army will redeploy its forces 75 km south of the Han River which runs through the capital, Seoul. In line with the worldwide shift in US military operations, former US Defence Secretary Donald Rumsfeld announced a reduction of 12,500 troops to be completed by 2008. The Department of Defence sought to reassure the Republic of Korea that this substantial reduction did not signal any diminution of the US commitment to the defence of Korea and that the improvements in US force structure and the modernization of the US armed forces would mean that the remaining forces in Korea would dispose of greater firepower than before the reduction. In May 2004, the United States redeployed 3,600 troops from Korea to Iraq. Another important change in relations between the armed forces of the ROK and the United States is the proposal to transfer wartime command of ROK forces to Korea (in place of the Korea–US combined forces command where all forces are commanded by the US commander in wartime). This change may take place some time around 2010.

Both the reductions, the redeployment and especially the change in wartime command have been viewed with some nervousness in Seoul and Pyongyang. The change in wartime command, while promoted by Roh Moo-hyun as a measure to reclaim the sovereignty of the ROK, is considered by many military leaders in Korea as premature and detrimental to the US security guarantee. The redeployment puts American forces beyond the reach of North Korea's artillery, thereby enhancing their capacity to respond to an attack. Of course US forces based in Korea continue to perform a 'tripwire function' and operational plans for a future war on the Korean peninsula rely on very substantial reinforcements, involving up to 500,000 troops (DoD 2001). The implementation of the operational plan (OPLAN 5027) raises two issues of concern for South Koreans. The first is that the substantial American troop commitments in Iraq and Afghanistan raise doubts about their viability. Privately South Korean specialists have expressed deep scepticism that reinforcements in the event of war would be on the scale necessary. Indeed, Michael O'Hanlon from the Brookings Institution estimates that 'we could cobble together a couple or three divisions I think, using equipment not in depot, from the 6–8 divisions here now (not in Iraq or Afghanistan). But it would be only about half of what the war plans call for' (O'Hanlon 2005, personal communication). The second issue is the timeliness of reinforcements, given that a surprise attack could very quickly create realities on the ground. Michael O'Hanlon and Mike Mochizuki have estimated that ground forces in Korea could be tripled within ten days. Within twenty to thirty days, eight SL-7 sealift ships could reach the Korean peninsula transporting a heavy army division based in the United States. The entire reinforcement operation envisaged by the operational plans could be completed within two to three months. The United States and the Republic of Korea have conducted large joint exercises, called 'Team Spirit', involving about 200,000 troops, and since the cancellation of 'Team Spirit' there has be a smaller annual Ulchi Focus Lens exercise involving 75,000 troops, so in principle they are well prepared. However, the long period required to complete the reinforcements means that decisive military engagements may have taken place before then.

Assuming the war plans can be implemented, the United States would deploy the equivalent of five modern heavy divisions (using TASCFORM criteria) and more than 15 fighter wings, exceeding North Korea's capabilities even without counting the formidable forces of the Republic of Korea. This assumes that the allies would not use nuclear weapons, which remains an option in extreme circumstances.

O'Hanlon and Mochizuki (2003) have conducted a detailed analysis of the prospects of a North Korean attempt to conquer the South, and this work has been built upon by the International Institute for Strategic Studies in their dossier on North Korean military capabilities. In the 1990s, it was assumed in the United States that a surprise attack by North Korea might be successful in capturing Seoul in the early phase of the conflict. Such a conflict would involve heavy artillery bombardment, the use of surface-to-surface missiles and the rapid movement of armoured forces across the DMZ. However, the combination of the continuing improvement of the capabilities of ROK and US forces and the decline of the resources available to the DPRK casts doubt on its ability to achieve even this objective despite the scale of the forces that it can muster. Military readiness has declined as the levels of training, equipment maintenance, provision of fuel and so on have plummeted. North Korean forces would face the bulk of the South Korean army across a 250 km front without any hope of either gaining air superiority or suppressing the artillery or air defences in the South. On the contrary, US and ROK air forces would establish air superiority for themselves very quickly. Thus the advancing forces would be extremely vulnerable because as they advanced their supply lines would be subject to interdiction. With about 500 aircraft, allied forces have the capacity to destroy several hundred enemy armoured vehicles every day. Moreover, much of the terrain is unsuitable for armoured vehicles, channelling the attacking forces into narrow corridors. In tank engagements with ROK armoured divisions, the more advanced forces of the South would prevail. Moreover, massive air attacks on targets throughout North Korea would begin with sea-based *Tomahawk* cruise missiles and heavy bombers based in Guam and Okinawa. Another decisive advantage for the allies are their all-weather day-and-night capabilities. Indeed, North Korea has nothing that matches allied reconnaissance capabilities which include joint surveillance and target attack radar system (JSTARS) aircraft, RC-7B reconnaissance aircraft and of course US space-based assets.

Although it is practically impossible for North Korea to conquer and absorb the South, it could inflict very serious damage on the South Korean population and economy, even without using chemical or biological weapons. Any conflict is likely to involve massive artillery bombardment of Seoul from beyond the DMZ. Although the ROK has the capability to track and locate artillery positions by radar and swiftly destroy them, it is not possible to prevent each artillery tube from firing at least five and possibly more shells before it is pulled back or destroyed. This means thousands of artillery shells could be fired at Seoul before all the artillery tubes are destroyed. The North Korean armies could also launch surface-to-surface missiles (e.g. Soviet era FROG missiles) at the capital or other targets throughout South Korea. Finally the possibility of the use of chemical weapons in the early phase of a conflict must be considered likely. These would not be effective against the ROK and US armies, but would have a devastating effect on the civilian population. This means it is virtually impossible to stop North Korea from causing large numbers of casualties (tens of thousands or more) and extensive economic damage (many billions of dollars).

While North Korea has little prospect of succeeding in a war to bring about reunification by force, the United States and the Republic of Korea also lack attractive military options for a pre-emptive attack against the DPRK. Any such attack would result in very heavy civilian and military casualties (not to mention the extraordinary chaos and economic dislocation in the aftermath, even if successful). Any attempt to conduct a campaign similar to Iraq 2003 will face great difficulties, as allied forces will try to cross through difficult terrain, facing forces that are much more capable and motivated than the

Iraqi army. Moreover, air strikes will be of limited value as many high-value targets, including command and control facilities, are deep underground.

Essentially it can be said that a stable system of deterrence exists on the Korean peninsula. For both sides the cost-benefit calculus of a war is such that neither has an interest in initiating conflict. Nevertheless the concentration of forces and the North Korean proclivity for brinkmanship and using the threat of war as a political tool means that a serious risk for the outbreak of a catastrophic conflict has to be considered real.

Nuclear programmes and missile technology

North Korea's involvement in the development of nuclear technology dates back to the 1950s when the DPRK was an ally of the Soviet Union which was then prepared to cooperate with other communist states in various aspects of industrial development, including civil nuclear technology. In 1956, North Korea and the Soviet Union signed two agreements on increased cooperation and North Korean scientists began to receive training on nuclear physics at the Dubna Joint Institute for Nuclear Research complex in the Soviet Union. In 1959, a research centre was set up with Soviet assistance on the bank of the Kuryong river close to the town of Yongbyon. It was called the 'furniture factory', presumably to keep its real purpose secret (Bermudez 1991). Programmes in nuclear technology were set up at the Kim Il-sung University and the Kimchaek College of Sciences. North Korea also began cooperation with China in the field of nuclear energy. In September 1961, at the fourth conference of the Korean Workers' Party (KWP), Kim Il-sung told scientists to work on the peaceful uses of nuclear energy.

A serious interest in the development of nuclear weapons emerged in the 1960s. The apparent capitulation of the Soviet Union in the Cuban Missile Crisis in October 1962 caused Kim Il-sung to reconsider North Korean security policy and in December 1962 he declared a new self-reliant military policy. In 1964, Kim Il-sung suggested in a letter to Mao Zedong that China and the DPRK should share nuclear weapons technology, given their partnership in the Korean War, but China refused, stating that such a small country did not need nuclear weapons. A similar request made in 1974 was likewise rejected (Oberdorfer 2001, pp. 252–3).

The core of North Korea's nuclear programme in the early stages was a small research reactor known as the IRT-2000 research reactor. This reactor was procured from the Soviet Union in January 1962 and construction began in 1963 under Soviet supervision. In Augusts 1965, the Soviet Union provided a critical assembly rated at 0.1 MWt and a reactor (the output of a nuclear reactor is measured either in terms of MWt (megawatts of heat produced) or MW(e) (megawatts of electricity generated)). The pool-type reactor that uses a mixture of uranium fuel elements of different levels of enrichment was designed to produce small quantities of isotopes for medical and industrial purposes. It became operational in 1965 with a power rating of 2 MWt (increased to 4 MW in 1974 and 8 MW in 1987).

North Korea's interest in nuclear technology initially involved civilian applications and clearly there was an interest in acquiring nuclear power stations as the DPRK had difficulty in generating sufficient electricity. It is not known exactly when the leaders of the DPRK decided to pursue a nuclear weapons programme, although this may well have been on Kim Il-sung's mind from the very beginning, an intention that firmed up after the Cuban Missile Crisis of 1962 and the deployment of US nuclear weapons in the Republic of Korea. According to North Korean defectors interviewed by Daniel Pinkston from the Monterey Institute of International Studies, Kim Il-sung gave a directive to develop nuclear warheads for missiles in 1966/67 (NTI Country Profile).

North Korea joined the International Atomic Energy Agency in 1974, although it did not at that point accede to the Nuclear Non-Proliferation Treaty. In 1978 it signed an INFCIRC/66 trilateral safeguards agreement with the IAEA to allow for the monitoring of the IRT-2000 reactor and the critical assembly. Choe Hak-kun was assigned as counsellor to the DPRK's office at the IAEA in Vienna, and reportedly spent his four years there using IAEA library facilities to acquire as much information as possible about nuclear reactor design and other aspects of nuclear technology. He became North Korea's atomic energy and industry minister in 1986.

In the late 1970s, the DPRK embarked on a substantial expansion of its nuclear programme. This manifested itself in the development of the nuclear infrastructure at Yongbyon as the first step in the establishment of a nuclear weapons programme. North Korean defectors reported that at that time a complex of nuclear facilities was constructed underground in the Pakchon area (22 km south-east of Yongbyon), where research to develop indigenous nuclear fuel enrichment technology and other aspects of nuclear weapons technology (including the design of a nuclear device) was undertaken. Other facilities constructed at Yongbyon during this period included a factory to refine yellow cake (U3O8) produced at the uranium milling factories at Packchon and Pyongsan and uranium metal fuel elements. North Korea has uranium ore deposits that could potentially yield 4 million tons of natural uranium.

In 1980, construction of an indigenous 5 MW(e) (20 MWt) gas-cooled, graphite-moderated reactor based on the British gas-graphite design of the 1940s, Calder Hall-type began. Construction of a second, larger reactor with an output of 50 MW(e) (200 MWt) commenced in 1984 (this reactor was detected by US observation satellites in 1989). The 5 MW(e) reactor went critical in August 1985 and began regular operations in 1986. Plans for the nuclear programme included a full-scale 200 MW(e) (800 MWt) power plant whose construction began in Taejon in 1989. However, only the original Yongbyon reactor has become operational, while the others remain unfinished projects. In addition, construction of a full-scale reprocessing plant to extract plutonium from the fuel rods, the so-called Radiochemistry Laboratory began around that time. The infrastructure developed at Yongbyon also included facilities to treat and store nuclear waste.

In 1985, the DPRK decided to join the nuclear non-proliferation treaty (NPT) in response to pressure from the

Soviet Union. The Soviet Union agreed to sell North Korea four light water reactors for the production of electricity in return, but the light water reactors were never delivered because after the Soviet Union put trade relations on a hard-currency basis using world prices, North Korea lacked the resources to pay for them. North Korea acceded to the NPT on 12 December 1985, and on 26 December 1985 the DPRK and the USSR signed an economic, scientific and technical agreement which included the provision of four light water reactors. Membership of the NPT requires states to submit to safeguards for all their nuclear materials and inspections by the IAEA. The implementation of safeguards, which took a very long time to get under way (36 months) due to administrative errors on the part of the IAEA, revealed discrepancies in North Korea's declaration that precipitated a dispute with North Korea. In time it became increasingly clear that North Korea was engaged in using its nuclear reactor to produce plutonium that might be used in fission weapons, contrary to its obligations under the NPT (Mazarr 1995; Wampler 2003).

The core of North Korea's programme is the 5 MW(e) reactor at Yongbyon which is designed to produce plutonium. Prior to the confrontation over the IAEA inspections in the early 1990s (the 'first North Korean nuclear crisis'), the reactor was shut down three times (1989, 1990, 1991) in order to permit the extraction of fuel rods. Plutonium could then be separated in the reprocessing facility at Yongbyon. Estimates of the amount of plutonium that North Korea is likely to have separated at that time varied between 8 and 24 kg. The Central Intelligence Agency calculated that North Korea could have obtained 12 kg of plutonium. These estimates cannot be fully verified because the IAEA was never permitted to verify the history of the reactor. Nevertheless, on the basis of the samples taken by IAEA inspectors in Yongbyon, satellite surveillance of the nuclear facilities and analysis of the discrepancies of North Korea's declaration to the IAEA yield a reasonable estimate of the amount of plutonium that North Korea could have separated (IISS 2004, pp. 47–8). According to a statement by the US Department of Energy in 1994, it takes about 4 kg of plutonium to make a nuclear fission weapon. This means that by 1991 North Korea might have accumulated enough plutonium for two to three weapons.

In 1994, the 5 MW(e) was shut down as part of the Agreed Framework that froze the plutonium programme until 2002. Some 8,000 spent fuel rods were removed from the reactor and stored without reprocessing. After the Agreed Framework broke down, North Korea began to remove the fuel rods from storage for reprocessing. It is estimated that the fuel rods may have yielded about 25 kg of plutonium, so that North Korea may have enough plutonium for eight fission weapons. There have been some claims that North Korea obtained plutonium from other sources (e.g. that 56 kg of plutonium were smuggled into the DPRK from Russia in 1992), but these are unsubstantiated. In addition, North Korea restarted the 5 MW(e) reactor in February 2003. Thus North Korea continues to produce more plutonium. In April 2005 the reactor was temporarily shut down, possibly in order to extract fuel rods for reprocessing. Analysts estimate that by the time of the shutdown, the fuel rods may have contained another 8–11 kg of plutonium (Pinkston and Diamond 2005). This shows that whatever the current state of North Korea's nuclear programme, as time passes it will acquire increasing quantities of weapons-grade fissile materials as long as the reactor remains in operation. Moreover, North Korea announced in 2005 that it was resuming work on the other (50 MW(e) and the 200 MW(e)) reactors.

In assessing North Korea's nuclear capabilities, we also need to consider the second path towards the bomb, namely the route using highly enriched uranium (HEU). During the final years of the Clinton administration, indications that North Korea was developing a clandestine uranium enrichment programme had begun to emerge. In 2001, US intelligence issued a secret assessment according to which North Korea had started a clandestine programme to produce HEU using centrifuge technology it had acquired from Pakistan in return for *Rodong* missiles. This approach is based on the concept of separating the various isotopes of uranium according to their different weight, using large numbers of high-performance centrifuges. The information on which this assessment was based had come from a variety of sources. Seoul informed Washington that North Korean scientists had visited Pakistan, and in March 1999 the Republic of Korea and the United States jointly prevented the purchase by North Korea of components for gas centrifuges in Japan. In 2001, a North Korean defector said that North Korea had been pursuing centrifuge technology for uranium enrichment for some time. Moreover, there was evidence that North Korea was seeking components such as certain types of aluminium tubes and equipment for uranium feed-and-withdrawal systems for which no other purpose appeared plausible. The conclusion was that since 1997 Pakistan had provided the DPRK with technical details of the process of enriching uranium, together with some equipment and design information on the nuclear warheads tested in 1998 that were based on an earlier Chinese design using HEU.

The provisional assessment of the CIA was that North Korea was constructing a uranium enrichment plant that would be able to produce HEU for two weapons annually once fully operational, possibly by 2005. The Defence Intelligence Agency, generally hawkish about North Korea (although its assessments have sometimes been proven to be incorrect), reported that in all likelihood North Korea had already produced some HEU warheads (globalsecurity.org). The IRT 2000 research reactor used uranium enriched to 80 per cent supplied by the Soviet Union, and North Korea could have diverted some of this material for weapons use (even though normally weapons-grade material is supposed to be enriched to over 90 per cent). The Republic of Korea and China were doubtful about the existence of an actual HEU programme. An analysis by experts from the International Institute for Strategic Studies in the United Kingdom, using the information that has come into the public domain, shows that, although no definite conclusions can be drawn, it seems unlikely that North Korea has an operational enrichment plan at present and may not have so for more than ten years. This tentative assessment is based on indications that North Korea is still seeking components for an enrichment plant, the difficulties of building other elements of the infrastructure required (i.e. a UF6 feeder plant), given what is known about North Korea's nuclear facilities, and the technical difficulties of successfully operating a uranium enrichment plant based on centrifuge technology. More recent internal South Korean assessments seem to broadly concur with the judgement that North Korea is not yet very close to possessing the capacity for producing HEU. Thus Kim Tae-woo from the Korea Institute for Defense Analyses suggests that the Khan Research Laboratory may have provided North Korea with a number of P-1- and P-2-type centrifuges, 50 kg of UF6 for calibration and technical information for the construction of enrichment stages and cascades. He concluded (as of the autumn of 2004) that North Korea most likely did not yet have any full-scale enrichment facilities or weapons-grade HEU, but that it might have laboratory-scale centrifuge facilities (Kim Tae-woo 2004). Of course these conclusions are based on estimates given the available information and the actual state of the uranium enrichment programme in North Korea remains unknown.

The production of weapons-grade materials is not yet the same, however, as the complete manufacture of nuclear warheads. The only certain way to establish the existence of working warheads is through testing. There have been claims that North Korea tested a nuclear warhead at an underground facility in 1993 or in Pakistan in 1998. These reports are unverified. It is rather doubtful that North Korea could have conducted an underground nuclear test without being detected, and closer analysis of the nuclear tests in Pakistan seems to confirm that these were Pakistani (HEU-based) warheads that were detonated. An American delegation to North Korea was allegedly shown nuclear weapons but could not verify the nature of the devices or whether they were functional (Hecker 2004).

The physical principles on which nuclear weapons are based are public knowledge but it is still a technically demanding task to make a weapon design work even if sufficient nuclear material is available. One of the key requirements for a functional warhead is a nuclear trigger using conventional high explosives designed to produce a geometrically perfect implosion that compresses the nuclear material into a critical mass necessary for a chain reaction. Between 1981 and 1991, North Korean engineers conducted about eighty high-explosive tests evidently designed to develop a nuclear trigger. The cessation of testing in 2001 may indicate that North Korea's weapons designers believed that they had finally achieved the results that they needed.

North Korea's policy on its nuclear status went from outright denial until the early 1990s to one of studied ambiguity. Until 2002, North Korea adhered to the principle that it did not seek to develop nuclear weapons. Once it restarted its nuclear activities, its representatives began to talk about its nuclear deterrent. On 10 February 2005, it announced that it had nuclear weapons but provided no evidence for this assertion. It was not until the underground nuclear test that North Korea conducted on 9 October 2006 that its capability to explode a nuclear fission device was confirmed. Although there is consensus that a fission device was detonated, it seems that the test did not go according to plan. Shortly before the test Pyongyang informed the Chinese government of the impending nuclear detonation and that it was supposed to have a target yield of 4 kT (that is, the kind of explosion that would be produced by 4,000 tons of conventional explosive). The precise yield is not known, but nevertheless there is consensus among expert observers that it was much lower (estimates vary between 0.2 and 1 kT) (Pinkston and Shin 2007). There are many possible reasons for the lower yield, from impurities in the plutonium, improper machining of the plutonium to problems with the conventional explosives that create the critical mass or the neutron initiator. Speculation that a second test would be required in order for North Korean nuclear specialists to be sure that these errors were corrected was supported by observations of renewed preparations close to the original test site in December 2006. It is also conceivable that North Korea will conduct another test at some time in the future to put further pressure on the United States to make concessions in the Six-Party Talks or other negotiations. It is also not yet clear to what extent North

Korea has developed a stockpile of deliverable nuclear devices. North Korea would need to create a device that weighs less than a ton in order to be able to use missiles to deliver it (the Nagasaki weapon weighed 4 tons and could not be delivered by North Korea's missiles or aircraft) (Garwin and von Hippel 2006).

Assuming that North Korea is in the process of assembling an arsenal of nuclear weapons, what can we say about the possible use of such weapons? Obviously the use of nuclear weapons on the Korean peninsula itself would have a devastating impact on South Korea, but at a prohibitive cost as it would invite retaliation from a nuclear superpower, the United States. Consequently the use of such weapons would undoubtedly be the end of the DPRK and most likely devastate the entire Korean nation. For this reason there is a persistent belief in South Korea, especially among the younger population, that North Korea would never use nuclear weapons against fellow Koreans. This view is not shared by some in the older generation with a more conservative outlook who see North Korea's nuclear weapons as a grave threat to the South. Nevertheless it is unclear that operational plans exist for the employment of nuclear weapons using specific types of delivery vehicles with particular targets. At the present stage of development, the nuclear capabilities have to be seen more as an existential nuclear deterrent, whose mere existence is supposed to discourage the United States and others from attacking the DPRK. But it has wider purposes than defence. By having acquired nuclear weapons, North Korea hopes to achieve equality with the US at the bargaining table. With the deep state of crisis that the country finds itself in, nuclear weapons are conceived as a form of leverage to elicit the cooperation North Korea thinks it needs on Pyongyang's own terms. North Korea is seeking nothing less than a US commitment to the national survival of the DPRK and normalization of relations, as well as significant support to stabilize the economy of the country. By creating the ultimate military threat, North Korea is essentially pursuing political, rather than military, purposes.

Chemical and biological weapons

North Korea's chemical weapons are in some way of even greater significance than the nuclear programme, given that these weapons may be used at the outset of any conflict on the Korean peninsula. For all their salience for the military balance, the details of the chemical weapons programme and capabilities are even more obscure than those of the nuclear programme, partly because production facilities are harder to identify and these capabilities have not aroused the same kind of international controversy. Nevertheless North Korea is believed to have one of the largest stockpiles of chemical weapons in the world, with estimates ranging from 2,500 to 5,000 tons of chemical agent. These reportedly include all the major classes of chemical agents, such as choking (phosgene), blister (mustard gas), blood (hydrogen cyanide) and nerve agents (sarin). According to a report by the US Department of Defence, North Korea began to develop and stockpile chemical weapons after the Korean War. In 1954, the Korean People's Army established nuclear, biological and chemical defence units on the same pattern as the Soviet armed forces. It is believed that North Korea's offensive chemical weapons programme received some assistance from China. During this period North Korea developed a substantial chemical industry, as called for in the first Five-Year Plan (1957–61). In 1961, Kim Il-sung issued a 'Declaration of Chemicalization' calling for the development of the chemical industry to provide for chemical weapons and a chemical bureau was established (from 1981 known as the Nuclear and Chemical Defence Bureau). In 1964, North Korea started to import agricultural chemicals from Japan which enabled Pyongyang to obtain chemical precursors for the synthesis of mustard gas and the nerve gas tabun, and at a later date organic compounds containing phosphorous and chlorine. When the Soviet Union resumed technical assistance to North Korea, the latter received nuclear, chemical and biological training materials. The DPRK also received small amounts of mustard gas and nerve agents from the Soviets. Production of chemical weapons most likely began in the 1970s. In the late 1970s, it was reported that North Korea was producing significant amounts of chemical agents, including cyanogen chloride as well as some mustard gas and tabun. This report seems credible even though the US Defence Intelligence Agency reported in 1979 that North Korea had developed protective measures against chemical weapons and that it was likely that it would proceed towards the production of offensive agents. In the following years there was continued speculation about North Korea's chemical weapons programme. The next official statement came from the South Korean Defence Minister, Lee Ki-baek, who stated on the basis of a defence ministry report that the DPRK had a stockpile of between 180 to 250 metric tons of chemical weapons. These included mustard gas and nerve gas. In January 1989, the foreign minister of the DPRK, Kim Young-nam, made a statement to the effect that North Korea did not produce or store nuclear or chemical weapons and did not seek to import such weapons. Around the same time it was reported that the North Korean inventory included mustard agents, hydrogen cyanide, adamsite, phosgene, tabun and sarin. In 1991, a military manual entitled *Offensive Warfare* (*Konggyokchon*) was published by Kim Il-sung Military University which codified the conduct of nuclear and chemical defence units. In February 1992, Kim Il-sung issued a directive to the effect that the entire population should be provided with protective masks and nationwide training in NBC defence. This was the first of many clear indications that Pyongyang expects a future war to be fought in a contaminated environment. In October 1992, South Korean Intelligence (then called the Agency for National Security Planning) claimed that North Korea had six centres for chemical weapons storage, each with a stockpile of 1,000 tons of agents, and that some chemical agents were kept by military units in artillery shells. In November, Pyongyang angrily denied that it had any chemical weapons, while at the same time accusing the United States of having a large stockpile in South Korea. The Republic of Korea signed up to the Chemical Weapons Convention (CWC) in 1993 as soon as it became open to signature and declared a small stock of chemical warfare agents which were then destroyed. North Korea repeated that it had no chemical weapons and declared that it adhered to international law in good faith, but declined to join the CWC despite being urged to do so by the Russian government.

In the mid-1990s, there were a number of defectors that confirmed the existence of an offensive chemical weapons programme and provided some details. On 18 March 1994 Yi Chung-kuk, a sergeant in the KPA Nuclear Chemical Defence Bureau, defected to the Republic of Korea. He said he defected in order to warn the world about North Korea's chemical weapons programme. Although he himself was involved in work on defence against chemical attacks, he claimed considerable second-hand knowledge about the DPRK's offensive chemical weapons and stated that the North had enough chemical weapons to destroy the South without the use of nuclear weapons. Moreover, he also claimed that North Korea could use *Scud* missiles to deliver chemical warheads (IISS 2004, p. 53). Yi provided detailed information about the 18th Nuclear and Chemical Defence Batallion and on Factory No. 279 and Research Institute No. 398 in Sokam-ri. According to him these facilities are responsible for the development and production of equipment for defence against chemical attacks. He also claimed that the February 8th Vinalon Complex is involved in the chemical weapons programme. Vinalon is a textile fibre and, according to Yi, the inventor of vinalon contributed to the research and development of chemical weapons. Choi Ju-hwal, a colonel in the KPA who served in the Ministry of Defence in Pyongyang from 1968 to 1995, when he defected. Choi only had second-hand information on North Korea's chemical weapons which he said he obtained from other officials. In 1997, he claimed that North Korea had a stock of over 5,000 tons of chemical agents, including hydrogen cyanide, cyanogens chloride, lewisite, mustard gas and various nerve gases such as sarin, tabun, soman and V agents (IISS 2004, p. 54). Some evidence comes from the high-level defector Hwang Jang-yop. Hwang was not in charge or directly involved with programmes relating to weapons of mass destruction, but he was one of the highest-level insiders of the regime and therefore is probably the most reliable source. On the basis of debriefing sessions with Hwang, the then foreign minister of the Republic of Korea, Yu Chong-ha, stated on 6 May 1997 to the National Assembly Unification and Foreign Affairs Committee that North Korea had about 5,000 tons of chemical weapon agents and operates eight plants capable of producing 5,000 tons of agent every year.

Missile technology

For over 30 years, North Korea has been involved in the production of ballistic missiles, developing a large infrastructure for their design, testing and manufacture. North Korea's ballistic missile industry is based primarily on Soviet technology and was developed with the help of the Soviet Union and China. Although there are significant uncertainties about the extent of North Korea's missile capabilities, it is estimated that the DPRK has about 700 ballistic missiles that can reach targets of up to about 2,500 km away.

Ballistic missiles are clearly the delivery system of choice for nuclear weapons, given the vulnerability of aircraft to air defence and the difficulties in executing a coordinated attack with strategic bombers. For this reason there seems to be an inextricable link between North Korea's nuclear ambitions and its ballistic missile programme. North Korean efforts to develop ballistic missiles go back to the mid-1960s. In 1965, the Hamhung Military Academy was opened, and departments were established where the design of missile engines was studied and taught. In 1968, the DPRK obtained FROG 5 short-range missile systems from the Soviet Union. These systems, with a range of up to 60 km and a payload of 400 kg, were capable of delivering conventional or chemical munitions into the Seoul metropolitan area from positions just behind the DMZ and therefore added to North Korean artillery. Moscow balked at providing North Korea with more advanced missiles as relations between the DPRK and the Soviet Union deteriorated in the context of a sharpening conflict between China and the USSR. Consequently, Pyongyang turned to Beijing to obtain access to more advanced missile technology. In 1971, China and North Korea concluded a military cooperation treaty that included missile technology transfer and the sale of missiles. In April 1975, when Kim Il-sung visited Beijing, a deal was concluded for North Korean participation in a Chinese missile development project. The *Dong feng 61* was conceived as a single stage tactical missile with a range of 600 km and a payload of 1000 kg based on Soviet *Scud* technology. The project did not come to fruition because when its main supporter, General Chen Xilian, was removed from the PRC government in 1978, it was cancelled. However, North Korean missile experts may have acquired a great deal of technical knowledge as a result of their participation that most likely assisted them when North Korea built its own version of the *Scud*.

After the end of the joint project with China, North Korea forged links with Middle Eastern countries, and Egypt and the DPRK began to collaborate on missile production. Egypt needed assistance because the relationship with the Soviet Union had collapsed in the wake of the 1978 Camp David accords. Cairo supplied Pyongyang with a few *Scud B* (R 11M) with its mobile launcher for the purpose of reverse engineering. By 1984, North Korea had successfully produced a number of *Scud B*-like prototypes, designated the *Hwasong-5*. This engineering effort involved the construction of a number of new facilities, including (according to defector reports) the Sanum-dong research and development facilities (also called the No. 7 Factory), the Sungni Automobile Factory where mobile launchers are produced, the No. 125 factory for missile assembly (located near Pyongyang) and the Musudan-ri missile testing facility (Hanyong province).

The *Hwasong-5* has a range of about 320–40 km (about 15 per cent greater than that of the original *Scud B*) and carries a payload of 1,000 kg. Serial production began in 1986 and continued until about 1991. The *Hwasong-5* was supplied to Iran during the Iran–Iraq war, where it experienced combat use that allowed DPRK engineers to gain valuable technical data. In the meantime North Korea developed another version of the *Scud* with a lower payload and a lighter airframe, extending the range to 500 km. This missile, called the *Hwasong-6*, started to be deployed in 1991.

By 1991, the entire Korean peninsula was within range of North Korean missiles, but the efforts to extend the range of the *Scud* had reached their limits. In the late 1980s, North Korea began the development of a medium-range missile that would have the capability to target Japan, with a range of 1,000–1,300 km and a payload of 700–1,000 kg. This missile, called the *Rodong*, was based on a design that required new engines and guidance systems to achieve the required performance characteristiscs. The concept design for the engine of the *Rodong* was developed by the Makeyev OKB in the Soviet Union (a design bureau that specializes in submarine-launched missiles) and consequently this missile bears some resemblance to the early designs of the SS-N-4 (R13) and SS-N-5 (R21). It seems that North Korea managed to overcome the challenges of developing new engines that require four times the thrust of a *Scud* engine, but it is suspected that North Korea had assistance from Soviet missile engineers. Indeed, the engine seems to be of similar design to the Isayev S-2.713M engine incorporated in the SS-N-4 and the missile itself is an intermediate design between the SS-N-4 and SS-N-5. Although the contribution of ex-Soviet missile engineers cannot be positively determined, it is known that 60 engineers from the Makeyev OKB were prevented from flying to North Korea in October 1992.

Details on the development and deployment of the *Rodong* are sketchy. In May 1990, a new missile that resembled what later became known as the *Rodong* was observed by US satellites at the Musudan-ri test launch facility. In May 1993, there was a successful launch from Musudan-ri into the Sea of Japan. The missile travelled a distance of about 500 km on a high-altitude trajectory designed to demonstrate warhead separation. This was the only test of the missile by North Korea ever reported, although Pakistan and Iran tested a number of *Rodong*-type missiles since 1998 and it may be assumed that North Korea obtained data from these tests. The IISS North Korea dossier estimates the CEP (circular error probable: a measure of accuracy) of the *Rodong* at 3–5 km; globalsecurity.org cites a report claiming a CEP of 2–4 km, but there are very limited data for such an assessment.

The timeline for production and deployment as well as the size of the *Rodong* force remain uncertain, and the programme suffered from various technical and financial problems. The construction of missile storage sites began in July 1995 and by October 1995 four launch sites had been built. Operational training of missile crews is believed to have started in 1995. The Ministry of Defence of the Republic of Korea declared the missiles to be operational in 1997, and South Korean sources claimed that by 1999 nine *Rodong* missiles had been deployed. The deployment rates and numbers remain guesses, but most observers believe that by 2002 the DPRK had between 100 and 200 operational *Rodong*. North Korea also exported the missile. The Pakistani *Ghauri* is practically identical to *Rodong*, and the Iranian *Shahab-3* was developed on the basis of the *Rodong* design with the assistance of North Korean engineers. It is believed that Iran purchased at least 10 complete *Rodong* missiles. Some *Rodong* were also exported to Libya. North Korea also exported about 500 *Hwasong-5/6* to Iran, Syria, Egypt and Libya.

Clearly, the strategic purpose of the *Rodong* is to hold Japanese cities, military installations and US forces in Japan at risk. The IISS dossier on North Korean military capabilities published in 2004 argues that because of its poor accuracy and low numbers the *Rodong* is not effective against hardened military targets and is therefore more likely a political rather than a military weapon, unless it is fitted with nuclear warheads. Of course the use of nuclear weapons would be suicidal for the Pyongyang regime. While it may be true that the effectiveness of the *Rodong* remains limited, it is clear that North Korea considers the capability to attack Japan and US forces in Okinawa a critical element of its defence posture. The deployment of the *Rodong* is probably considered to be only a first step until more advanced and accurate missiles become available.

This became evident when on 31 August 1998 North Korea launched a new kind of missile in an attempt to place a small satellite into orbit. This missile was called *Taepodong-1* by US analysts (after the area from where it was launched), although the North Korean name is believed to be *Paektusan-1*.

Although the satellite launch failed, the launch alarmed analysts because it demonstrated the capability to manage the technical problems of building a missile with three stages. The *Taepodong* thus demonstrated the potential for developing missiles of intercontinental range (ICBMs).

The *Taepodong-1* missile (in distinction to the space launch vehicle) is a two-stage missile. The first stage is based on a modified *Rodong* while the second stage is a *Scud B/C*. This combination is estimated to have a range of 2,000–2,200 km and a payload of 700–1,000 kg. The space launch vehicle had a third stage consisting of a small ellipsoid-shaped solid motor designed to lift the satellite into orbit. The Korean Central News Agency reported that

> the rocket was launched at 12:07 on 31 August 1998 at a launching station in Musudan-ri, Hwadae county, North Hamgyong province. The satellite was put into orbit at 12 hours, 11 minutes, 53 seconds. The process of placing it into orbit took 4 minutes, 53 seconds. The rocket used to launch the satellite comprised three stages. The first stage separated from the rocket in 95 seconds and fell into the Sea of Korea, 253 km from the launching station (40 degrees 51 minutes north latitude, 139 degrees 40 minutes east longitude). The second stage separated from the rocket within 266 seconds and fell into the Pacific Ocean, 1,646 km from the launching station (40 degrees 13 minutes north latitude, 149 degrees 07 minutes east longitude). The third stage placed the satellite into orbit within 27 seconds after separating from the second stage. The satellite is currently in an oval orbit that runs 218.82 km nearest to the earth, and 6,978.2 km furthest from it. One revolution of its orbit around the earth takes 165 minutes 6 seconds. The satellite is equipped with necessary sounding instruments and is currently transmitting melodies of North Korean revolutionary hymns in 27 MHz. Its purpose is to: (1) contribute to North Korean scientific research for peaceful use of outer space; (2) confirm the calculation basis for future satellite launches; and (3) encourage the Korean people in the efforts to build a powerful socialist state under the wise leadership of General Secretary Kim Jong Il.

This was evidently a prepared statement and the North Korean government did not want to report that in fact the launch had failed. The first stage fell into the Sea of Japan and the second stage into the water near the Sanriku coast. The third stage fired but an unknown malfunction resulted in the failure of the satellite to achieve orbit.

Although it is now generally accepted that North Korea attempted to launch a satellite, the launch provoked considerable reaction due its trajectory which was perceived as demonstrating a threat to Japan. The Japanese government denounced the event as a missile launch and stated it would reconsider its contribution to the light water reactors under the Agreed Framework, although in the end Japan resumed its support. The event also gave further impetus to collaboration with the US on theatre missile defence, and on 20 September the United States and Japan reaffirmed their commitment to conduct joint research on ballistic missile defence.

In the face of international criticism and political pressure, North Korea negotiated an agreement with Washington in September 1999 whereby in return for the lifting of a range of sanctions North Korea imposed a moratorium on long-range missile tests. This moratorium was extended more than once and remains in force, even though, after the collapse of the Agreed Framework, Pyongyang indicated it would resume space launches and in early 2005 threatened the resumption of missile tests if no progress were made in nuclear talks. On 5 July 2006, North Korea made good on this threat, conducting a series of missile launches that resulted in the imposition of sanctions by the United Nations (Cordesman 2006).

The key strategic question is if and when North Korea will be able to acquire an intercontinental missile capability that can strike at targets on the continental United States. According to the IISS analysts, the three-stage version of the TD-1 could deliver a small payload (100–200 kg) to targets on the US mainland, not enough for a crude nuclear device and probably not enough for a chemical warhead that could cause significant numbers of casualties. North Korea's plans for an ICBM capability therefore rest on the development of a larger missile, designated *Taepodong-2*. According to a North Korean defector, development of the *Taepodong-2* began in 1987 on direct orders of Kim Jong-il. The missile is believed to exist in a two-stage or three-stage variant (the latter being a space launch vehicle). The second stage is believed to have the engine from the *Rodong*, with a substantially larger first stage that can deliver a great deal more thrust. Various analysts, including US intelligence reports, have described the first stage as similar to the first stage of the CSS/DF-3, although it is to be expected that it will be based on systems that North Korea has already developed. The IISS dossier describes the first stage as a cluster of four *Rodong* engines. Estimates of the range for the missile vary between 3,500–6,000 km, with a payload of about 1,000 kg. The 1995 US National Intelligence Estimate (NIE) gave a range estimate of 4,000–6,000 km, and concluded that no country other than the declared nuclear powers would be able to attack the continental United States for at least another 15 years. The *Taepodong-2* would be able to reach Alaska or Hawaii at best.

It is generally believed that testing will be required for further missile development. This might mean that until testing is resumed, further development of long-range missiles will remain constrained. The tests in July 2006 were a political demonstration without significant technical value. In the case of the *Rodong*, Pyongyang essentially outsourced its testing to its customers in Pakistan and Iran, although those tests were few in number and therefore confidence in the reliability of *Rodong* must remain limited (especially as about 50 per cent of the tests appear to have been failures). A test of the *Taepodong-2* engine is believed to have taken place in 2001. The test in 2006 resulted in the early explosion of the missile, so the data this test provided must have been very limited. It is reported that North Korea initiated talks with Iran on exporting components of the *Taepodong-2* to Iran where they would be assembled by North Korean engineers. In 2004 it was again reported that Iran was considering purchasing the *Taepodong-2* as the basis for an intercontinental ballistic missile and also that Russian missile engineers were assisting a solid-fuel design team at the Shahid Bagheri Industrial Group in Iran to develop two long-range missiles with a range of 5,000 km and 10,000 km respectively. These missiles could be the *Shahab-5* and *Shahab-6*, although Teheran has indicated that its missile developments would end with the *Shahab-4*. The *Shahab-4* is a satellite launch vehicle possibly based on the *Taepodong-1*.

In any case, it is unclear how much progress North Korea has made towards the development of an ICBM. Such a missile would require not only a new kind of engine and air-frame, but also an improved guidance and control system. In order to achieve intercontinental range, the so-called re-entry vehicle that houses the warhead is projected into space and has to re-enter the atmosphere. The achievement of even modest accuracy (measured by the CEP – circular error prob-able) is a very considerable engineering challenge.

In September 2003, there were reports of sightings by US intelligence satellites of a new type of missile that seemed to be similar to the Soviet SS-N-6 (originally a submarine-launched missile) at Mirim airbase. On 9 September 2003, just prior to the celebrations for the fifty-fifth anniversary of the foundation of the DPRK, about ten missiles and five launchers were sighted at the base (the preparation site for parades), but the missiles never appeared at the public parades. Subsequently some analysts have expressed the view that these were merely mock-ups and that this unknown missile, which has never been flight-tested and about whose development there had been no prior information, does not exist. However, information that construction on two under-ground missile sites in Yangdok County, South Pyongan province, and Hochon, Hamgyeong province was under way seemed to substantiate the view that there might be more to this new missile programme. The ROK government seems to believe that the missile is real; on 7 July 2004 in testimony due the National Defence Committee of the ROK National Assembly, then Defence Minister Cho Young-kil confirmed that North Korea had deployed this new missile with a range of 2,750–4,000 km.

If it is a real missile, it is suggested that it is based on the engine of an SS-N-6 with a *Rodong* re-entry vehicle and inter-stage element, thus resulting in a missile body with a diame-ter of 1.5 m (equal to that of the SS-N-6) but of somewhat greater length than the original Soviet missile (12 m as opposed to 9.65 m) (Yu 2004). (The dimensions of the missile cited here differ from those reported by the IISS where a diameter of 1.65 m and a length of just under 10 m is given (IISS 2004, p. 81).) The missile has not yet been flight-tested and so there is no information on its performance characteristics other than extrapolations from what is known of the SS-N-6. If the estimates for the range of the missile are correct, then it could target American bases in Okinawa and Guam. Unlike the other missiles, this new system is deployed on mobile launchers. The original SS-N-6 was tested for deployment on surface ships as well as submarines, and there are fears that North Korea might seek to deploy the missiles in this mode, thereby potentially increasing the target range, although surface ships would be very vulnerable to interception.

In conclusion, a few observations can be made on the North Korean missile programmes and their implications for international security. North Korea has pursued the development of ballistic missiles since the 1970s, based on first-generation Soviet missile technology. It has developed and deployed a substantial force of short-range missiles capable of delivering conventional, chemical or nuclear munitions on any target in the Republic of Korea. It has also developed the *Rodong* that can reach all of Japan, including American bases in Okinawa. Having a few hundred deployed missiles and more in reserve provides North Korea with an important augmentation of its long-range artillery capabilities, enabling strikes in the rear and interdiction of reinforcements. The longer range missiles in particular have an important political function – without them the deterrence and intimidation based on North Korea's emerging 'nuclear deterrent' would have much less salience. It is not known whether any non-conventional munitions are deployed on missiles at present. Of course, the missiles also have come to play a significant economic role as one of North Korea's most successful export industries. It seems safe to conclude, however, that the military significance of the long-range missiles is very limited. North Korea does not yet have a missile capable of delivering a nuclear warhead to the continental United States. However, given time and effort it seems to be well within the capabilities of the DPRK to develop missiles with greater range and payload. Once it can demonstrate the capability to attack the United States with nuclear weapons, the strategic situation on the Korean peninsula will have shifted decisively. This is an argument for the view that the United States cannot simply accept a nuclear North Korea and the issue of North Korean WMD needs to be resolved sooner rather than later.

9 Understanding the Security Dilemma on the Korean Peninsula

There is no scarcity of proposals for solutions to the crisis on the Korean peninsula. Most of these revolve around the creation of multilateral security regimes, involve the elimination of nuclear weapons from the peninsula and the establishment of a whole range of military confidence-building measures as well as economic support for the North and closer inter-Korean relations. The South Korean government is banking on political and economic engagement, in the hope of preserving stability and bringing about gradual reform in the North. The North Korean government itself sees the key to its security in an end to American hostility to its regime. Exactly how the 'American threat' could be credibly removed is unclear, but elements that the DPRK has demanded include the establishment of diplomatic relations, a peace treaty or at least a non-aggression treaty, the elimination of sanctions and a deal involving the abandonment of the nuclear programme in return for a whole range of economic benefits.

But the security dilemma on the Korean peninsula is of a different nature than the classic security dilemma and there is a nagging doubt that the various instruments to mitigate the perception of the external security threat or the creation of regional security and arms control regimes can really address the sources of insecurity on the Korean peninsula.

There are two different classes of theoretical approaches that scholars use to understand or explain foreign policy behaviour. The first of these involves system-level theories that emphasize the structural constraints of the international system as opposed to the strategies and motivations of agents. From this perspective the relative power position is the critical factor that explains foreign policy behaviour and internal factors, such as the type of political system or the actions of individuals, are not significant. The second type of theoretical approach emphasizes domestic and social factors that explain the action of states.

Neorealism, or structural realism, was given its classic systematic exposition by Kenneth Waltz in *Theory of International Politics* (Waltz 1979) and has been developed further by various scholars, including John Mearsheimer in his *The Tragedy of Great Power Politics* (Mearsheimer 2003). Although in Waltz's conception it is not a theory of foreign policy as such, it has been widely used as a conceptual basis for interpreting foreign policy behaviour. It is based on the assumption that the international system consists of states that can be described as rational actors. This system is anarchic, i.e. it has no central authority, and its units are independent and sovereign. In order to ensure their survival, states acquire offensive military capabilities. Thereby they can increase their relative power in the international system, but they also provoke mistrust and the strengthening of the military capabilities of other states. This problem is described as the *security dilemma*. The desire of states to maximize their power results in arms races and alliances. International relations are shaped by the *balance of power*. States differ primarily in their capabilities. Their balancing behaviour is a function of the structure of the system (the distribution of power).

On the face of it, structural realism seems to offer a plausible explanation of North Korean behaviour, as Kenneth Waltz himself intimated at a meeting of the American Political Science Association in 2000. Indeed, much of North Korean behaviour and public utterances seem to suggest that they themselves strongly believe that they face a serious and persistent security threat. According to North Korean official statements, the main threat to their security is the hostile attitude of the United States which is using sanctions and military threats to support its policy of regime change in the North. If only the United States would abandon its hostile policy, accord the DPRK diplomatic recognition, lift sanctions and end its military threats (preferably through a non-aggression pact or even a peace treaty), North Korea would not need nuclear weapons or long-range ballistic missiles.

The structural realist perspective on the basis of which North Korean foreign policy behaviour is explained simply as a consequence of the DPRK's security dilemma has many adherents in the Republic of Korea and some in the academic community. Tim Beal has described North Korea's foreign policy as 'the struggle against American power' and provides an extensive defence of the North Korean position which sees the United States as the main source of the conflict (Beal 2005). This kind of viewpoint finds considerable resonance in South Korea, especially among the younger generation. More sophisticated versions of this approach have been developed by Selig Harrison and Bruce Cumings. Harrison argues for a disengagement of the United States from Korea and seeks to demonstrate in minute detail how North Korea's policies are explained on the basis of US actions that create a sense of threat in Pyongyang (Harrison 2002). He envisages the possibility of a neutral unified Korea in the future.

Looking at the history of the Korean peninsula since 1945, something seems to be amiss with this picture of the security dilemma. Although part of the North Korean threat perception is accurate, in so far as the United States would like to see a regime change in the North and the South would like to see a united democratic Korea at some point in the longer term, there is no clear evidence of a coordinated policy to bring this about. Quite to the contrary, it has become abundantly clear that there is a consensus in the United States that the use of military force against North Korea has to be ruled out except in very extreme circumstances of North Korean military aggression. There is a profound ambiguity about the development of North Korea's advanced military programmes. While on the one hand it is claimed that missiles and nuclear weapons are designed to deter an American attack, on the other hand the fact that North Korea appears to be willing to bargain them away against political assurances and economic support seems to raise the question of their military significance in the first place. It seems that a country that is so suspicious of the outside world and perceives the external threat to be so acute is unlikely to settle for political declarations and an exchange of ambassadors as the basis of its security.

The other paradox of the Korean situation is that the weakest state in north-east Asia has been so successful in its negotiations with other powers. In the 1990s, North Korea obtained almost everything it wanted in negotiations with the United States, although it was less successful during the Bush administration which did not seem to care how high North Korea raised the level of threat. China refuses to 'punish' North Korea for 'bad behaviour' and the Republic of Korea is in many respects behaving as the weaker partner, frequently giving in to North Korean demands for aid and political concessions while often facing North Korean refusals to honour its agreements or reciprocate. This kind of asymmetrical bargaining, where the weakness of the North Korean state is in fact one of its principal assets, has no place in the structural balance-of-power theory. As Samuel Kim and Alexander George have pointed out, it is necessary to distinguish between aggregate structural power and power that is usable with regard to specific issues and situations. This would help us to understand why powerful states often do less well than weaker states in armed conflicts or trade disputes (George 1993, p. 111; Samuel Kim 1998, p. 11). In the Korean case, this can be understood in terms of the particular form of deterrence that North Korea employs. Deterrence is based on a threat of action that is wholly unacceptable to the other side. In order for deterrence to be effective, the threat must be credible. This means that the capability to implement the threat must exist and the willingness to carry out the threat must be believed (Freedman 2004). The main threat that North Korea employs is that it would initiate a war on the Korean peninsula that would result in large-scale casualties (many millions) and the complete destruction of the Republic of Korea, even though such a war would result in the demise of the North Korean regime itself. Although it remains uncertain under what circumstances North Korea would carry out this threat, its official statements are designed to convey the impression that the threshold of the transition to full-scale war is rather low and that certainly any attack on its nuclear facilities, for example, would provoke such a response. The enormous concentration of its forces close to the DMZ and especially the large number of artillery pieces that have the range to attack Seoul provide the physical military capability to carry out such a threat at short notice. An essential element of this form of deterrence is the suggestion conveyed through the various ways in which Pyongyang engages in brinkmanship that somehow North Korea is less deterred than the other side, i.e. it is more willing to risk its own annihilation.

Nevertheless, the strategic situation on the Korean peninsula means that deterrence is both mutual and stable up to a point. But this stability is fragile because of the nature of the North Korean security dilemma. The main threat to North Korean security is internal because the perpetuation of the regime requires, at least in the belief of its leaders, continued tight social control in the presence of severe economic deprivation, and the regime has been unable to reverse the catastrophic economic collapse it experienced in the 1990s. The challenges to the government are such that in any country that is less tightly controlled the regime would have already collapsed. This means that deterrence is not enough; the regime needs to extort external support in order to deal with the failing economy. Ratcheting up the military threat with the nuclear and missile programmes has been at the core of this strategy. The other threat that North Korea employs very effectively is that of sudden regime collapse (although this is never explicitly acknowledged in official statements). It is the latter that has the most impact on the policies of China and South Korea towards the DPRK.

The dilemma that this situation represents for the stronger power is fully expressed in the American political discourse on North Korea. Leon Sigal has demonstrated the extent of the critical commentary, both from leading politicians and political commentators, towards any form of compromise with North Korea to achieve a termination of the nuclear programme in the 1990s (Sigal 1998). This was based on an incoherent mixture of a structural realist understanding of power in international politics and a moralistic approach that labelled North Korea as a 'rogue state' because it refused to conform to international norms; it rejected compromise as rewarding North Korea's violation of its international commitments and essentially giving in to blackmail. The problem was that the United States did not have any instruments to compel North Korea effectively without incurring unacceptable risks.

This indicates that the neorealist approach does not provide a sufficient analytical framework for understanding the crisis on the Korean peninsula. Neither the distribution of power in the international system nor the general concept of anarchy are sufficient to understand how North Korea's threat perceptions are generated. Although on the surface North Korea fits the classic neorealist paradigm, closer analysis shows that the constructivist approach to international relations, which is based on the notion that power in international politics is socially constructed, is a more appropriate framwork of analysis. In the constructivist approach, elements of social reality such as perceptions of identity, norms and values, interests, fears and culture have a significant impact on the interactions of units (i.e. states) in the international system. In other words, they are not given in nature or determined by material factors alone, and consequently can be altered by human practice. In the words of Alexander Wendt: 'The effects of anarchy are contingent on the desires and beliefs states have and the policies they pursue' (Wendt 1999, p. 146). We can go further than that and state that the effects of anarchy are constrained by shared norms. Although the international system is anarchic in the sense that there is no world government and each state is considered to be sovereign, in reality many aspects of the interactions between states, in particular the use of force and international trade, are highly regulated by treaties as well as international regimes and institutions. This is what gives rise to the concept of the 'rogue state'. Western leaders have described a 'rogue state' as one that is seeking weapons of mass destruction, supporting terrorism, is ruled by an unaccountable and unelected elite and threatens other states. In other words, it is not constrained by international norms; it is behaving as if the international system were anarchic. Asymmetry of normative behaviour as a defining characteristic of asymmetric conflict has undoubtedly become a significant factor in international security in the age of global terrorism, suicide bombers and *jihad* and also clearly seems to be useful in the analysis of relations between North Korea and the United States. Nevertheless, the concept of a 'rogue state' has been criticized on the grounds that the various states such as Syria, Iraq (prior to 2003) and Iran that have been included in this category have very different interests and foreign policy behaviour.

Similarly, the neorealist paradigm has clear limitations in explaining the policy of the Republic of Korea towards the North, especially since 1998. It could be argued that the policy of engagement that involves eschewing political and military pressure on the North, provision of economic support reducing pressure on the regime and incentives to comply with demands from the international community regarding its military programmes, along with a weakening of the alliance with the United States which provides a security guarantee to the ROK, is far from what a structural realist approach would predict. Every bargain the Republic of Korea makes with the DPRK seems to result in absolute and relative gains for the North, a total inversion of the principles of cooperation according to neorealism. Indeed, one could argue that the 'sunshine policy' of Kim Dae-jung is best understood on the basis of constructivist principles as an attempt to bring about a long-term change in the values, threat perceptions and identity of North Korea.

All of this suggests that the Korean security dilemma cannot be fully understood without considering domestic political factors. The significance of domestic sources in explaining international politics has long been debated by the scholarly community. Two assumptions of structural realism are open to question – one is that the units have similar characteristics (i.e. liberal democracies behave in the same way as totalitarian dictatorships) and the other is that they behave as rational actors. The reasons to question the first assumption become apparent when we consider the example of the conflict between the Soviet Union and the United States in the

Cold War. Structural realism interprets it merely as a competition between two major powers. In this account it resulted in a structure of the international system which is called bipolar. The two 'superpowers' acted like the sociopolitical equivalent of magnetic poles with other states aligning their foreign policy behaviour in accordance with one pole or the other. While this description of the Cold War system is useful in some respects, it leaves out various other factors, such as Marxist-Leninist ideology, authoritarian or totalitarian governments and the shared values in the West including personal freedom, human rights and democracy. It can be argued that a theory that ignores the major salient factors that determine how the agents think about the power relationships that they are involved with, and how they define their interests and goals, is not complete. In other words, structural realism simply ignores what must be a major part of the story. The fact that structural realism does not allow for the possibility that international regimes or changing norms and identities could themselves change the structure of the international system may account for its failure to explain the timing and the manner in which the Cold War ended. Indeed the fairly rapid collapse of the bipolar structure of the international system was a surprise to scholars and policymakers alike. From a different analytical perspective that takes into account the nature of the regime and the domestic structure of power, the East–West conflict cannot be understood simply as the natural rivalry between two great power systems. It was a more fundamental antagonism involving the legitimacy of different types of socioeconomic organization and the legitimacy of certain political elites for which the pursuit of Great Power interests was an essential instrument to perpetuate their own existence and ambitions. The notion that different regime-types lead to different behaviour regarding international cooperation and the use of force has received greater attention due to the 'democratic peace theory'. This states that liberal democracies do not go to war with each other. This is based on the observation that not only have there been no wars between liberal democracies but neither are they perceived to threaten one another and the balance of power between liberal democracies has been relevant only in the context of responses to other external threats. Some IR scholars have expressed the view that 'the absence of war between democratic states has come as close as anything we have to an empirical law in international relations' (Kim 1998, p. 14). The extent to which the empirical evidence supports the 'democratic peace theory' depends on how one defines the term 'liberal democracy'. Among the conditions for the theory to be applicable, there must be a shared value system which includes the acceptance of international norms and the existence of institutional mechanisms for the resolution of conflicts. Other factors may explain the 'democratic peace theory', such as the more diffuse nature of political power in liberal democracies that makes it difficult to sustain military conflicts unless they are relatively limited in time and their objectives are widely accepted by the population. This generally rules out the acquisition of territory by force owing to the difficulties of absorbing hostile populations in the political system and the violation of political norms involved. It also means that domestic consent to a war depends highly on the nature of the regime against which war is to be conducted – i.e. it has to be credibly described as an aggressive and authoritarian (non-democratic) regime.

It would be fair to say that the Republic of Korea and the DPRK are good examples for the 'democratic peace' and the 'realist' paradigms respectively. The ROK has become a democratic state, has fully integrated into the international community and does not represent a military threat to anyone. Indeed, there would be strong opposition to any military attack on North Korea along the full spectrum of the political elite and political opinion in the South. The armed forces have become a defensive force and are now taking their rightful place in society. The DPRK, on the other hand, is despite its name a totalitarian state and the 'military first' policy, whereby the military receives full priority in the distribution of available resources, is part of an attempt to resolve its security dilemma in a manner consistent with a realist understanding of international relations (Kim Chul Woo 2000).

If we concede that the type of regime is important in determining foreign policy behaviour, we need to examine more closely what the nature of the regime is and how its structure, the way in which the state defines its own identity and the ideology that legitimates it impact on foreign policy.

North Korea traces its roots back to the Old Choson dynasty of the fourth and third centuries BCE. North Koreans use the word *Choson saram* (Choson people – the word Choson means 'morning calm'), whereas the people from the Republic of Korea (*Taehan Minguk*) refer to themselves as *Hanguk saram* (Han is the Chinese name for Korean people). The Korean expression for 'Democratic People's Republic of Korea' is *Choson Minjujuui Inmin Konghwaguk*, while South Koreans refer to it as *Pukhan* (North Korea). This shows that North Koreans describe their Korean identity in different terms and how they see themselves as representing the pure heritage of the Korean people. The philosophy on which Kim Il-sung sought to build the Korean nation can be described as a mixture of Confucianism, socialism and totalitarianism which was developed into the philosophy of *juche*. The Confucian element is important for the adoption of a hierarchical social order in which Kim Il-sung took the part of the Confucian emperor, the supreme leader apart from the people. It must be remembered that the people of the DPRK have never known anything resembling a democracy. The Korean Workers' Party plays a role similar to the *yangban* nobility of the Choson dynasty. The people are taught not to think for themselves or question anything, but follow the guidance of their leaders. Ideological truth is not subject to debate but its truth is considered self-evident. Paradoxically this hierarchical structure has been imposed on a society which has been developed on the basis of strict egalitarian principles (Oh and Hassig 2000, pp. 9–11). Another critical element that influenced Kim Il-sung's vision for Korea was his experience as a guerila in Manchuria. He saw life as an incessant struggle, requiring the constant mobilization of the people. This explains the centrality of militarism in North Korean society. Power is based on military force, the purpose of the state is to wage war and the economy must provide the means for waging war (Buzo 1999, p. 241). Diplomacy and foreign policy is one way in which the conflict with the outside world is conducted. This would explain why North Korean foreign policy embodies many elements described by neorealist theory, where it sees negotiations and bargaining as zero-sum games in which both the absolute and relative gains are critical. It would also explain how, within the narrow confines of its ideological preconceptions, North Korean leaders are unable to correctly assess the policies and intentions of the states that they see as implacable adversaries. Ralph Hassig and Kongdan Oh have articulated this problem in the following terms:

> North Korea is a land of illusions. An ideology that places the leader above the people and the nation. An economy built on the assumption that people can lead selfless, communitarian lives. A ruler and his top policymakers who rarely travel outside the country or meet foreigners. A military that boasts of being the mightiest in the world. A social control system that seeks to keep 23 million people isolated from the outside world. And a foreign policy based on the premise that by threatening other nations North Korea can become a respected member of the international community. (Oh and Hassig 2000, p. 10)

In foreign policy analysis, models of decision-making have been developed that question the rational expectations theories that are at the root of system-level theories of international relations. A pioneering study by Graham Allison and Philip Zelikow on the 1962 Cuban Missile Crisis, called *The Essence of Decision,* proposed three alternative models for the study of decision-making: the rational actor model, the organizational behaviour model and the governmental politics model (Allison and Zelikow 1999). The rational actor model is based on the assumption that governments are the primary actor in foreign policy, that they set a series of goals based on their assessment of the national interest and then devise policies to achieve them. The organizational behaviour model is based on the observation that the bureaucratic organization of governments places limits on and influences the implementation of policy to the extent of sometimes determining the

final outcome. Organizational processes, based on set proce-
dures and previous experience, are used to implement policy.
In a crisis, due to time and resource limitations governments
do not necessarily examine all possible courses of action, but
often settle on the first proposal that seems to deal with the
issue. Often there is not a wholistic approach to a problem,
but it is broken up and assigned to the different parts of the
bureaucracy that deal with it in accordance to established
processes rather than in terms of the overall desired outcome.
The governmental politics model acknowledges that the government is not necessarily a unitary actor, but that differences
of interests and points of view exist within a government.
Moreover, foreign policy may not necessarily be designed to
serve the interests of the state, but rather to serve the political
interests of sections of the government or other vested interests in society and be wholly unrelated to the national interest
in foreign policy.

There is no doubt that the organizational behaviour model
and the governmental politics model can be used to develop a
rich narrative to explain the foreign policy of the Republic of
Korea, especially since the end of the military dictatorship.
There has been considerable debate in the literature of
whether and how such models can be applied to North Korea.
This is due to the fact that Kim Il-sung and now Kim Jong-il
appear to have a very tight control over the government and
the population so that internal debate over policy can only
take place within tightly restricted parameters. There seems to
be clear scope for the organizational behaviour model to yield
important insights, because totalitarian governments typically
exhibit a very formalistic bureaucratic behaviour. What is less
clear is to what extent there are different loci of power within
the North Korean elite. It is often suggested that the military
leadership or the security services constrain the freedom of
action by the government. Indeed, North Korean negotiators
at times told their American counterparts that the military
would not accept their proposals. More recently, the agreement to reconnect rail services between South and North
Korea was alleged to have been vetoed by the North Korean
military. A recent study published by the International

Institute for Strategic Studies documented the existence of a struggle between reformers and hardliners in North Korea, which manifested itself primarily with respect to economic reforms (Carlin and Wit 2006). A particularly instructive example is the issue of cellphones. The reformers were able to get support for a policy of permitting the selective availability of mobile phones, only for the security services to reverse that decision later. Economic reform was postponed in order to continue the focus on the external security environment by maintaining heavy investment in military industry until the year 2001, when finally the first clear signs of economic reform became evident. Even if the analysis by Carlin and Wit is accepted, however, it is clear that the parameters of real political debate are very restricted and in the end the decision of Kim Jong-il prevails. Indeed, social control throughout North Korea is so extensive and has been organized down to the neighbourhood level that there is no institution that can act as a channel for mass dissent, nor is there evidence of the reformation of factions or differing institutional interests. Indeed, the entire system is geared to suppress any sign of dissent with extraordinary brutality. The only institution that could act as a power centre itself is the military, but by promoting a large number of younger generals Kim Jong-il has ensured the loyalty of the armed forces. This analysis leads to several conclusions. First of all, in view of the mechanisms of central control bureaucratic politics and organizational behaviour decision-making models are unlikely to have any relevance except as second-order explanations of policy. The rational actor model will provide a better fit for explaining North Korean decision-making than in most other political systems.

Conceptualizing the sources of insecurity on the Korean peninsula

At the root of the crisis on the Korean peninsula is the bitter struggle about the future of the Korean nation and the resolution of its division into two states, one of which is becoming increasingly unsustainable while the other is prospering. As David Kang has put it:

> Both North Korea and South Korea are mired in a zero-sum battle for the Korean nation. An almost total absence of linguistic, ethnic and religious cleavages leaves no simple way to 'divide the pie', and the relatively constricted geographical situation, lacking natural barriers to conflict, intensifies an already acute security dilemma between the two sides. The result is not surprising: North and South Korea view each other as dangerous and illegitimate states, and each views compromise as tantamount to surrender. (Kim 1998, p. 166)

As we have seen, however, the dynamics of the confrontation and hence the sources of insecurity have changed over the decades. In the period following the Korean War, North Korea enjoyed security guarantees from the Soviet Union and China, its economy was stronger than that of the South and its military capabilities superior. The greatest source of insecurity was North Korean power, the totalitarian nature of the regime and the ambitions of Kim Il-sung to reunite the two Koreas by force. The end of the superpower conflict and the dramatic shift in the correlation of forces between the two Koreas has altered threat perceptions of North and South. Northern leaders articulate the threat as emanating from the 'hostile attitude' of the United States. This threat has a political and a military component. The political component consists in the rejection of the legitimacy of North Korea, the unwillingness of the United States to open diplomatic relations with the DPRK and the various indications that Washington would like to see a regime change in North Korea. Some of the language used by the Bush administration, such as including North Korea in the 'axis of evil' and Bush's personal dislike of Kim Jong-il, the attacks on North Korea's human rights records and its missile exports and the maintenance of sanctions are all part of this image of an implacably hostile United States that might seek any opportunity to attack it. The Bush national security doctrine with its emphasis on pre-emptive attack adds to this perception. The military component consists of the presence of US forces in Korea and Japan as well as the global military power projection capabilities which include tactical and strategic nuclear weapons. This portrayal of the threat, however, is clearly exaggerated. In fact the DPRK has sufficient military capabilities to render any military attack option for the United States exceedingly unattractive. While the assurances from the United States that it has no intention to launch a military strike against North Korea are credible, it is also true that not only the United States, but the Western world as a whole would like to see North Korea disappear as an entity in the future and the Korean peninsula be united as a Republic of Korea. With the collapse of communism in eastern Europe, its weakening to the point of irrelevance as an ideology in China and increasing globalization, the international community has by and large abandoned the ideas and values that underpin the social system in North Korea. While it is undeniable that the disapproval of much of the international community does constitute a threat to the DPRK, this threat does not translate into an intention to collapse or attack the North Korean state. Indeed the possibility of a sudden collapse of the DPRK is in itself perceived by other states as a serious threat. The reality is that North Korea could negotiate agreements to mitigate any external threat, including political and military confidence-building measures, reductions in the military deployments at the DMZ (arms control) and economic aid for relatively minor concessions on its part. The problem is that none of these solutions address the fundamental security dilemma that the DPRK faces. This dilemma resides in the paradox that the regime cannot survive in the longer term without fundamental reform, but fundamental reform will destroy the regime. This is true for several reasons. First of all the regime's entire claim for legitimacy is based on the principles of its social, economic and political organization. Without it, there would be no reason for the DPRK to exist; it could just become another South Korea and unification could take place without preconditions. Secondly, national survival is equated with the survival of its ruling dynasty. This places very strict constraints on reform because the hierarchical and social control that is inherent to the sociopolitical organization of the country is necessary to achieve it. As Han S. Park has put it:

> One must realize that North Koreans believe for good reason that system change means system collapse. Therefore, their resistance to change is in fact their resistance to collapse. Viewed from this perspective, it is not hard to understand why the North Korean leadership has refused to compromise its stance on the question of reforms and opening to the outside. It is a huge dilemma for North Korea that it cannot participate in the global market to make best use of its high-quality labor force, rich mineral resources, and strategically placed geographical location, which may well bring the necessary comparative advantage in market competition. This fixation on survival constrains the choice of acceptable strategies and tactics for the goal of system identity. The identity of the system cannot be easily altered from an ideological (*Juche*) system to a pragmatic system without losing the legitimacy war with the South, thereby risking system survival. (Park 2002, p. 149)

The severe obstacles in the path of fundamental reform have been further elucidated by Adrian Buzo:

> The central paradox remains that while the overwhelming majority of the population still appears to direct its loyalty to the state, large sections of this population are destitute, malnourished, exhausted and cynical. Their education is largely inappropriate to the modern world, they have no sense of rights as a citizenry, and they continue to be indoctrinated with a harsh, fearful, often utterly mendacious view of the modern world outside the DPRK's frontiers. Politically they are schooled only in obedience and economically they have only known an extreme version of economic commandism. The regime has done enormous damage to the national psyche and has given its citizens little in the way of intellectual or material resources with which to make their way in the modern world. Its archaic and primitive economic infrastructure is almost useless as a basis on which to develop an economic system which can serve even the basic needs of the country. There are no exile movements, no dissidents, and no models for building new social and economic institutions except those in the demonized ROK. (Buzo 1999, p. 147)

In other words, the essence of the security dilemma on the Korean peninsula is that the North Korean state is doomed. It can only survive if it loses the essence of its identity, but then there is no reason for it to continue to exist. However, this does not mean that it will collapse any time soon. It is held together with enormous force, with all the control instruments of a totalitarian society and with total disregard to the well-being of its citizens except for a small elite. It does mean, however, there is no solution for the North Korean security dilemma, because the primary threat it faces is not external, but rather derives from the very essence of the regime itself.

North Korea's threat to the world

The military threat posed by North Korea's conventional build-up and its unconventional weapons has to be assessed in the light of the basic security dilemma on the Korean peninsula and what we can discern about the intentions of the North Korean leadership. The total concentration of economic resources on the military and the enormous build-up of forces at the DMZ went beyond the needs for defence from a possible attack by US and ROK forces; it was designed to support a strategy of unification on Pyongyang's terms if the situation was right. Although in the first two decades after the Korean War the conventional forces of the North posed a serious threat by sheer weight of numbers and were superior to the forces of the ROK, the alliance with the United States which was supported by the presence of US forces with nuclear weapons deterred a full-scale attack. As the Republic of Korea developed its economy while the economy of the DPRK stagnated and then went into precipitous decline, the military balance changed as North Korea had to make do with old and obsolescent military equipment based on Soviet technology, whereas the South acquired more and more state-of-the-art US military equipment. Nowadays the Republic of Korea would most likely win a (non-nuclear) war with the North, even without direct US involvement (although US forces are still in Korea and committed to be engaged if the

ROK came under attack). Although North Korea could not win a war with the South, and its regime would not survive such a war, it could nevertheless inflict unacceptable damage on the South due to the large number of artillery pieces that can target the capital Seoul and its longer range missiles which can target any point on the peninsula. North Korea can also target US forces in Japan with some of its missiles. There is no doubt therefore that North Korea has a robust deterrent capability that means that the United States has no plausible military option, nor would South Korean governments want to risk any war on the peninsula. As far as North Korea's unconventional arsenal is concerned, it is militarily less significant than is sometimes supposed. The chemical weapons significantly enhance the DPRK's capacity to cause civilian casualties in the South, but do not necessarily redress the military balance as South Korean and American forces are equipped and trained to operate in a contaminated environment. Increasingly North Korean missiles can target US forces in Japan or Japan itself. The analysis of the military balance shows that the strategic situation on the Korean peninsula can be best characterized as a stable deterrence relationship. Nevertheless, there are significant dangers. North Korea's threat to international security comes in two ways. The first is the threat of proliferation. As a major source of ballistic missile technology for Iran and Pakistan, the DPRK has provided potential nuclear delivery vehicles to states in crisis regions, a development that significantly affects the interests of the United States. From the American perspective, the acquisition of long-range ballistic missiles by anti-Western states such as Iran and Syria is one of the major emerging threats to international security. Moreover, Pyongyang has hinted that it might engage in the proliferation of nuclear weapons materials and technology. This threat of proliferation will persist as long as North Korea has non-conventional weapons programmes. The second is the longer term threat of North Korea's emerging capabilities. Although at present no operational missiles of intercontinental range have been deployed, that could change over the next decade or two. North Korea has not yet demonstrated that it has operational nuclear devices and can mount nuclear warheads on long-range missiles. However, as missile development and the accumulation of fissile material continues apace, it cannot be excluded that in the medium term such a strategic threat to the continental United States could emerge. This would transform the strategic situation.

At the core, the reason why North Korea represents a threat to international security is that its military capabilities constitute the main leverage it perceives it has with regard to the United States. Consequently, as North Korea fails to achieve its objectives, it escalates the military threat. This is exacerbated by the myopia of North Korean leaders that leads them to have an exaggerated perception of the threat they are facing. Provocative missile launches, exchanges of fire between soldiers across the DMZ – these kinds of incidents demonstrate the high risk of an inadvertent escalation to a catastrophic war. Since the underlying source of North Korea's insecurity cannot be resolved, its belligerent behaviour is likely to continue. This is likely to be the case even if the agreement reached at the Six-Party Talks results in a period of reduced tension and increased cooperation between the DPRK and the United States. Despite the apparent strategic stability, therefore, there are present and emerging risks which the international community cannot afford to ignore (Chang 2006).

Korea and the future of north-east Asia

What is at stake is not just the future of the Korean people, but the geopolitical configuration of the entire region. The United States and China are involved in a major strategic rivalry in the Asian-Pacific region. The optimal long-term scenario for the US would be a united, democratic Korea which is a strong alliance partner. For China this outcome is not desirable, nor would China like to be confronted with the chaos of a collapsed state which would generate an enormous refugee and security problem. China currently provides all of North Korea's oil and about a third of its food imports and has resisted US pressure to use its economic influence to force

Pyongyang to make concessions. China's strategy towards North Korea is centred around the Six-Party Talks in order to constrain North Korea's nuclear and missile ambitions and reduce tension between the DPRK and the United States by facilitating a direct dialogue between the two sides. The hope in Beijing is that North Korea will embark on economic reform following the example of China and become an economically viable and less autocratic state. In this way North Korea would remain a buffer between the pro-American South where US forces are based and China itself. If some time in the distant future the two Koreas were to unite, China intends a united Korea to be leaning closer to China than the United States. China since the early 1990s has established good relations with South Korea which focused primarily on economic cooperation. The approach taken by the Bush administration to North Korea had the result that US policy became increasingly dependent on China. This could give China more leverage in relation to other issues, such as relations with Taiwan (Shambaugh 2003; Wu 2005).

Another critical power in the region is Japan. Japan has supported a policy of engagement with North Korea and has provided substantial aid. It was also a major contributor to KEDO. The substantial North Korean community in Japan has been a major source of hard currency for the DPRK. In the mid-1990s, Japan embarked on a process of normalization of relations with North Korea which was derailed when 26 North Korean commandos entered the South using a submarine. The test of a *Taepodong-1* missile whose third stage fell into the sea off Japan in 1998 was seen as a major provocation against Japan and has prompted Japan to collaborate with the United States for the development of theatre missile defences. Relations were also affected by the unresolved issue of Japanese citizens who had been abducted and brought to North Korea. Since then relations have fluctuated as North Korea sought to bargain concessions against further aid. Under the leadership of Koizumi, the alliance between Japan and the United States has strengthened even further. Japan takes part in the Six-Party Talks and is anxious that the nuclear issue is dealt with. In 2006, relations between Tokyo and Pyongyang reached a new low as a result of an abortive attempt to resolve the issue of the abductees and the missile launches in July. The latter prompted Tokyo to impose strict sanctions on the DPRK and for the first time seriously seek to interdict the flow of private funds from Japan (Kim and Rhee 2000). Relations between Seoul and Tokyo are not as close as they could be. This is a consequence of the history of the occupation which still evokes anti-Japanese feelings, sometimes stirred up by politicians, and a minor territorial dispute about an island called Dokdo by the Koreans. Nevertheless, it is clear that the US–ROK alliance in practice also includes Japan, although Japan's constitution is interpreted to prohibit direct military assistance to another country. In principle, Japan has supported both the containment and engagement of North Korea. Dealing with the DPRK's missile and nuclear programmes is a central issue of national security for Japan. At the same time, major instability on the Korean peninsula would likewise constitute a serious threat. In the longer term Japan has a vital stake in any unification process, which must be peaceful and result in a friendly Korea whose principal alliance is with the United States.

Finally, Russia is another player in the geopolitical game in north-east Asia. Although the Soviet Union enabled the creation of the DPRK and was Pyongyang's principal source of external support until the end of the 1980s, it lost virtually all its influence when President Gorbachev decided to switch from Pyongyang to Seoul as its main Korean partner and cut off all of its aid (especially subsidized fuel deliveries) for the DPRK. Since the early years of the Russian Federation when many in Moscow saw South Korea as a possible economic model for Russia itself, the Russian government decided to rebalance its relations with the Korean peninsula and develop greater collaboration with Pyongyang. The success of this policy has been limited because Russia has neither the resources nor the will to provide North Korea with the kind of aid that it needs. Pyongyang needs fuel and would like access to Russian missile technology. But Russia insists on world prices for its fuel and it is prevented by the missile technology control regime from collaborating with North Korea in the development of missile technology. As a member of the Six-Party Talks, Russia is involved in the effort to eliminate North Korea's nuclear programme. At the talks Russia tends to take a position supportive of China and weaken American efforts to impose more sanctions on the DPRK. There is a certain commonality of interests between China and Russia. Like China, Russia would like to see economic reforms in North Korea so that it can integrate with the economies of north-east Asia. As far as the long-term future is concerned, Russia would not want to see a geopolitical shift that would strengthen the position of the United States, which is a likely outcome of unification on Seoul's terms.

In terms of the geopolitics of the region, the crisis on the Korean peninsula has two important aspects. The first one, which dominates most of the discussions about Korea, is the security risk posed by the present situation. The other powers are aware of the serious risks posed by the possibility of a collapse of the North Korean state or the outbreak of conflict. The second relates to the long-term future of the Korean peninsula and the possible impact on the geopolitics of the region where all regional powers have a stake on how this turns out.

Engaging North Korea

In the early 1990s there was widespread belief that the collapse of the North Korean state was imminent. Officials in the South Korean presidential office told me they thought that they had perhaps another three years before the disaster. Since then a regional consensus has emerged that a sudden collapse is not desirable. A 'hard landing' for the DPRK could have disastrous consequences. The desirable outcome is a 'soft landing' through gradual reform, but no one really knows how it can be brought about, nor is there agreement about what kind of North Korea would emerge from such a process. South Korea's 'sunshine policy' consists of economic aid and investment to facilitate economic reform that it is hoped will bring about social and political change. In principle this policy seems sound, and the experience of the policy of détente in Europe during the Cold War provides a convincing example of this approach. There are some criticisms of its implementation in so far as South Korea has eschewed using the leverage that the North's increasing dependence on the South should provide and has until recently adopted an almost subservient posture towards Pyongyang in the face of severe provocation. There are two major caveats, however. One is that the leaders of the DPRK are fully cognizant of the potential dangers of going along with the South Korean policy of engagement. Despite their desperate need for economic aid, they have again and again forgone economic benefits in order to limit any impact on their control over the country. Nevertheless, there are some indications of at least a slight relaxation of central control as evidenced by the limited economic reforms introduced by Kim Jong-il. North Korea's urban youth seems to have a positive view of the South; clothing items made in the Republic of Korea fly off the shelves and samizdat videotapes of South Korean soap operas are being passed around. But there is no sign of an emerging opposition. One serious political problem for the regime is the fact that the matter of the succession has not yet been addressed. The sudden death of Kim Jong-il could result in a crisis that might destabilize the regime. The other caveat is that there are serious questions about whether the system can be reformed sufficiently to make it viable. The gap between the DPRK and the Republic of Korea is now such that it will take enormous resources and a long time to bridge it. Assuming that it is possible, then at some point the changes will be so far-reaching that they amount to a change of regime. This obviously is the desired outcome, but this process could create a degree of instability that will either cause retrenchment by a leadership desperately clinging to power and/or bring about a total collapse as there are no roots for civil society or an alternative political leadership. In other words, long-term gradual change involves similar risks to sudden regime change.

There is no easy solution to the crisis on the Korean peninsula. Fortunately the strategic situation is stable at present and there is no imminent risk of war. But there are real risks and dangers which must be assessed realistically. The best policy to mitigate these risks is one based on political and economic engagement, together with a robust policy of deterrence and containment. The primary objective must be to avoid a conflict on the Korean peninsula itself. Another critical objective should be the prevention of the proliferation of missile and nuclear weapons technology. The two Koreas will eventually be unified. But there is a long and dangerous road still ahead.

References

Aesop (1998) *The Complete Fables*, Penguin Classics.

Albright, David and Paul Brannan (2006) *The North Korean Plutonium Stock Mid-2006*, ISIS.

Albright, David and Kevin O'Neill (eds) (2000) *Solving the North Korean Nuclear Puzzle*, ISIS.

Allison, Graham T. and Philip Zelikow (1999) *The Essence of Decision*, Longman.

Bae, Jong-Yuan and Chung-in Moon (2003) 'The Bush Doctrine and the North Korean Nuclear Crisis', *Asian Perspective (Special Issue on the Bush Doctrine and Asia)* 27 (4): 9–45.

BBC News, www.news.bbc.co.uk accessed 22 December 2006.

Beal, Tim (2005) *North Korea – The Struggle Against American Power*, Pluto Press.

Becker, Jasper (2005) *Rogue Regime*, Oxford University Press.

Bennett, Bruce (2004) 'Weapons of Mass Destruction: The North Korean Threat', *The Korean Journal of Defense Analysis* XVI (2) Fall: 170–98.

Bermudez, Joseph S. (1991) *Jane's Intelligence Review* (September): 405.

Bermudez, Joseph S. (2001) *The Armed Forces of North Korea*, I. B. Taurus.

Bluth, Christoph (1992) *Soviet Strategic Arms Policy Before SALT*, Cambridge University Press.

Bluth, Christoph (2004) 'The Eagle Resurgent – National Security in the Second Bush Administration', *The World Today* (December): 2–4.

Bluth, Christoph (2005) 'Face Reality: Why Six-Party Talks Must Fail', *The Korea Herald*, 9 May: 6.

Buzo, Adrian (1999) *The Guerilla Dynasty*, I. B. Tauris.

Campbell, Kurt, Derek Mitchell and Carola McGiffert (2002) *Conventional Arms Control on the Korean Peninsula*, Center for Strategic and International Studies.

Carlin, Robert L. and Wit, Joel S. (2006) *North Korean Reform*, Adelphi Paper 382, IISS/Routledge.

Carpenter, Ted Galen (2004) 'A Hedging Strategy is Needed Toward North Korea', *Korea Journal of Defense Analysis* XVI (1) (Spring): 7–23.

Cha, Do-hyeogn (2004a) 'Challenges and Opportunities: The Participatory Government's Policy Toward North Korea', *East Asian Review* 16 (2) (Summer): 97–110.

Cha, Do-hyeogn (2004b) *The Future of the ROK–U.S. Alliance: Toward the Evolution of a Strategic Cooperation Alliance*, The KIDA Papers, No.7 (December).

Cha, Victor D. and David C. Kang (2003) *Nuclear North Korea – A Debate on Engagement Strategies*, Columbia University Press.

Chang, Gordon G. (2006) *Nuclear Showdown – North Korea Takes on the World*, Hutchinson.

Cordesman, Anthony H. (2006) *North Korea's Missile Tests: Saber Rattling or Rocket's Red Glare*, CSIS.

Cossa, Ralph A. (ed.) (1999) *US–Korea–Japan Relations: Building Toward a Virtual Alliance*, CSIS Press.

Cumings, Bruce (1981) *The Origins of the Korean War, Volume I: Liberation and the Emergence of Separate Regimes, 1945–1947*, Princeton University Press.

Cumings, Bruce (1990) *The Origins of the Korean War, Volume II: The Roaring of the Cataract, 1947–1950*, Princeton University Press.

Cumings, Bruce (1997) *Korea's Place in the Sun – A Modern History*, W. W. Norton.

Daalder, Ivo H. and James M. Lindsay (2003) 'Where Are the Hawks on North Korea ?', *American Prospect*, 1 February.

Daalder, Ivo H. and James M. Lindsay (2005) *America Unbound: The Bush Revolution in Foreign Policy*, Wiley.

Dallin, David (1961) *Soviet Foreign Policy After Stalin*, J. B. Lippincott.

Department of Defense (2001) *Quadriennal Defense Review*, Arlington, VA.

Downs, Chuck (1999) *Over the Line – North Korea's Negotiating Strategy*, American Enterprise Institute Press.

Eberstadt, Nicholas (1999) *The End of North Korea*, American Enterprise Institute Press.

Eberstadt, Nicholas and Richard J. Ellings (eds) (2001) *Korea's Future and the Great Powers*, University of Washington Press.

Economist, The (2004) *North Korea – Through a Glass Darkly*, 11 March 2004.

Freedman, Lawrence (2004) *Deterrence*, Polity.

French, Paul (2005) *North Korea – The Paranoid Peninsula: A Modern History*, Zed Books.

Gallucci, Robert L., Daniel B. Poneman and Joel S. Wit (2004) *Going Critical – The First North Korean Nuclear Crisis*, Brookings Institution Press.

Gallucci, R. L. and Mitchell B. Reiss (2005) 'Dead to Rights', *Foreign Affairs* 84 (2) (March/April): 142–5.

Garwin, Richard L. (2005) 'HEU Done It', *Foreign Affairs* 84 (2) (March/April): 145–6.

Garwin, Richard L. and Frank N. von Hippel (2006) 'A Technical Analysis: Deconstructing North Korea's 9 October Nuclear Test', *Arms Control Today* (November).

George, Alexander L. (1993) *Bridging the Gap: Theory and Practice in Foreign Policy*, US Institute of Peace Press.

globalsecurity.org, *Rodong Design Heritage*, http://www.globalsecurity.org/wmd/world/dprk/nd-1.htm

Han, Woo-Keun (1970) *The History of Korea*, East–West Center Press.

Han, Yong-sup and Levin, Norman D. (2002) *Sunshine in Korea*, RAND Corporation.

Harrison, Selig S. (2002) *Korean Endgame*, Princeton University Press.

Harrison, Selig S. (2005a) 'Did North Korea Cheat?', *Foreign Affairs* 84 (1) (January/February): 99–110.

Harrison, Selig S. (2005b) 'Harrison Replies', *Foreign Affairs* 84 (2) (March/April): 146–8.

Hastings, Max (1988) *The Korean War*, Simon and Schuster.

Hecker, Siegfried S. (2004) *Visit to the Yongbyon Nuclear Research Center in North Korea*, Senate Committee on Foreign Relations Hearing.

Hickey, Michael (1999) *The Korean War – West Confronts Communism 1950–1953*, John Murray.

Huh, Moon-Young (2006) '60th Anniversary of Korea Liberation: Current Status of Inter-Korean Relations and Future Direction', *International Journal of Korean Unification Studies* 15 (1): 66–105.

Huntley, Wade L. (2004) 'Ostrich Engagement: The Bush Administration and the North Korea Nuclear Crisis', *The Nonproliferation Review* 11 (2) (Summer): 81–115.

Huntley, Wade L. (2006) 'Rebels Without a Cause: North Korea, Iran and the NPT', *International Affairs* 82 (4): 723–42.

Hwang, Jaeho (2006) 'Measuring China's Influence over North Korea', *Issues and Studies* 42 (2) (June): 205–32.

Hwang, Jang-yop (1999) *I Saw the Truth of History*, Hanwul.

IISS (International Institute for Strategic Studies) (2004) *North Korea's Weapons Programmes*, Palgrave.

Jan, Suk (2002) *Study on General Kim Jong Il's National Unification*, Pyongyang Publishing House.

Jung, Yeon Bong (2005) 'The US Response to the North Korea Nuclear Issue', *The Korean Journal of Defense Analysis* XVII (2) (Fall): 63–86.

Kahn, Joseph (2003) 'Korea Arms Talks Close With Plan for a New Round', *New York Times*, 30 August.

Kang, Chol-Hwan and Pierre Rigoulot (2001) *The Aquariums of Pyongyang*, Basic Books.

Kihl, Young Whan (2005) *Transforming Korean Politics*, M. E. Sharpe.

Kim, Byungki (2006) 'The Role of State Institutions, Organizational Culture and Policy. Perception in South Korea's International Security Policymaking Process: 1998–Present', *International Journal of Korean Unification Studies* 15 (1): 106–31.

Kim, Chul Woo (2000) *General Kim Jong Il's Military First Politics*, Pyongyang Publishing House.

Kim, Do-tae (2004) 'US–North Korea Nuclear Talks: Pyongyang's Changing Attitude and US Choice', *East Asian Review* 16 (1): 3–20.

Kim Il-sung (1982) *Kim Il Sung Works, Vol. 9: July 1954–December 1995*, Pyongyang: Foreign Languages Publishing House.

Kim, Jae Ho (2000) *Kim Jong Il's Strategy to Build a Strong and Rich Nation*, Pyongyang Publishing House.

Kim, Jina (2005) 'An Endless Game: North Korea's Psychological Warfare', *The Korean Journal of Defense Analysis* XVII (2): 153–82.

Kim, Keun-sik (2004) 'The North Korean Nuclear Crisis and Inter-Korean Relations', *East Asian Review* 16 (1): 21–36.

Kim, Samuel S. (ed.) (1998) *North Korea Foreign Relations in the Post-Cold War Era*, Oxford University Press.

Kim, Samuel S. (ed.) (2004) *Inter-Korean Relations*, Palgrave.

Kim, Samuel S. (2006) *The Two Koreas and the Great Powers*, Cambridge University Press.

Kim, Sung-han (2003) 'AntiAmerican Sentiment and the ROK-US Alliance', *The Korean Journal of Defense Analysis* XV (2) (Fall): 105–30.

Kim, Tae-hyo and Sang-woo Rhee (eds) (2000) *Korea–Japan Security Relations*, Oruem Publishing House.

Kim Tae-hyo and Woosang Kim (2004) 'A Candle in the Wind: Korean Perceptions of ROK–US Security Relations', *The Korean Journal of Defense Analysis* XVI (1): 99–118.

Kim, Tae-woo (2003) *Living with North Korean Bomb? Current Debates in and Future Options for South Korea*, KIDA Paper 2 (June).

Kim, Tae-woo (2004) 'North Korean Nuclear Politics at the Crossroads', *The Korean Journal of Defense Analysis* XVI (2) (Fall): 27–47.

Korean Institute for National Unification (2006) *White Paper on Human Rights in Korea*.

Laney, James T. and Jason T. Shaplen (2003) 'How To Deal with North Korea', *Foreign Affairs* 82 (2) (March–April): 27–45.

Lankov, Andrei (2002) *From Stalin to Kim Il-sung: The Formation of North Korea 1945–60*, Hurst and Company.

Lee, Hoi Chang (2000) 'Remarks made by Grand National Party President Lee Hoi Chang at press conference in Seoul, June 19, 2000'.

Lee, Chung-Hoon and Chung-in Moon (2003) 'The North Korean Nuclear Crisis Revisited: The Case for a Negotiated Settlement', *Security Dialogue* 34 (2): 135–51.

Lee, Suk (2006) 'Reliability and Usability of the DPRK Statistics: Case of Grain Statistics in 1946–2000, *International Journal of Korean Unification Studies* 15 (1): 132–72.

Lee, Nae-young and Jeong Han-wool (2003) 'Anti-Americanism and the US–ROK Alliance', *East Asian Review* 15 (4) (Winter): 23–46.

Lehrman, Thomas D. (2004) 'Rethinking Interdiction. The Future of the Proliferation Security Initiative', *The Non-Proliferation Review* (Summer) 11 (2): 1–45.

Lintner, Bertil (2005) *Great Leader, Dear Leader*, Silkworm Books.

Lott, Anthony D. (2004) *Creating Insecurity*, Ashgate.

Martin, Bradley K. (2004) *Under the Loving Care of the Fatherly Leader – North Korea and the Kim Dynasty*, St Martin's Press.

Maull, Hanns W. (2002) *Nordkorea: Ein Staat vor dem Aus?*, Trier University.

Mazarr, Michael J. (1995) *North Korea and the Bomb*, St Martin's Press.

Mearsheimer, John (2003) *The Tragedy of Great Power Politics*, W. W. Norton.

MND (Ministry of National Defense) (2000) *Defense White Paper*, Ministry of National Defense, Seoul, Korea.

MND (Ministry of National Defense) (2003) *Participatory Government Defense Policy 2003* Ministry of National Defense, Seoul, Korea.

MND (Ministry of National Defense) (2004) *Defense White Paper*, MND, Seoul.

Moltz, James C. and Mansourov, Alexandre Y. (eds) (2000) *The North Korean Nuclear Program*, Routledge.

Moltz, James Clay and C. Kenneth Quinones (2004) 'Getting Serious about a Multilateral Approach to North Korea', *The Nonproliferation Review* (Spring): 136–44.

Moon, Chung-in and David Steinberg (eds) (1999) *Kim Dae-jung Government and Sunshine Policy: Promises and Challenges*, Yonsei University Press.

Moon, Chung-in (2004) 'The North Korean Nuclear Problem and Multilateral Cooperation: The Case of the Six Party Talk', *Whitebook on the Korean Economy*, Korea Institute for International Economic Policy, Seoul 2004.

Nam, Koon Woo (1974) *The North Korean Communist Leadership, 1945–65: A Study of Factionalism and Political Consolidation*, University of Alabama Press.

Nanto, Dick K. and Raphael F. Perl (2006) 'North Korean Counterfeiting of US Currency', CRS Report for Congress, Order Code RL33324, March 22, 2006..

Natsios, Andrew (2001) *The Great North Korean Famine*, USIP Press.

Noland, Marcus (2000) *Avoiding the Apocalypse – The Future of the Two Koreas*, Institute for International Economics.

Noland, Marcus (2003) *Famine and Reform in North Korea*, Institute for International Economics.

Noland, Marcus (2004) *Korea after Kim Jong-il*, Institute for International Economics.

NTI Country Profile, DPRK, Nuclear, http://www.nti.org/e_research/profiles/NK/index.html

O'Hanlon, Michael and Mike Mochizuki (2003) *Crisis on the Korean Peninsula*, McGraw-Hill.

Oberdorfer, Don (2001) *The Two Koreas*, Basic Books.

Oh, Kongdan and Ralph C. Hassig (2000) *North Korea: Through the Looking Glass*, Brookings Institution.

Paik, Haksoon (2005) 'What is the Goal of the US Policy toward North Korea: Nonproliferation or Regime Change?', Nautilus Policy Form Online, 7 April, www.nautilus.org

Palais, James B. (1975) *Politics and Policy in Traditional Korea*, Harvard University Press.

Park, Han S. (2002) *North Korea: The Politics of Unconventional Wisdom*, Lynne Rynner.

Park, Ihn-hwi (2004) 'Toward an Alliance of Moderates: The Nuclear Crisis and Trilateral Policy Coordination', *East Asian Review* 16 (2) (Summer): 23–42.

Park, Sun Song (2004) 'Reform or Military Buildup: North Korea's Economic Policy 1994–2004', *East Asian Review* 16 (2) (Summer): 3–22.

Perry, William (1999) *Review of United States Policy Toward North Korea: Findings and Recommendations*, http://www.state.gov/www/regions/eap/991012_northkorea_rpt.html

Pinkston, Daniel A. (2006) *North Korea's Nuclear Weapons Program and the Six-Party Talks*, NTI Issue Brief, http://www.nti.org/e_research/e3_76.html#fn31

Pinkston, Daniel A. and Phillip C. Saunders (2003) 'Seeing North Korea Clearly', *Survival*, 45 (3) (Autumn): 79–102.

Pinkston, Daniel A. and Andrew F. Diamond (2005) *Special Report on the Shutdown of North Korea's 5 MW(e) Nuclear Reactor*, Monterey Center for Non-Proliferation Studies, http://cns.miis.edu/pubs/week/pdf/050428.pdf

Pinkston, Daniel A. and Shin Sungtack (2007) *North Korea Likely to Conduct a Second Nuclear Test*, Center for Non-Proliferation Studies, MIIS, cns.miis.edu

Quinones, C. Kenneth and Joseph Tragert (2003) *Understanding North Korea*, Alpha Books.

Rees, David (1964) *Korea: The Limited War*, Penguin.

Sagan, Scott (1996) 'Why Do States Build Nuclear Weapons?', *International Security*, 21 (3): 54–86.

Samore, Gary (2003) 'The Korean Nuclear Crisis', *Survival* 45(1) Spring: 7–24.

Saunders, Phillip C. (2004) *Military Options for Dealing with North Korea's Nuclear Program*, http://cns.miis.edu/research/korea/dprkmil.htm

Scobell, Andrew (2004) *China and North Korea: From Comrades-in-Arms to Allies at Arm's Length*, Strategic Studies Institute, US Army War College.

Shambaugh, David (2003) 'China and the Korean Peninsula: Playing for the Long Term', *Washington Quarterly* 26 (2) (Spring): 43–56.

Sheen, Seongho (2004) 'Preempting Proliferation of WMD – Proliferation Security Initiative (PSI) and its Challenges', *The Korea Journal of Defense Analysis* XVI (2) (Fall): 109–30.

Shorrock, Tim (1986) 'The Struggle for Democracy in South Korea in the 1980s and the Rise of Anti-Americanism', *Third World Quarterly* 8 (4) (October): 1195–218.

Sigal, Leon (1998) *Disarming Strangers*, Princeton University Press.

Sigal, Leon (2006) 'Building a Peace Regime in Korea: An American View', *International Journal of Korean Unification Studies* 15 (1): 30–52.

Smith, Hazel (2005) *Hungry for Peace: International Security, Humanitarian Assistance, and Social Change in North Korea*, United States Institute of Peace.

Snyder, Scott (2002) *Negotiating on The Edge – North Korean Negotiating Behavior*, United States Institute of Peace Press.

Snyder, Scott (2005) 'South Korea's Squeeze Play', *The Washington Quarterly*, 28 (4): 93–106.

Strohmaier, James G. (2003) *Extorting Cooperation: A Case Study of the Negotiation and Implementation of the 1994 US–DPRK Agreed Framework*, PhD Dissertation, University of Kentucky.

United Nations Security Council (1994) 'Presidential Statement on US–North Korea Agreed Framework', 4 November.

US White House (2001) Statement by the President, 13 June 2001, www.whitehouse.gov/news/releases/2001/06/200010611–4.html

Waltz, Kenneth (1979) *Theory of International Politics*, Random House.

Wampler, Robert A. (ed.) (2003) *North Korea and Nuclear Weapons: The Declassified Record*, National Security Archive Electronic Briefing Book No. 87.

Weathersby, Kathryn (1993) *Soviet Aims in Korea and the Origins of the Korean War 1945–50*, Cold War International History Project Working Paper No. 8.

Wendt, Alexander (1999) *Social Theory of International Politics*, Cambridge University Press.

Wu, Anne (2005) 'What China Whispers to North Korea', *The Washington Quarterly* 28 (2): 35–48.

Yeo, In-Kon (2006) 'Search for Peaceful Resolution of the North Korean Nuclear Issue', *International Journal of Korean Unification Studies* 15 (1): 53–65.

Yu, Yong-won (2004) 'North Deploys New 4,000 km-Range Missiles, *Chosun ilbo* (English edition) May 4.

Yuan, Jing-dong (2006) 'China New York Korea Diplomacy', *Asia Times*, 14 November.

Index ───────────────────────────